Fun with the Family™ in Colorado

Praise for the *Fun with the Family™* series

"Enables parents to turn family travel into an exploration."
—Alexandra Kennedy, Editor, *Family Fun*

"Bound to lead you and your kids to fun-filled days,
those times that help compose the memories of childhood."
—Dorothy Jordon, *Family Travel Times*

Help Us Keep This Guide Up to Date

Every effort has been made by the author and editors to make this guide as accurate and useful as possible. However, many changes can occur after a guide is published—establishments close, phone numbers change, hiking trails are rerouted, facilities come under new management, etc.

We would love to hear from you concerning your experiences with this guide and how you feel it could be improved and be kept up to date. While we may not be able to respond to all comments and suggestions, we'll take them to heart, and we'll make certain to share them with the author. Please send your comments and suggestions to the following address:

The Globe Pequot Press
Reader Response/Editorial Department
P.O. Box 480
Guilford, CT 06437

Or you may e-mail us at: editorial@globe-pequot.com

Thanks for your input, and happy travels!

FUN WITH THE FAMILY™

in COLORADO

HUNDREDS OF IDEAS
FOR DAY TRIPS WITH THE KIDS
FOURTH EDITION

DORIS KENNEDY

The
Globe
Pequot
Press

GUILFORD, CONNECTICUT

The prices, rates, and hours listed in this guidebook were confirmed at press time. We recommend, however, that you call establishments to obtain current information before traveling.

Fun with the Family is a trademark of The Globe Pequot Press.
Text design by Nancy Freeborn
Maps by M. A. Dubé

ISSN 1543-1231
ISBN 0-7627-2677-6

Manufactured in the United States of America
Fourth Edition/First Printing

This book is dedicated to my husband and fellow traveler, professional photographer Gary Kennedy, who patiently encouraged and consoled me through research and deadlines; to my wonderful dad, James Clark, who blessed me with sensitivity, honesty, and an endless love for animals; to my forever friends, Peggy Moran and Lynn Reamer; and to my countless other friends whose steadfast support I can never repay.

My sincere thanks to Jeannine and Brad Crooks, internationally published travel writer and photographer team, for their congenial assistance with this edition. Their meticulous research helped establish this book as an accurate, dependable resource for fun with *your* family.

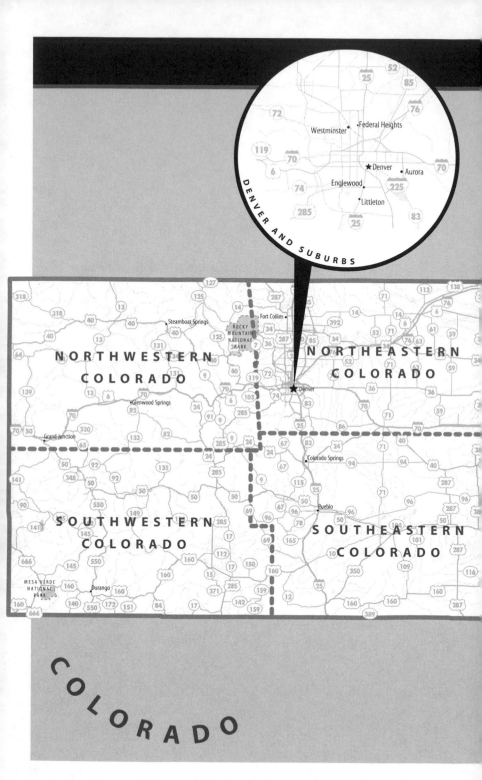

DENVER AND SUBURBS

52
85
25
76
72
Westminster • Federal Heights
119
70
6
74
Englewood
285
Littleton
Denver
Aurora
70
225
83
25

318
127
125
287
113
138
318
13
14
Fort Collins
76
40
Steamboat Springs
14
40
40
131
125
ROCKY MOUNTAIN NATIONAL PARK
34
392
52
71
14
6
59
64
13
40
7
287
34
NORTHWESTERN COLORADO
131
9
40
119
72
NORTHEASTERN COLORADO
52
34
139
70
6
Glenwood Springs
70
82
103
74
Denver
36
36
50
330
Grand Junction
82
133
91
285
83
70
71
59
70
50
65
24
86
70
50
92
285
9
24
67
83
24
40
141
348
135
24
67
Colorado Springs
94
94
40
50
92
285
9
115
287
50
50
50
50
67
25
71
90
550
149
285
69
96
Pueblo
96
96
141
SOUTHWESTERN COLORADO
17
96
50
78
287
38
666
145
550
112
69
165
SOUTHEASTERN COLORADO
101
287
145
550
150
10
350
109
116
MESA VERDE NATIONAL PARK
160
15
17
160
25
160
160
Durango
285
159
12
160
666
140
550
172
151
84
17
142
159
389
287

COLORADO

Contents

Introduction

I have lived in Colorado for more than thirty years and have traveled extensively throughout the state. After visiting nearly every city, town, resort, attraction, park, and nook and cranny, I am delighted to share my finds with you. In this book you will discover where to dig for dinosaur bones, ski on sand dunes, walk through ancient cliff dwellings, fish for trout in Gold Medal Waters, find Buffalo Bill's grave, slide down snow-covered mountains on custom-made tubes, go dogsledding, ski downhill and cross-country, and visit Santa's North Pole almost any day of the year. You will find family-friendly lodging and eateries; encounter an alligator farm and a wolf reserve; and explore a gold mine, underground caves, and a bug museum. I hope you enjoy *Fun with the Family in Colorado*. It was written with you and your family in mind.

Colorado Fast Facts

- **Colorado:** A Spanish word meaning red.
- **Population:** Approximately 5 million.
- **Nickname:** Centennial State (admitted to the Union in 1876).
- **Highest Point:** Mt. Elbert at 14,433 feet.
- **State Flower:** The lavender-and-white Rocky Mountain columbine, adopted in 1899.
- **State Bird:** Lark bunting, designated in 1931.
- **State Song:** "Where the Columbines Grow" by A. J. Flynn, adopted in 1915.
- **State Animal:** Rocky Mountain bighorn sheep, designated in 1961.
- **State Tree:** Colorado blue spruce, adopted in 1939.
- **State Fossil:** Stegosaurus, designated in 1982.
- **State Insect:** Colorado hairstreak butterfly, adopted in 1996.

HOW TO USE THIS BOOK

A tremendous amount of travel, research, and thought have gone into the writing of this book, making it comprehensive but by no means all-inclusive. New activities, attractions, accommodations, and eateries continually sprout up; therefore, you will find some pleasant surprises along your journey. If you discover something of interest that I have missed and you think other families would appreciate knowing about, please let me know by writing to the publisher.

For your ease the state has been divided into five sections: Metropolitan Denver and Suburbs, Northeastern, Southeastern, Northwestern, and Southwestern. You will find a map at the beginning of each chapter pinpointing the towns mentioned in that chapter, plus lists of the best attractions and festivals for that part of the state. At the back of the book is an alphabetical index of all places and attractions. In addition, there is an activities index to help you find the perfect attraction to delight your family.

In many areas within the state of Colorado, callers must dial ten digits (the area code plus the regular number) when making local phone calls. All numbers with a 303 or 720 prefix are in this category. The 970-prefix communities of Berthoud, Dillon, Estes Park, Frisco, Greeley, La Salle, Mead, Platteville, and Wiggins also require ten-digit dialing for local calls. Regions with a 719 area code are not affected by this new system.

I have listed lodging and dining recommendations that I feel are apropos for families. Please keep in mind, however, that in most locations there are many other options in addition to those mentioned.

Rather than give dollar amounts for the cost of attractions, activities, lodging, and dining, I have used the following guide:

Attractions and Activities
(per adult; fees for children are often less)

$	up to $5.00	$$$$	more than $20.00
$$	from $6.00 to $10.00	Free	if there is no charge for any-
$$$	from $11.00 to $20.00		one, regardless of age

Lodging
(one-night stay for two adults)

$	up to $75
$$	from $76 to $100
$$$	from $101 to $150
$$$$	more than $150

Meals
(one complete adult meal)

$	up to $10
$$	from $11 to $15
$$$	from $16 to $20
$$$$	most more than $20

Neither the author nor the publisher will be held responsible for injury or harm resulting from any activity described in this book. Care should be taken and rules followed when traveling in the backcountry or engaging in recreational activities. When traveling to high-altitude areas, it is advisable to gradually (over a period of several days) ascend to your destination. For instance, plan to stay a day or two in Denver, at a 5,280-foot altitude, before continuing on to an altitude of 8,000 or more feet so that your body can adjust to the higher elevation.

Attractions Key

The following is a key to the icons found throughout the text.

 Swimming

 Animal Viewing

 Boating / Boat Tour

 Food

 Historic Site

 Lodging

 Hiking / Walking

 Camping

 Fishing

 Museums

 Biking

 Performing Arts

 Amusement Park

 Sports / Athletic

 Horseback Riding

 Picnicking

 Skiing / Winter Sports

 Playground

 Park

 Shopping

 Plants / Gardens / Nature Trails

Farms

Metropolitan Denver and Suburbs

The Denver area is often mistakenly considered to be in the mountains when, actually, it is against the foothills, along the front range of the Rocky Mountains. The climate is also often misunderstood. To be sure, the region is blanketed with a heavy snow now and then throughout the winter, but it lies just east of a high mountain barrier and far distant from any moisture source, resulting in a mild and arid climate. Annual precipitation ranges between 8 and 15 inches (about the same as Los Angeles), and Denver area residents bask in approximately 300 days of sunshine a year—more annual hours of sun than received by residents of San Diego, Honolulu, or Miami Beach. When snow does fall, it usually melts within a few days.

Doris's Top Picks in Denver and the Suburbs

1. Butterfly Pavilion and Insect Center, Westminster
2. Denver Mint, Denver
3. Denver Museum of Nature and Science, Denver
4. Denver Zoo, Denver
5. Ocean Journey, Denver
6. Six Flags Elitch Gardens Amusement Park, Denver
7. Wings over the Rockies Air & Space Museum, Denver

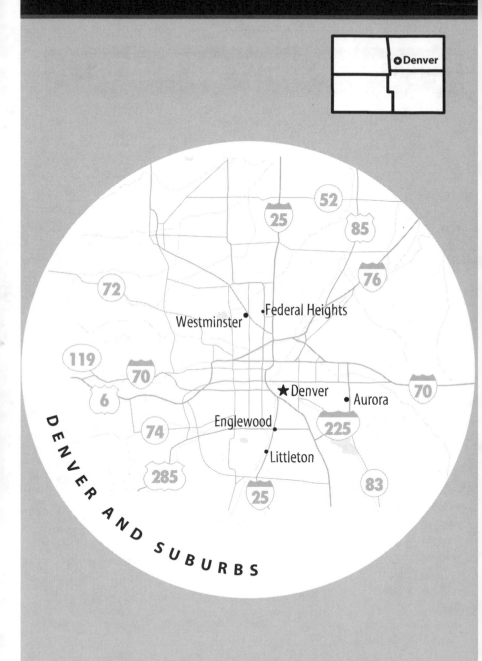

DENVER AND SUBURBS

Denver

Home to a world-class amusement park and a 50,000-seat baseball stadium in the center of the city, Denver boasts more than 200 parks and four major-league sports teams—the NHL Stanley Cup–winning Avalanche, NFL Super Bowl champions the Denver Broncos, the NBA Nuggets, and the National League Colorado Rockies. The Denver International Airport is deemed to be the safest, most high-tech air facility in the world.

 COLORADO STATE CAPITOL BUILDING (ages 5 and up)

1475 Sherman Street, Denver 80204; (303) 866–2604. Tours available year-round, except on holidays, Monday through Friday. Also open Saturday, June through August. Times vary. Best to phone. Stairs to the dome open 9:00 A.M. to 3:30 P.M. **Free**.

Elegance prevails at Colorado's State Capitol Building, where priceless wainscoting of rose-onyx marble sheathes the walls; bronze work glistens on stairway balusters and at the base of floor-to-ceiling pillars; rich woods glow under glittering chandeliers; and striking, hand-painted murals tell the history of Colorado in picture and verse.

Construction began in 1886 and took twenty-two years to complete. The dome was originally covered in copper, but when citizens complained that copper was not a primary metal in the state, Colorado miners contributed a total of 200 ounces of pure gold to cover its surface.

Although preschool children may not be thrilled with touring the State Capitol Building, those ages five and above usually are impressed by the splendor. They are sure to enjoy the challenge of climbing the ninety-three stairs, beginning on the third floor, to the gleaming gold dome rising 272 feet above the ground. From here they will get a wonderful bird's-eye view of the entire city and the Rocky Mountains beyond.

The elevator, which serves all levels except the dome, is located in the east wing behind the rotunda. There are a cafeteria and souvenir shop in the basement. The stairway to the basement is behind the grand staircase in the center rotunda.

Free forty-five-minute tours begin at the Tour Desk near the north entrance (Colfax Avenue) on the first floor. Or ask for a *Visitor's Guide* at the desk and explore on your own.

COLORADO HISTORY MUSEUM (ages 6 and up)

13th Avenue and Broadway, Denver 80203; (303) 866–3682; www.colorado history.org. Open Monday through Saturday 10:00 A.M. to 4:30 P.M. and Sunday noon to 4:30 P.M. $

Getting around Denver

Three standouts in Denver's public transportation system can make getting around town easy—and fun! Regional Transportation District (RTD) information: (303) 299–6000; www.rtd-denver.com.

LIGHT RAIL

Light rail began service in 1994. The Central Corridor line runs right through downtown. On Denver's south side, a large Park-n-Ride at I–25 and Broadway makes it easy for riders to leave their cars (Free parking). Purchase train tickets (under a dollar on weekends and off-peak hours) from vending machines at the station. The tracks are ground level, and trains come every ten minutes midday, every six minutes during rush hour. Consider riding it with your children just to let them experience another form of transportation.

16TH STREET MALL SHUTTLE

It's Free—and frequent! The shuttle runs along the otherwise free-of-traffic pedestrian mall, from the Civic Center to LoDo (lower downtown). The electric buses are scheduled so closely that there's usually one in sight. So if the kids start to whine about the walk as you sightsee along the mall, just hop on the shuttle.

CULTURAL TROLLEY

One of the best ways to experience Denver's most popular tourist attractions is to climb aboard the Cultural Connection Trolley (303–289–2841). From Memorial Day through Labor Day, RTD provides this special bus service. The thirty-stop route includes such diverse interests as the Denver Museum of Nature and Science, Botanic Gardens, Cherry Creek shopping, and Coors Field. For the price of one ticket ($) you can ride all day, getting on or off as many times as you like. The Visitors Center and the Market Street or Civic Center bus depots have maps, schedules, and tickets. Or you can purchase tickets on the bus itself. The eye-catching red-and-green "trolley" picks up passengers at bus stops marked "CC Trolley Stop" every half hour, seven days a week.

True to its name, the Colorado History Museum presents early life in Colorado. It is a good stop for a quick look at the Native Americans, pioneers, trappers, traders, and cowboys who shaped the state.

The Irma Bartels exhibit usually interests kids. Irma was born in Denver in 1888. When she died suddenly from pneumonia at age twelve, her parents gathered her favorite possessions—toys, clothes, books, even some schoolwork—into a large trunk. The trunk was passed down through the family and donated to the museum in 1975. The objects and photographs in this exhibit represent a typical childhood in Colorado at that time.

Peek into the Broadway Classroom to see what a typical schoolroom looked like at the turn of the twentieth century. And be sure to ask about the museum's special exhibits. They often run for an extended period, and the topics are intriguing.

DENVER PUBLIC LIBRARY (all ages)

10 West 14th Avenue Parkway and Broadway, Denver 80204; (303) 640–6200; www.denver.lib.co.us. Open Monday through Wednesday 10:00 A.M. to 9:00 P.M., Thursday through Saturday 10:00 A.M. to 5:30 P.M., and Sunday 1:00 to 5:00 P.M. **Free**.

Designed to reflect the shapes and colors of other buildings around Civic Center Park, the seven-story Denver Public Library houses 1.5 million books on 47 miles of shelves and includes a world-class western history and art collection. Once a day, a **Free** one-hour tour gives visitors an overview of the facility. An orientation video runs continuously near the east entry.

The Children's Library has a self-guided tour laid out as an adventure game. Ask the librarian for a form. "Family Weekends" offer **Free** activities each Saturday and Sunday. Sample topics include Sign Language, Drumming, and Bugs! Bugs! Bugs! Schedules are available by the month.

The library is located between the history museum and the art museum, so it's an easy quick stop. Look for fossils embedded in the floor and walls on the main floor and in the outdoor stonework. Just outside the Children's Library, *The Yearling*, a sculpture by Donald Lipski, is sure to elicit comments from each family member.

DENVER ART MUSEUM (all ages)

100 West 14th Avenue Parkway, Denver 80204; (303) 640–4433; www.denver artmuseum.org. Open Tuesday and Thursday through Saturday 10:00 A.M. to 5:00 P.M., Wednesday 10:00 A.M. to 9:00 P.M., and Sunday noon to 5:00 P.M. $

Easy to spot, this building has been described as an Italian castle wrapped in aluminum foil. Two seven-story towers display the largest art collection between Kansas City and the West Coast. This family-friendly museum offers an amazing array of **Free** activities for children. Eye Spy games enliven every floor, and many exhibits include interactive stations. Kids Corner, in the first-floor lobby, has a new art project each month. Directions and materials are ready and waiting.

If you visit on a weekend, from 10:30 A.M. to 4:00 P.M. on Saturday and from noon to 4:00 P.M. on Sunday, check out a family back-pack, full of hands-on games and activities that lead you through the galleries. Along the way, you're likely to encounter several Art Stops, places where you can pick up and handle art objects and talk to museum interpreters. On the first Saturday of each month, the art museum presents family workshops—gallery games and art activities designed for families with children ages five to nine. Check out the museum's family fun on the Web at www.wackykids.org for art projects they can print and do at home.

Fun Facts

Due to its elevation of 5,280 feet, Denver is known as the "Mile High City." Consequently, visitors to the state capitol often photograph the step on the west side of the building, which is marked as being ONE MILE ABOVE SEA LEVEL. In 1969, however, students from the engineering school at Colorado State University found the measurement to be incorrect. As a result of their finding, a geodetic survey plug was placed three steps above the original marker and now serves as the accurate "mile high" designation.

The bronze sculpture of an Indian hunter standing over a buffalo on the east lawn of the capitol grounds was created by sculptor Preston Powers, and the cast was made by artisans in Florence, Italy. Before arriving in Denver, the masterpiece was displayed at the 1893 Chicago World's Fair.

The Colorado rose-onyx marble wainscoting, located throughout the capitol building, contains more than a thousand designs that resemble animals, objects, and faces of famous people. Among those easily recognized are George Washington, Molly Brown (Denver socialite and *Titanic* heroine), and Franklin Delano Roosevelt.

The gift shop carries an assortment of books, games, and trinkets for kids, along with items for shoppers on a bigger budget. While Palettes Restaurant is a bit upscale for a relaxing meal with young ones, Palettes Express offers tasty salads, sandwiches, desserts, and beverages in a deli setting.

Home Cookin' Down on the Farm

White Fence Farm, 6263 West Jewell Avenue, Lakewood 80232, between Sheridan and Wadsworth Boulevards (just twenty minutes from downtown Denver); (303) 935–5945; www.whitefencefarm.com. Open Tuesday through Saturday 4:30 to 8:30 P.M. and Sunday 11:30 A.M. to 8:00 P.M. Closed Monday and the month of January.

The motto of the White Fence Farm restaurant in Lakewood, a western suburb of Denver, is "The best food in town is down on the farm." And so is one of the nicest dining experiences. Come early, give your name to the hostess, and then stroll the beautifully landscaped grounds. Let your children climb the ladder to a handsome Bavarian-style tree house with shutters, flower boxes, and shake roof. Walk through the trellised rose arbors, sit a spell in the gazebo, or borrow a croquet set for a game before dinner. Then take your children to the barn to see the chickens, goats, horse, cow, and woolly sheep. Step into the Country Store for a memento or two. And when you are called to dinner, sit down to a family-style meal of delicious fried chicken, salads, mashed potatoes and gravy, and homemade pies like only Grandma could make. This is like Sunday dinner used to be, but you don't have to do the dishes.

DENVER MINT (ages 4 and up)

320 West Colfax Avenue (between Cherokee and Delaware Streets), Denver 80204; (303) 405–4761; www.usmint.gov. Open year-round, Monday through Friday. Entry to the mint by guided tour only; the visitors' entrance is on Cherokee Street. Security is tight, and many regulations apply since September 11. Visitors are advised to check www.usmint.gov for instructions on how to obtain admission for touring the facility. Permission to tour must be obtained at least two weeks before your visit. The mint is usually closed for yearly inventory the last week of June and the first week of July; call to confirm the actual dates. Free. The Mint Gift Shop, located at 333 West Colfax Avenue, across the street from the mint, is open Monday through Friday from 9:00 A.M. to 3:00 P.M. It offers money-related items for the entire family, from numismatic collectibles to toys, games, and clothing.

If you want to prove to your kids that money doesn't grow on trees, take them for a tour of the Denver Mint. Here they will see the various steps in minting coins. While soundproofing cubicles around each stamping machine diminish the view, you still see shiny copper-clad pennies tumbling into carts. Looking down on an estimated half-million dollars' worth of coinage, adults and kids gape into the weighing and bagging area. Using handheld sewing machines, workers close cloth bags of coins and neatly stack them onto pallets. From here all the coins are shipped to Federal Reserve Banks.

The final stop on the tour, the salesroom, provides an opportunity to purchase souvenir coin sets, commemorative coins, and other numismatic treasures. For a quarter, mint personnel place a blank in an old press, and *you* push the button to strike a souvenir medal. Every child in your family will want one. For a color catalog showcasing gift items, phone (202) 283–2646.

DENVER FIREFIGHTERS MUSEUM (ages 2 and up)

1326 Tremont Place, Denver 80204 (across from the Denver Mint); (303) 892–1436; www.colorado2.com/museum. Open year-round, except on holidays, Monday through Saturday. Summer months open from 10:00 A.M. to 4:00 P.M.; winter months open from 10:00 A.M. to 2:00 P.M. $

What kid, big or little, wouldn't love the opportunity to climb aboard a gleaming white fire truck, ring the bell, take hold of the steering wheel, and pretend to race the vehicle to a raging fire? Kids can do this and a whole lot more at Old Firehouse No. 1, a Denver landmark with a listing on the National Register of Historic Places. Youngsters are invited to try on firefighters' coats, hats, and boots; listen as the tour guide relates harrowing stories about blazes of long ago; and watch a video about fire safety featuring Jimminy Cricket and Donald Duck. Among the fire-fighting apparatus you will see are hand-drawn hook-and-ladder carts, buckets once used for bucket brigades, horse-drawn pumpers, and wonderful old fire trucks. Be sure to take a peek upstairs to see the former sleeping area and the "fire laddies'" old metal cots. A pair of boots sits on the floor beside each bed.

16TH STREET MALL (all ages)

The 16th Street Mall, a mile-long, outdoor pedestrian promenade, runs through the heart of Denver, connecting the Civic Center to LoDo. **Free** shuttle buses leave each end of the mall. Hop on and off as often as you please for easy access to shopping, restaurants, and attractions.

Pedal Pleasures

Bicycling Magazine named Denver one of the top-ten best cities in the nation for bicycling. And it's no wonder—there are more than 450 miles of biking trails in the Denver metro area. Maps (including descriptions of the routes and rankings from easy to difficult) are free at the Denver Metro Convention and Visitors Bureau. Commercial pamphlets and books are available at metro Denver bookstores.

A good place to start is at Confluence Park in downtown Denver. You can follow the creek all the way to Cherry Creek Reservoir (16^1/$_{10}$ miles one way) or just traverse the distance that works best for all members of your family. This is a gentle ride, avoiding traffic via bike underpasses. Or perhaps you'd like to cycle through City Park. A 3½-mile jaunt will take you leisurely past Duck Lake, City Park Lake, tennis courts, playing fields, the Museum of Nature and Science, and the southwest side of the zoo. Pause beside the zoo to listen for the cries of the peacocks and other assorted animal calls. This is an easy ride, with lots of opportunities for stopping to rest along the way.

DENVER PAVILIONS (all ages)

Mid-downtown Denver, along the 16th Street Mall; (303) 260–6000; www. denverpavilions.com.

The Denver Pavilions complex—offering entertainment facilities, restaurants, and retail shops—covers 2 entire mid-town city blocks. At this polestar of energy and activity, you'll find numerous restaurants, including the Wolfgang Puck Cafe and the Hard Rock Cafe. You can snack at the Corner Bakery and the 16th Street Deli, chow down at Margarita Mama's Mexican Cantina, and dine in style at Maggiano's Little Italy. You can browse the dozens of specialty shops, including the GAP Kids store, Nike Town (as much an entertainment center as it is a retail outlet), Barnes and Noble's two-level bookstore, and Virgin Megastore, the most successful music merchandiser in the world. When it's time to rest, you can choose a family-appropriate movie at the two-level United Artists theater featuring thirteen screens and 3,500 seats.

DENVER CENTER FOR THE PERFORMING ARTS (ages 4 and up)

1245 Champa Street, Denver 80204; in mid-downtown Denver. The box office is located at the corner of 14th and Curtis Streets; (303) 893–4100 or (800) 641–1222; www.denvercenter.org. Open Monday through Saturday 10:00 A.M. to 6:00 P.M. Daily performance information: (303) 893–3272. $$$–$$$$

The Denver Center for the Performing Arts (DCPA), with nine theaters that cover 4 square blocks, is the second-largest complex of its kind in the nation, surpassed only by New York City's Lincoln Center. "The Plex," as it is known locally, features music, opera, theater, and ballet. Always popular with families, *The Nutcracker Suite* ballet is an annual event.

Operating within the DCPA is the Denver Center Theatre Company (DCTC), a nurturing ground for new plays, a national training school for actors, and the site of some of the most dynamic live theater in the Rocky Mountain West. The largest resident professional theater company between Chicago and the West Coast, the DCTC includes four theaters plus the Denver Center Theatre Academy, with classes in acting, voice, creative dramatics, playwriting, and stage taught by working professionals. For information phone (303) 893–4000.

Also operating within the DCPA is the Wilbur James Gould Voice Center (V.C.), with an extensive voice laboratory that conducts research on the human and synthetic voice, assists persons with voice disorders, and hosts **Free** voice workshops designed to prevent vocal problems. The V.C. is funded by a grant from the National Institute of Deafness and Other Communication Disorders.

Day-Tripper: Downtown Adventure

Explore the Mile High City's downtown area without worrying about driving and parking. Leave your chariot in the **Free** Broadway Park-n-Ride at I–25 and Broadway. Board the light rail for a short ride into the city. Watch for the 16th Street Mall stop.

The outdoor pedestrian mall is lined with shops and restaurants—something for everyone. Corporate giants such as Nike Town, Media Play, and the Hard Rock Cafe intermingled with artisan carts and chess players make this an interesting stroll. Walk west until the mall ends at Market Street, or jump on the **Free** shuttle that runs up and down the mall.

A short walk along Market Street brings you to Coors Field, home of the Colorado Rockies, where you can take the one-hour ballpark tour. When you finish exploring, take the light rail back to the Broadway station to retrieve your car.

If you're ready for dinner, the Blue Bonnet Cafe is just a mile north at 457 South Broadway. This family-run restaurant has been pleasing Denverites with great Mexican food for more than thirty years. It's popular, so go early.

Part of the Plex, the National Theatre Conservatory Library harbors a sizable collection of scripts, criticism, periodicals, and books about theater. The general public is welcome to use the library by appointment. For information call (303) 446–4869.

SKI TRAIN (ages 2 and up)

The Ski Train departs Union Station at 17th and Wynkoop Streets in lower downtown Denver (LoDo) (303–296–4754; www.skitrain.com). Saturday and Sunday, mid-December to early April; additional days during holidays, February, and March. The train leaves Denver at 7:15 A.M., arriving back at Union Station at 6:45 P.M. Summer hours are 8:00 A.M. to 6:00 P.M., mid-June to mid-August. Generous discounts are available on children's fares in summer, and passengers may buy discounted lift tickets on board the train. $$$$

In the winter, the Ski Train takes skiers, and those who just like to ride trains, from Denver's historic Union Station for a day at Winter Park.

Departing early in the morning, the train glides through 56 miles of breathtakingly beautiful mountain vistas while climbing 4,000 feet in elevation. It skirts sheer cliff walls; travels high above roaring, ice-banked rivers; and burrows through twenty-nine tunnels, including the Moffat Tunnel, the highest passenger train tunnel in the United States. The ride takes two and a half hours in each direction. Passengers relax in reclining seats and watch the pristine wilderness slide past their windows. Three snack cars and two cafe lounge cars provide food and beverages for purchase.

 ## COORS FIELD (all ages)

20th and Blake Streets; (303) 762–5437 or (800) 388–7625; www.colorado rockies.com. Game tickets $–$$$$, depending on location; tours $6.00 adults, $4.00 children 5 and older and seniors 65 and older. Phone for times.

Built in the classic style of Fenway Park and Wrigley Field, Coors Field is an old-fashioned ballpark almost in the center of town. The red-brick exterior, live organist, and "muscle board" (scoreboard changed by hand) hark back to the good old days. The wide, tree-lined perimeter of this park edges LoDo, Denver's hottest place to be. Art galleries, boutiques, bistros, and sports bars attract crowds along the surrounding streets, day and night.

The Rockies encourage families to come on out to the ballgames. Youngsters merit special attention on the Buckaroo's concourse. Here, a fast-food stand with lower counters offers them smaller portions at smaller prices. Madeline's, an ice-cream shop, serves the world's best ice cream—at least according to Madeline, granddaughter of Rockies owner Jerry McMorris. For those under 4 feet tall, there's a playground where Dinger, the Rockies mascot, often visits. In designated family-seating sections, no alcohol is allowed.

*B*aseball on a Budget

To make a major-league ballgame an affordable family adventure, purchase seats in the Rockpile and pack a picnic. Many games at Coors Field are sold out; however, an allotment of Rockpile (straightaway centerfield) seats goes on sale two and a half hours before game time. Cost for Rockpile seats is $4.00 for adults, $1.00 for children twelve and younger and seniors fifty-five and older. A lenient food-and-beverage policy throughout the park allows fans to bring their own treats.

Even if the Rockies are on the road or it's winter, Coors Field is a great stop. A one-hour tour will take you into the visitors' locker room, a luxury box, the press box, and out to the home team's dugout.

Be sure to examine *Evolution of the Ball,* just outside the park. It's a tongue-in-cheek sculptured arch paying homage to the ball—including gumball, eyeball, and Lucille Ball.

CENTRAL PLATTE VALLEY

Along the South Platte River from Colfax Avenue north to 23rd Street.

In 1858 a prospector spotted flakes of gold near the confluence of Cherry Creek and the South Platte River, and the rush was on.

Once the location of Denver's first crude buildings and gold-rush-incited tent city, the Central Platte Valley today attracts those seeking sports and entertainment. Paved paths along both the river and creek bring in-line skaters, cyclists, joggers, and parents pushing strollers to Confluence Park. Six Flags Elitch Gardens Amusement Park; the Ocean Journey aquarium; playgrounds; the Children's Museum; and the Pepsi Center, Denver's newest arena for professional hockey and basketball, draw visitors of all ages. Just to the west stands Invesco Field at Mile High, home to the Denver Broncos and an REI (Recreation Equipment Incorporated) mega-store providing outdoor enthusiasts the opportunity to try out climbing equipment, bicycles, and kayaks before buying. Again, the rush is on.

SIX FLAGS ELITCH GARDENS (ages 2 and up)

Six Flags Elitch Gardens is located in Denver's Platte Valley, near I–25 and Speer Boulevard; (303) 595–4386. Open May through October, weather permitting, varying days and hours. Water park open Memorial Day through Labor Day, 11:00 A.M. to 7:00 P.M. Admission includes entry to both the amusement park and the water park. $$$–$$$$, depending on age. Admission is Free for ages 3 and younger or 70 and older. Parking $7.00.

In 1890 John and Mary Elitch turned their small vegetable farm and apple orchards into picnic areas and ball fields and opened them to the public. Over the years a theater that hosted such luminaries as Sarah Bernhardt, Edward G. Robinson, and Grace Kelly was added, along with amusement rides, extensive gardens, and a dance pavilion. In 1995, after continual operation for more than 104 years, the park was relocated near the center of the city.

This park features seemingly endless major attractions, including the 300-foot-tall Total Tower with an observation platform. The vista offers a perfect orientation to the park plus views of downtown Denver and three of the Rocky Mountains' 14,000-foot peaks (Pikes Peak, Mt. Evans, and Longs Peak).

Exciting rides include the Tower of Doom, a controlled free-fall from twenty-two stories in the sky; Disaster Canyon, where riders experience the thrill of white-water rafting while they whirl through churning, surging rapids; and X-C.A.P.E., an interactive ride that lets you, as pilot, escape the bounds of earth by controlling the altitude and angle of your flight, even allowing you to dive from dizzying heights of 100 feet. Other attractions include the 100-foot-high Ferris wheel and the spinning teacups. A 1905 carousel, fully restored in 1995, features sixty-seven exquisitely hand-carved animals and chariots—a park highlight for visitors of every age.

Coaster aficionados find three choices for their ultimate thrill. Twister II, a wooden coaster in the classic style, reaches nearly 100 feet at its highest point. A steel coaster, Sidewinder, blasts passengers twice through a giant loop, forward and in reverse. On Mind Eraser riders hang suspended, feet dangling, from the looping, iron-clad track soaring ten stories skyward before plummeting at 60 miles per hour.

The park has approximately 84,000 square feet of garden space and extensive landscaping that includes acres of lawn and flowerbeds and nearly 3,000 trees. Of special note are the topiary carousel horses and other figures placed throughout the grounds.

The $4 million StarToon Studios complex contains twelve kid-size rides in a cartoon-studio setting. The centerpiece of this interactive playland is the Foam Factory, where thousands of colorful foam balls fly hither and yon, scoring hits on participants and spectators alike. Children enter a three-story-high enclosure where flashing lights and sirens heighten the excitement as cannons fire foam balls, and huge baskets at the top of the cage rain their cargos of spongy spheres down upon players far below. This incredible cage of chaos appeals to all kids, from toddlers to teens.

At the Turntable Arcade your family will find ten different games, including state-of-the-art video games from around the world. This is a good place to cool off on a hot summer day by entering the Water Wars Battle Zone and catapulting water balloons onto your opponent's battle station. Count on getting wet. If you end up the loser (and that means getting soaked), this may become your kids' favorite game.

Included in your admission to Six Flags Elitch Gardens is Island Kingdom, an expansive tropical paradise packed with water adventures for the whole family. Here you will find dozens of twisting and turning water slides; a five-story water play structure with more than seventy-five interactive features; a huge treehouse anchored in the center of Hook's Lagoon; a meandering, peaceful river to float down; soaking pools; and sunning spaces.

Ice-Cream Breaks

There's nothing like an ice-cream cone to lift the spirits. Squelch that backseat squabbling or refresh tired sight-seers with a simple treat. No matter what end of town you're in, you're not far from a delicious delight.

Bonnie Brae Ice Cream, *799 South University Boulevard, Denver 80206; (303) 777–0808.*

Cold Stone Creamery, *14233 West Colfax Avenue, Golden 80401; (303) 215–9364.*

Lik's Ice Cream Parlor, *2039 East 13th Avenue, Denver 80206; (303) 321–2370.*

Maggie Moo's Ice Cream and Treatery, *735 South Colorado Boulevard, Denver 80246; (303) 722–9991.*

Soda Rock Cafe, *2217 East Mississippi Avenue, Denver 80210; (303) 777–0414.*

OCEAN JOURNEY (all ages)

700 Water Street, Denver 80211. Located in the Platte Valley just east of the Children's Museum, exit 211 from I–25; (303) 561–4450 or (888) 561–4450; www.oceanjourney.org. Open every day except Christmas, 10:00 A.M. to 6:00 P.M. Last ticket sold at 5:00 P.M. Open Thanksgiving 10:00 A.M. to 2:00 P.M. Last ticket sold at 1:00 P.M. $$–$$$; parking $$.

After a sixty-five-million-year absence, the ocean returns to Denver. This state-of-the-art aquarium takes visitors on river journeys from the Continental Divide to the Sea of Cortez and from an Indonesian rain forest (complete with two very real Sumatran tigers) to the Pacific Ocean. Standing on the boardwalk in River Otter Cove, you'll find your-selves entertained by otter antics. In the Sea of Cortez visitors walk through an acrylic tube while the fish swim over, under, and around. Temperature changes, scents, recorded sounds, and special lighting effects enhance the realistic presentations. And there are touch tanks!

Put this stop on your "don't miss" list. But be advised that officials are anticipating one million visitors a year, and that's a conservative projection. Plan on a crowd and leave the stroller at home. Borrow (free) a museum backpack and tote your wee ones at a level where they can easily see the exhibits.

 CHILDREN'S MUSEUM (all ages)

At I–25 and 23rd Street, exit 211; 2121 Children's Museum Drive, Denver 80211; (303) 433–7444; www.cmdenver.org. The teal-and-raspberry building is easy to spot. Open Tuesday through Friday 9:00 A.M. to 4:00 P.M. and Saturday and Sunday 10:00 A.M. to 5:00 P.M.; also open Monday, June through August. Toddler hour Tuesday and Thursday 9:30 to 10:30 A.M. $

For kids who love to touch—and what kid doesn't? This hands-on facility has been a favorite with Denver kids for more than twenty-five years, celebrating curiosity and creativity. The Children's Museum, a nonprofit facility, provides stimulating ideas and learning experiences for children and their families. With innovative, hands-on exhibits, the-ater performances, educational programs, and special events, the museum encourages youngsters to create, explore, discover, imagine, and just plain have fun. The museum is geared to those ages two through twelve, but older siblings are welcome to tag along.

The museum's Science Lab provides guided experiments and demon-strations in biology, chemistry, and physics. CompuLAB allows users to manipulate, explore, and create computer programs and to access the Internet. At StormCenter 4, a mock television weather studio, kids can produce videos on weather and geography. Children learn about length, width, weight, and height through a basketball theme at the Starwise exhibit. Here they test how high they can jump, play basketball using regulation and miniature-size hoops, and try on shoes and jerseys from members of the Denver Nuggets basketball team.

Toddlers through kindergartners won't want to leave Play Partners, a whimsical "Goldilocks and the Three Bears" playhouse with child-size furniture and an upstairs loft.

Toddler's Morning Out

Want to spend some special time with the toddler in your life? One stop offers a morning of activities. The Children's Museum has a special toddler hour every Tuesday and Thursday from 9:30 to 10:30 A.M. Afterward hop aboard the Platte Valley Trolley and watch for wildlife along the river. Bring a snack or lunch to enjoy while romping at the Gates Crescent Park playground, especially toddler-friendly with soft landing surfaces. It will be nap time before you realize it.

BLACK AMERICA WEST MUSEUM AND HERITAGE CENTER (ages 5 and up)

3091 California Street, Denver 80205; (303) 292–2566. Open daily May through September, 10:00 A.M. to 5:00 P.M. October through April, Wednesday through Friday 10:00 A.M. to 2:00 P.M. and Saturday and Sunday noon to 5:00 P.M. $, children 4 and younger **Free**.

The former home of Dr. Justina Ford, the first African-American female doctor in the state of Colorado, is now a museum. Housing a remarkable collection of memorabilia and artifacts, this is one of the most comprehensive sources of historic materials representing African-American western pioneers.

The assemblage began as a personal hobby of Paul Stewart, an African American who was forced as a child to always take the role of the Indian when playing cowboys and Indians with his white friends, because his chums insisted that there had never been a "black cowboy." Imagine his surprise when, as an adult, he met exactly that—a black cowboy who had led many a cattle drive at the turn of the twentieth century. That was all Stewart needed. He became a self-taught historian and curator, determined to search out and make known the African-American influence on the settlement of the West.

Paul Stewart's personal collection became the nucleus for today's museum, opened in 1971. He unearthed letters, photographs, documents, and oral histories proving that nearly a third of the cowboys who helped settle the West were black. It may not be recorded in history books, but documents on display at the museum reveal that black families came west in covered wagons and established all-black towns, filling the necessary positions of merchant, blacksmith, doctor, teacher, and banker. African Americans were among the West's earliest millionaires, owning vast amounts of real estate and prominent businesses. At the museum you can see saddles, spurs, rifles, and vintage photographs—hundreds of items pertaining to the black influence on the Old West.

 MUSEUM OF MINIATURES, DOLLS AND TOYS (ages 4–12)
1880 Gaylord Street, Denver 80206; (303) 322–1053; www.coloradokids.com/ miniatures. Open Tuesday through Saturday 10:00 A.M. to 4:00 P.M. and Sunday 1:00 to 4:00 P.M. $

Although the Museum of Miniatures, Dolls and Toys is for the most part a no-touch museum, children, especially little girls, love wandering through its eight galleries. Permanent and changing exhibits include scale-model dollhouses, a teddy bear closet, and a wonderful collection of Steiff stuffed animals.

Located in the 1899 Dutch Colonial Revival–style Pearce-McAllister Cottage, the museum showcases more than 10,000 miniatures, toys, and dolls. The house is listed on the National Register of Historic Places and contains one room filled with the priceless antique furnishings of the former owners, Phebe and Henry McAllister.

One entire gallery of the museum, the fourth largest of its kind in the United States, is devoted to Southwestern miniatures. A nine-room adobe dollhouse features hand-woven wool Native American rugs, authentic Santa Clara Pueblo pottery, hand-woven Papago baskets from Arizona, hand-carved furniture, kiva fireplaces, and hanging *ristras* (decorative swags) of tiny red chilies.

Holding court in another chamber, the Kingscote Dollhouse is an exact replica of a circa-1839 Carpenter Gothic mansion that still stands in Newport, Rhode Island. The three-story, 1-inch-scale house is 6½ feet long, weighs 250 pounds, and boasts sixteen rooms. The floors are oak, teak, cherry, and Brazilian rosewood parquet. The Chippendale dining-room furniture, made of lustrous cherrywood, was imported from England. The dining-room table is set with eighteen-karat-gold flatware, hand-painted porcelain dishes, and handsome crystal stemware rimmed in fourteen-karat gold. A sterling-silver candelabra serves as the centerpiece.

Of special note are the nineteenth-century Dutch and German "cabinet houses" in a cupboardlike enclosure. These are the forerunners of today's dollhouses and once belonged to extremely wealthy women of the period.

DENVER CITY PARK (all ages)

Located north of 17th Avenue, between Colorado Boulevard and York Street.
Free.

City Park is home to the Denver Zoo and the Museum of Nature and Science. But it's also a large park with three lakes, a formal rose garden, athletic fields, and a public golf course. There are two playgrounds, paddleboats for rent, and lots of picnic areas. Be sure to stop at the playground just outside the zoo's west entrance. Your kids' eyes will light up when they see the massive community-built layout. An appealing gorilla sculpture, carved from a tree trunk, overlooks the area.

DENVER MUSEUM OF NATURE AND SCIENCE

2001 Colorado Boulevard, Denver 80205 (in City Park); (303) 322–7009 or (800) 925–2250; www.DMNS.org. Open daily 9:00 A.M. to 5:00 P.M. Summer extended hours, Tuesday 9:00 A.M. to 7:00 P.M. and Sunday 10:00 A.M. to 7:00 P.M. IMAX additional fee; combination tickets available. $$

"Entertain your brain" is its motto, and it's well deserved. From the moment a giant tyrannosaurus greets you at the main entrance, you'll be hooked. Try on mule deer ears (not real!) to see how they funnel sound. Push the button to smell what attracts a doe to a buck. Feel the fuzz on antlers. The Edge of the Wild is just one of many interactive exhibits that fascinate children (and grown-ups) with the wonders of the natural world. From the hoofprints in the floor to the recorded animal sounds, you'll be immersed in this western habitat.

In Coors Mineral Hall visit Tom's Baby, Colorado's largest gold specimen, which is displayed in a safe. Glow-in-the-dark rocks, birthstones, and diamonds intrigue kids here.

Of particular interest to children is the permanent **Prehistoric Journey** exhibit, where they can experience prehistoric times through an extraordinary display of fossils, interactive technology, videos, touchable specimens, and time stations.

The most ambitious exhibit in the museum, Prehistoric Journey was six years in the making. Designed to stimulate, excite, and satisfy the curiosity of children and adults, the $7.7-million, 17,000-square-foot dis-

Raindrops Keep Falling on My Head

Denver, a city that boasts 300 days of sunshine a year, still gets a little rain. Even on the sunniest summer days, the clouds often roll in during the afternoon, delivering a brief thunderstorm. So where can you take your kids until our perfect weather returns?

The Denver Museum of Nature and Science is not the stuffy, dead-bones sort of museum you may remember from childhood. DMNS is loaded with dinosaurs, glow-in-the-dark rocks and minerals, an interactive Hall of Life, and the IMAX Theater. There's decent food in an informal setting, and the gift store has quality, yet affordable, souvenirs.

The zoo is usually a sunny-day destination, but the Denver Zoo also has many indoor exhibits. Wandering through climate-controlled Tropical Discovery or Bird World, you'll forget the rain. The Hungry Elephant provides indoor dining, right next door to the gift shop.

play encompasses a working fossil laboratory with public viewing areas, more than 500 real fossil specimens, and a total of twelve dinosaur skeletons, seven dinosaur skulls, and two fleshed-out dinosaurs enhanced by innovative lighting and astonishing sound effects.

You begin your journey with a time-travel theater production where you are taken back 4.5 billion years to the origins of Earth and then brought up to 3.5 billion years ago, when the first forms of life are said to have appeared. Next you move from the theater into the sights and sounds of ancient worlds. You pass by natural habitat scenes and walk through "enviroramas."

When you arrive at the Nebraska Woodland Envirorama, you will witness Nebraska as it was twenty million years ago. A giant dinohyus appears on a distant ridge in pursuit of a herd of small camels, and a salivating, vicious-looking carnivore resembling a giant wild boar (nicknamed the "Terminator Pig") grunts menacingly. From the distance is heard the sound of rumbling thunder.

Space Odyssey, which opens in 2003, will be the museum's most ambitious project in its one-hundred-year history. It will establish the Denver Museum of Nature and Science as the leading space-science resource in the Rocky Mountain region. State-of-the-art technology and participatory experiences will provide visitors with the feeling that they are traveling across the universe without ever leaving the ground.

Plan to spend at least an hour in **The Hall of Life,** where interactive stations will help you learn more about your body. What's good for you, what's not? As you enter you'll receive a plastic card that will activate exhibits on fitness, the five senses, stress, reproduction, drugs, and alcohol. Since this hall is so popular with local families and school groups, you might try to visit at an off time—late afternoon on a weekday.

The **IMAX Theater** is not your typical neighborhood movie house. The screen is nearly five stories high, the surround sound is state-of-the-art, and the film subjects are spectacular. You can call ahead to reserve tickets for specific show times.

Where Are They? Elves, Yoda, and Galileo can be found by eagle-eyed observers in the museum dioramas, paintings, and murals. Spotting the elves painted into the Kent Pendelton backgrounds is a favorite activity for Denver children. Places to search include Edge of the Wild, Explore Colorado, and Prehistoric Journey. If you want help, Guest Services will provide a "Museum Secrets" guide sheet. In the IMAX lobby check out the large Tom Buchannon painting for hidden *Star Wars* images. The search will make detectives out of all of you.

DENVER ZOO (all ages)

Located on 23rd Avenue, between Colorado Boulevard and York Street (in City Park); (303) 376–4800; www.denverzoo.org. Open daily year-round, October through March, 10:00 A.M. to 5:00 P.M.; April through September, 9:00 A.M. to 6:00 P.M. It's important to note that Bird World and Tropical Discovery close at 4:00 P.M., and snack stands sometimes close early, so don't wait too long to take care of the hungries. Push chairs, little red wagons, and strollers are available for rent. $–$$, depending on age; children 3 or younger Free. *Check for free days during the off-season.*

Founded in 1896, the Denver Zoo features more than 3,500 animals representing 642 species. An accredited member of the American Zoo and Aquarium Association, it draws visitors from coast to coast. It gained worldwide attention by successfully hand-raising two polar bear cubs.

Primate Panorama, a five-acre, $10-million facility, houses more than twenty-five species of primates, from tiny squirrel monkeys to 400-pound gorillas, all in environments that resemble their natural habitats. Visitors enter the area through an African village setting with bamboo and thatch-roofed structures and view the primates from special blinds that allow them to stand as close as 15 feet to a gorilla with seemingly nothing in between. Thick vegetation, outdoor streams, and waterfalls simulate a tropical setting.

Wildlights Each December the Denver Zoo turns into a spectacular winter wonderland when thousands of sparkling lights in animal shapes enhance the pathways and animal enclosures for the nightly Wildlights extravaganza. Bundle the kids up in scarves, mittens, and caps, and participate in this festive tradition. Here's an opportunity to view the animals at night, when many species are more active. Music, caroling by local choirs, and roasting chestnuts add to the holiday atmosphere. In the Northern Shores area Santa listens to wish lists. Visitors are encouraged to bring along a nonperishable food item to be distributed to the less fortunate. Wildlights takes place the month of December. Call the zoo for exact times (303-376-4800). $; no charge for children three or younger.

Artists, biologists, curators, veterinarians, architects, and horticulturists helped design and construct this fascinating facility, which contains one of the country's largest outdoor habitats dedicated to the endangered lowland gorilla. According to Clayton Freiheit, director of the Denver Zoo, "Primate Panorama replicates primate habitats to such a degree that we can establish normal social groups, increase breeding potential, and explain to our visitors the vital role of modern zoos as leaders in global conservation efforts. Primate Panorama's mission concentrates on caring for the animals' needs and stimulating normal social behaviors by creating spacious naturalistic habitats."

The zoo's Bird World, with spacious indoor and outdoor habitats, contains more than 500 birds, including threatened and endangered species from around the world. The endangered African black-footed penguin, the Bali mynah, and the black palm cockatoo, along with numerous other species, are involved in the zoo's highly specialized breeding programs. A colony of six endangered Humboldt penguins resides in a replica of a Chilean intertidal coastline, complete with rocky cliffs for nesting. Chilly water and faux sea kelp make this area seem like home to the penguins.

Another not-to-miss attraction is Tropical Discovery, a 45-foot-tall glass pyramid where you can view more than 1,200 animals in a rain-forest environment. You'll see venomous and nonvenomous snakes, vampire bats, alligators, and a capybara, the world's largest rodent.

Be sure to check out the Pachyderm Habitats, the indoor-outdoor Giraffe House, and Bear Mountain. Northern Shores houses sea lions, polar bears, and other Arctic wildlife. Don't forget to stop by the nursery to check if there are any new zoo babies to observe. Wildlife Theater, with animal shows, and a Komodo dragon exhibit are both popular attractions.

For a nominal fee hop aboard the open-air Zoo Liner; a narrated spin around the park can help you plan your visit. Or take a lift when legs are beginning to tire and little feet have taken too many steps. Ride with your youngsters on the zoo's Pioneer Train, the first natural gas-powered train ride in the country.

Day-Tripper: City Park Adventure

Pack a picnic lunch and head to City Park. Here the Denver Zoo and the Museum of Nature and Science offer hours of family fun. Choose one or do both. The park itself has lots of areas to run and play games, and you can rent paddle-boats during summer months. The community-built playground, just outside the zoo's west entrance, is exceptional; picnic tables are close by.

Just 6 blocks east of the park at 23rd Avenue and Dexter, you'll find Scones and Cones, a good place for a late afternoon pick-me-up. Ice-cream cones for the kids, a muffin and latte for you?

If you're about ready for dinner, Cherry Tomato is a great pick. Also located at 23rd Avenue and Dexter, this neighborhood corner restaurant is owned and operated by four families. You'll be very comfortable with kids here as you enjoy a delicious Italian meal (303-377-1914).

If you need a little exercise after dinner, there's a small playground across the street. Or take a walk in this lovely old neighborhood.

MOLLY BROWN HOUSE (ages 6 and up)

1340 Pennsylvania Street, Denver 80203; (303) 832–4092; www.mollybrown. org. Open Monday through Saturday 9:30 A.M. to 4:00 P.M. and Sunday noon to 4:00 P.M. Closed on Monday September through May and on all major holidays. $–$$, children 5 and younger Free.

If your children's history lessons have included the voyage and sinking of the *Titanic,* they may be interested in seeing the former home of the "Unsinkable Molly Brown." Molly Brown is credited with taking command of one of the *Titanic*'s lifeboats and suppressing a panic.

Located in Denver's historic Capitol Hill District, the three-story home is filled with priceless antiques, many of which were once owned by the spirited Molly. Political activist, philanthropist, and suffragist, Molly received her "Unsinkable" moniker as the result of her remark following the *Titanic* incident. According to Molly, her survival was "typical Brown luck. We're unsinkable."

Tours of the museum, lasting approximately forty minutes, are led by costumed guides who entertainingly reveal Molly's rags-to-riches story, her remarkable bravery during the *Titanic* disaster, and the house's resident ghosts.

 DENVER BOTANIC GARDENS (all ages)
1005 York Street, Denver 80206; (720) 865–3500; www.botanicgardens.org. Open daily 9:00 A.M. to 5:00 P.M.; open until 8:00 P.M. during summer months, Saturday through Tuesday. $$

Vegetable Garden, Scripture Garden, Romantic Garden, Windsong Garden, or Monet Garden, to name just a few—the Denver Botanic Gardens presents plants in their special environments. Whether you stop in for a relaxing stroll or come to learn about xeriscaping or endangered plants, you'll appreciate this spot of greenery in Denver.

All ages enjoy the Tropical Conservatory. Look for fossils embedded in the walls. Ride the glass elevator into the treetops for a bird's-eye view.

In summer, sip a cool drink and enjoy a salad at the Cafe Monet, adjacent to the Monet Garden and open 9:00 A.M. to the gardens' closing. Or dine al fresco at the Three Tomatoes Cafe, open 11:00 A.M. to 3:00 P.M.

On weekends check out a family fun pack at the information desk. These backpacks are filled with science activities designed for families to do together while visiting the gardens.

Walk through the outdoor gardens. Tucked in the northwest corner is the Japanese Garden and Teahouse, a good place for some reflec-

***B*lossoms of Light** The Denver Botanic Gardens also celebrates the holiday season with a blaze of lights. Join the visitors strolling through the outdoor gardens, oohing and aahing over festive light displays. There's hot chocolate and cider for sale inside, and the indoor gardens are also decorated.

The Denver Zoo and the Botanic Gardens encourage you to see both light displays. When you purchase tickets at one stop, you receive a discount coupon ($2.00 off) for tickets at the other.

tive moments, even with a four-year-old. The Alpine Rock Garden is a good place to see and identify the plants found in our Rocky Mountains.

Cheesman Park borders the Botanic Gardens on the west side. It's one of Denver's most attractive urban parks and has a playground.

A Lark in the Park

Washington Park is a local favorite in a neighborhood by the same name. Restricted traffic and the choice of several paths through the park make it easy to share this space with walkers, joggers, skaters, and dogs. Two ponds attract anglers, ducks, and geese. The excellent playground makes a good rest stop. And to top it all off, within a few blocks of Washington Park, there are two great places to get an ice-cream cone. Choose Bonnie Brae Ice Cream, 799 South University Boulevard, Denver 80206 (303–777–0808); or Soda Rock Cafe, 2217 East Mississippi Avenue, Denver 80210 (303–777–0414). Reward yourselves for all that exercise!

CHERRY CREEK SHOPPING CENTER (all ages)

3000 East 1st Avenue, Denver 80206; (303) 388–2522; www.shopcherrycreek. com. Open Monday through Friday 10:00 A.M. to 9:00 P.M., Saturday 10:00 A.M. to 7:30 P.M., and Sunday 11:00 A.M. to 6:00 P.M. Some store and restaurant hours may vary.

Denver is the shopping capital of the Rocky Mountain West, and the Cherry Creek Shopping Center is top of the line. Neiman Marcus, Saks Fifth Avenue, and Tiffany—this center is lined with luxury shopping. Sculptures, skylights, and plenty of open space make shopping here a pleasant experience. Comfy seating areas entice shoppers to rest tired feet and regroup.

You'll have no trouble finding Kids' Kourt, the playground area with a breakfast theme. Just follow the kids. There are not many places where you're allowed to play in a giant bowl of shredded wheat, slide down a piece of bacon, or stomp on a waffle, so don't miss this opportunity.

Even if your children don't recognize the status of Neiman Marcus, they won't soon forget their visit to Build-A-Bear (303–320–9888; www. buildabear.com), where they can choose an animal priced between $10 and $30, stuff it, give it a heart, dress it, name it, and make a birth certificate for it. The shop also carries already-stuffed animals, accessories, and a selection of fashions for your child's pet bear that celebrate the various holidays throughout the year.

Hungry? Paul's Place (a locally owned way-better-than-the-chains hamburger place) and Salmagundi's (soup and salad buffet) are good choices for a quick but tasty meal at moderate prices. There's likely to be a wait at Rain Forest Cafe, which offers more than a meal.

TATTERED COVER BOOK STORE (all ages)

*Two locations: 2955 East 1st Avenue, Denver 80206; (303) 322–7727 or
(800) 833–9327; www.tatteredcover.com. Open Monday through Saturday 9:00
A.M. to 11:00 P.M. and Sunday 10:00 A.M. to 6:00 P.M. 1628 16th Street, Denver 80202; (303) 436–1070. Open Monday through Thursday 9:00 A.M. to
9:00 P.M., Friday and Saturday 9:00 A.M. to 11:00 P.M., and Sunday 10:00 A.M.
to 6:00 P.M.*

The Tattered Cover Book Store began as a small, intimate bookshop
in 1974. The cozy atmosphere, attention to customer needs, and an
eclectic selection of books soon attracted a faithful following of book-
lovers. Alas, bookshelves hold only so many volumes, so owner Joyce
Meskis had to expand, eventually settling into a four-story building at
1st Avenue and Milwaukee Street in the Cherry Creek North district and
a second location on 16th Street in Denver's LoDo area. Miraculously,
by designing cozy nooks with reading lamps and large, overstuffed
couches and chairs, plus providing the hospitality and customer service
that was always available at her original shop, she has maintained the
same warm, welcoming ambience created more than two decades ago.
That's quite an accomplishment when you consider the fact that the
two stores now contain a total of 150,000 titles and 750,000 volumes.

Children are encouraged to indulge in the wonderful assortment of
books in the kids' area. Here parents sit on the floor, youngsters in laps,
and read aloud. Or often the reverse happens, as children read to their
parents. Overheard in the children's section: "I love it here. Our whole
family loves this bookstore. It's our favorite place to spend an afternoon."

At the Cherry Creek store, on Tuesday at 11:00 A.M. and Saturday at
10:30 A.M., guest authors, storytellers, and staff host a thirty-minute
children's story time. Listen right along with your kids, or browse the
books from nearby shelves. Afterward, relax with a beverage and pastry
in the bookstore's cafe. At the LoDo store the children's staff will read
stories anytime. Just ask.

FOUR MILE HISTORIC PARK (all ages)

*715 South Forest Street, Denver 80246; (303) 399–1859; www.stepintohistory.
com/states/CO/Four_Mile.htm. Open April through September, Wednesday
through Sunday 10:00 A.M. to 4:00 P.M. Closed Monday and Tuesday. Inquire
about summer day camps and year-round special events. $, children 5 and younger
Free. Horse-drawn rides $1.00.*

This fourteen-acre living-history museum is located 4 miles southeast of downtown Denver, hence its name. Spanning a period between
1859 and 1883, the farm park consists of the Four Mile House, a for-

mer tavern and wayside inn that once welcomed travelers on the Chero-kee Trail, plus a reconstructed bee house where former owner Millie Booth kept her beekeeping equipment, three barns and a corral housing chickens and draft horses, a summer kitchen, and a privy.

Docents in period clothing lead visitors through the Four Mile House and are stationed around the grounds demonstrating nineteenth-century farm life. Children like the horse-drawn rides—stagecoach, hayride, or sleigh ride. You are welcome to visit the fragrant rose garden, check on the crops in the vegetable garden, and spread a blanket under a shade tree for a family picnic. There's a small gift shop in the bee house. Sunday is special-events day designed with the family in mind. Call for the latest schedule, which includes seasonal and holiday celebrations along with western heritage events.

Shopping "Only in Denver"

Like every town, Denver has its hometown favorites—the locally owned stores that make this town great. You can shop at national chains anywhere, but here are a few standouts for families that you'll find only in the Mile High City:

Kazoo & Company. *2930 East Second Avenue, Denver 80206, in Cherry Creek North; (303) 322–0973 or (800) 257–0008; www.kazootoys.com.* "Toys That Play with the Imagination" is the theme here—two floors invitingly full of quality items. Need a stuffed camel, zebra, or warthog? Larger animals lounge on a park bench, while an outstanding assortment of others fills shelves along one wall. Stop in the Travel Section for something new to do in the car: Toddlers to twelve-year-olds will find puzzles, books, art supplies, and games for traveling.

There is a large section for your wee ones, a special area for horse-lovers, and a Dress-up Section (glittering shoes, pink tutus, magic wands) sure to enchant your little girls. The staff is knowledgeable and kid-friendly.

If you're going to be in town long-term, ask for a schedule of Kazoo KidShops (art, crafts, science workshops for two- to twelve-year-olds). Be forewarned: It's really hard to get kids out of Kazoo!

The Bookies. *4315 East Mississippi, Denver 80210 (2 blocks east of Colorado Boulevard); (303) 759–1117. Open Monday through Saturday 10:00 A.M. to 6:00 P.M. and Sunday noon to 5:00 P.M.* A favorite haunt for parents and teachers, The Bookies is floor-to-ceiling fun for kids. An amazing collection of books (fiction and nonfiction, picture books, learn-to-read, chapter books) shares space with animals (cute, fuzzy characters from stories to rubbery, scientifically accurate invertebrates), games, puzzles, and art supplies. Curriculum guides, workbooks, and an assortment of teaching aids draw educators.

This store is overflowing, but the inventory is well organized, and the atmosphere is casual and friendly. There's always a bowl of pretzels to munch. The staff really know their stuff!

Caboose Hobbies. *500 South Broadway, Denver 80209; (303) 777–6766; www.caboosehobbies.com. Open Monday through Friday 9:30 A.M. to 6:00 P.M., Saturday 9:00 A.M. to 5:30 P.M., and Sunday noon to 5:00 P.M.* The family-owned Caboose Hobbies train store was established in 1938 and remains the world's largest model-railroad hobby shop. The 18,000-square-foot store contains 300,000 train-related items, including the largest selection of N scale items in the United States. The book department claims to have more than 1,000 titles and 300 different videos. Children will be fascinated by the displays of moving trains plunging in and out of tunnels, speeding through the countryside, and chugging past towns and villages. They also will be pleased to find toy locomotives, striped engineer caps, and train stickers and books.

 WINGS OVER THE ROCKIES AIR & SPACE MUSEUM (ages 2 and up)
7711 East Academy Boulevard, Denver 80230; (303) 360–5360; www. dimensional.com/-worm/. Open Monday through Saturday 10:00 A.M. to 5:00 P.M. and Sunday noon to 5:00 P.M. $, children 5 and younger **Free**.

Thanks to the enthusiasm of dedicated volunteers and the foresight of Russell Tarvin, a retired Army Air Corps colonel, this museum has an outstanding collection of irreplaceable aviation artifacts and lore. Beginning in 1982, Tarvin and like-minded followers used their military clout to save a score of outdated airplanes and other aviation items from the scrap heap. Civic leaders, recognizing the importance of preserving Tarvin's collection, won approval from the U.S. Department of Defense for the acquisition of two gigantic hangars located on the former Lowry Air Force Base to serve as a home for the new museum.

A visit to the museum is a wonderful opportunity to get close to some mighty impressive aircraft, such as a rare BIA Bomber, predecessor to the Stealth Bomber; a circa-1930 B-18 Bomber; and a T-33, America's first jet fighter plane. Especially popular with kids is the giant H-21 Helicopter, known as the "Flying Banana." Other prize aircraft include a Fokker D7, one of several German fighters from World War I; an Eagle Rock biplane from the 1920s; and a one-person glider used in the

1920s by the Germans after the Versailles Treaty banned them from the use of powered flight.

Other exhibits of note include the Frederic Howard collection of model aircraft with wingspans of 2 feet or more and controls that respond to the maneuvering of the control stick, photographs and artifacts from the China-Burma-India theater of World War II, and an extraordinary display of World War I fighter pilot uniforms placed on mannequins. Your kids can pick out inexpensive aviation pins and patches and attractive T-shirts in the small gift shop.

One day every other month, visitors are allowed into the cockpits of an Fl-ll, F4, B-57, and a helicopter. The aircraft are inside the hangar, so be sure to bring a flash unit for your camera to get a shot your child will cherish. Call for exact dates.

This place is a dream come true for aviation buffs. Visitors return time after time, usually bringing friends back with them to share in the experience. Watch for the huge B-52 Stratofortress, which is parked outside the hangar. It's too large to store inside the five-acre hangar and makes an ideal landmark.

Denver Suburbs

 ## LAKESIDE AMUSEMENT PARK (ages 2 and up)

4601 North Sheridan Boulevard, Denver 80211; (303) 477–1621; www.lake sideamusementpark.com. Open late April through May, weekends only; June through Labor Day, open daily. The main park hours are Monday through Friday 6:00 to 11:00 P.M.; Saturday, Sunday, and holidays noon to 11:00 P.M. (Hours subject to change. Best to phone.) Kiddies Playland open daily 1:00 to 10:00 P.M. It's best to arrive early with little ones, when the atmosphere is most suited to families with young children. **Free** *parking. $$–$$$*

This old-fashioned, circa-1908 amusement park appears somewhat like a movie set. The park's bell tower, currently housing refreshment booths and arcade games, is a Denver landmark.

The carousel, with its hand-carved wooden animals, is original to the park. Serious coaster-lovers come from far and wide to ride Cyclone, ranked as one of the top classic wooden roller coasters in the world. Built in 1940, the Art Deco station and cars are a throwback to another era.

Also of special interest are "Puffing Billy" and "Whistling Tom," two miniature, coal-burning, steam-engine trains acquired from the 1904 St. Louis World's Fair and also original to the park. Both trains, among the last in the country that burn coal for power, are still in operation today.

A diesel streamliner also shares the scenic 1¼-mile track that leads around the park and skirts Lake Rhoda.

The Kiddies Playland comprises fifteen rides sure to please the preschoolers in your family, and the Cyclone Roller Coaster will no doubt thrill your teenagers.

BUTTERFLY PAVILION AND INSECT CENTER (ages 3 and up)

6252 West 104th Avenue, Westminster 80020; (303) 469–5441; www. butterflies.org. Open daily Memorial Day through Labor Day, 9:00 A.M. to 6:00 P.M.; open 9:00 A.M. to 5:00 P.M. the remainder of the year. Closed Thanksgiving and Christmas. $–$$, children 3 and younger **Free**. *Maximum of two free child admissions per paid adult.*

This fascinating, 16,000-square-foot facility has a 7,800-square-foot glass conservatory housing a tropical forest with free-flying butterflies. Here you can walk among butterflies of every color from all over the world. Beautiful flowers and foliage, a goldfish pond, and a rippling stream create a desirable environment for as many as 2,000 butterflies. A special viewing area reveals how the adults eventually emerge from the chrysalis.

One section of the center features tarantulas, crayfish, giant centipedes, huge cockroaches, and all sorts of other creepy-crawlers that your kids will absolutely love. Volunteers are on hand to remove an insect or two from their enclosures so that youngsters can carefully stroke and pet them. The volunteers are well versed in the habits and habitats of insects and are excellent with children.

HYLAND HILLS WATER WORLD (ages 2 and up)

1800 West 89th Street, Federal Heights 80260; (303) 427–7873. Open daily Memorial Day until late August, 10:00 A.M. to 6:00 P.M. $$$, children 3 and younger **Free**.

Located only twenty minutes from downtown Denver, this sixty-acre park has more than three dozen aquatic attractions. Ride the whitewater rapids of River Country. Or pile into a five-person raft to float past the lair of a sea monster and through the earthquake cavern for an up-close encounter with the giant T-Rex, king of the underground on the Voyage to the Center of the Earth. The Lost River of the Pharaohs will take you on a wild ride into an ancient Egyptian pyramid. Wally World, a miniature water park, is just the right size for toddlers. Older children and their parents will love the 4-foot-high waves of Thunder Bay. Many of the rides are family oriented and can accommodate the entire family on the same craft.

Although food, from blueberry funnel cakes and chocolate chip cookies to pepperoni pizzas, is readily available, you are allowed to bring in your own picnic lunches (no glass bottles or jars, please). It's wise to bring along some sort of bathing footwear, because the cement pathways can be hot and slippery.

CHERRY CREEK STATE PARK (all ages)

4201 South Parker Road, Aurora 80014; information, (303) 699–3860; campsite reservations, (303) 470–1144 or (800) 678–2267; www.parks.state. co.us/cherry_creek. Open daily April through October, 5:00 A.M. to 10:00 P.M.; daily November through March, 6:00 A.M. to 7:00 P.M. Park facilities (marina, concessions, etc.) are open Memorial Day through Labor Day. Park passes, $; campsites, $$.

This suburban oasis contains more than one hundred campsites and as many picnic sites. The 3,915-acre recreational area boasts full-service camping, stables for renting horses, guided nature walks, an extensive trail system for biking and horseback riding, and a paved model airplane field. An 880-acre reservoir attracts water enthusiasts for boating, water-skiing, Jet-Skiing, windsurf-

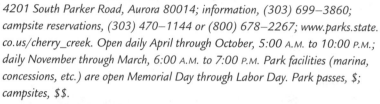
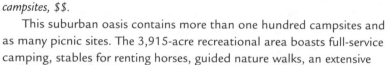

When Thunderclouds Appear During summer in Colorado, white, puffy thunderclouds often turn dark and threatening. This usually occurs in the afternoon, sometimes forcing water and amusement parks to close. For this reason it is always best to arrive in the morning hours in order to give your children plenty of time to experience all the rides and attractions.

ing, and fishing. Boat rentals are available at the marina on the west side of the lake. The swim beach provides a sandy roped-off area for swimmers, plus a bathhouse, food concessions, and a first-aid station. Campsites fill quickly on summer weekends, so advance reservations are a must.

BELLEVIEW PARK (all ages)

On West Belleview Road between Broadway and Windemere, Englewood. Children's Farm and Train open Memorial Day through Labor Day, Tuesday through Saturday 10:00 A.M. to 4:00 P.M. and Sunday 11:00 A.M. to 4:00 P.M. Almost **Free** *(50 cents per person).*

Picnic tables under shady old cottonwoods, lots of grass, a stream, and a playground make this a good stop for all families. But those with younger children will think this place is too good to be true: There's also a Children's Farm and a miniature train. The Lions Club International operates the train. Tracks loop through the park, crossing a trestle over Big Dry Creek. At the Children's Farm, you'll find a changing selection of animals, on loan from area farmers. It's all refreshingly low-key.

LITTLETON HISTORICAL MUSEUM (all ages)

6028 South Gallup Street, Littleton 80120; (303) 795–3950. Open Tuesday through Friday 8:00 A.M. to 5:00 P.M., Saturday 10:00 A.M. to 5:00 P.M., and Sunday 1:00 to 5:00 P.M. **Free.**

Take your family back, way back, to the early days of Littleton. The 1860s homestead farm and the 1890s farm are two separate living-history museums on this property. Interpreters work the farm sites, run the blacksmith shop, and teach in the school (Littleton's first one-room schoolhouse).

Cows, sheep, horses, pigs, chickens, ducks, and geese ensure that your kids will like this place. Those too young to understand the history can work on math or language skills. What does the sheep say? How many pigs are wallowing in the mud? Take a moment to try out the old wooden swing hanging from the willow. Have a picnic on the front lawn under the old cottonwoods. A rooster or pheasant may join you.

The main building of this museum houses three galleries with changing exhibits. Ask about year-round special events ranging from evening concerts during the summer to a pioneer Christmas celebration.

Where to Eat

Bella Ristorante. *1920 Market Street, Denver 80202; (303) 297–8400. Open for lunch Monday through Friday, daily for dinner. Also on the southwest corner of I–25 and Arapahoe Road. (303) 768–8400. Open daily for lunch and dinner.* Their spinach lasagna is the best! Lots of good choices, ample portions, and a pleasing atmosphere make this a good spot. Several entrees can be ordered in family portions, designed to be shared. $$$

Blue Bonnet Cafe. *457 South Broadway, Denver 80209; (303) 778–0147. Open Monday through Saturday 11:00 A.M. to 11:00 P.M. and Sunday noon to 9:00 P.M.* Unbelievably popular Blue Bonnet wows Denverites with award-winning Mexican food. It's family owned and has been at this location for more than thirty years. Affordable prices and fast service make this a good family stop. $

Bonnie Brae Tavern. *740 South University Boulevard, Denver 80206; (303) 777–2262. Open Tuesday through Sunday.* The Dire family has been serving pizza on this spot for more than sixty years. Considered a neighborhood treasure, Bonnie Brae is usually filled with a mix of singles, young families, and older folks. Televisions keep patrons tuned to the latest sports events. It's noisy and crowded but friendly and unpretentious. Their menu includes nightly specials, but try their award-winning pizza. $

Casa Bonita. *6715 West Colfax Avenue, Lakewood 80214; (303) 232–5115. Open daily for lunch and dinner.* Folks don't come to the Casa Bonita restaurant for quiet, sophisticated dining. On the other hand, it is sure to become one of your kids' favorite eateries. While cliff divers plunge 30 feet from the top of a waterfall into a pool of water and the sheriff engages bad guy Black Bart in a shoot-'em-up, youngsters can indulge in a Piñata Plate of cheese enchiladas, tacos, refried beans, rice, and a sopapilla from the "Little Amigos" menu.

This is a lively, fun place, with serenading mariachis, puppet shows, magicians, and fire jugglers. Kids delight in exploring the dark passages of Black Bart's mysterious, secret hideout. **Free** chips, chili con queso, salsa, and homemade sopapillas come with each dinner. $

The Cherry Tomato. *4645 East 23rd Avenue, Denver 80205 (near City Park); (303) 377–1914. Open for dinner Tuesday through Sunday.* Head to this delightful Italian cafe in Denver's Park Hill neighborhood. It was started by four couples in a former drug store. You still walk on

the original black-and-white tile floor. Butcher paper covers the tables, and crayons keep the kids happy. Great food will keep *you* happy. $$

Denver Buffalo Company. *1109 Lincoln Street, Denver 80203; (303) 832–0880. Open for lunch and dinner, from 11:00 A.M. to 9:00 P.M. Monday through Thursday and from 11:00 A.M. to 10:00 P.M. Friday and Saturday. (The deli, gallery, and trading post open at 10:00 A.M.)* Flavorful buffalo, high in protein and lower in fat and cholesterol than any other meat, chicken, or fish, is the star of the show. Denver Buffalo Company raises its own herd on its ranch in eastern Colorado. Surrounded by western artifacts and memorabilia, enjoy your buffalo as steaks, prime rib, or stir-fry. "The Great Buffalo Hunt" on the kids' menu/activity sheet encourages youngsters to locate five special items around the restaurant. When all are found, a surprise awaits in the Trading Post.

Before or after your meal, spend some time in the Trading Post and Gallery. From salsas to sculptures, you'll find an assortment of apparel, jewelry, foods, and original art. During the day a friendly weaver, using buffalo-hair yarn, welcomes guests to watch and ask questions. She loves to share her knowledge of buffalo and western history, especially with children. Items made from the weavings and buffalo leather products are for sale.

Sandwiches or salads from the deli can be eaten in or taken out for an al fresco lunch—Civic Center Park is just 5 blocks away. The Market features fresh buffalo meat and sausages. Gift boxes are available. $$–$$$$

Where to Stay

Hotel Monaco. *1717 Champa Street at 17th Avenue, Denver 80202; (303) 296–1717 or (800) 397–5380; www. monaco-denver.com.* "Please send up an extra set of towels and a goldfish." If the kids miss the animals left at home, they can borrow a pet goldfish, complete with name and bowl, during their stay at Hotel Monaco. Or you can bring the family dog or cat to this hotel. Weekend rates are especially family friendly for a great "city escape" with the kids. Hotel Monaco's spacious suites, quality food, and convenient location make it a comfortable choice. $$$–$$$$

Inverness Hotel & Golf Club. *I–25 south at exit 192, 200 Inverness Drive West, Englewood 80112; (303) 799–5800; www.invernesshotel.com.* This is "Denver's only Resort Hotel." Inverness is a AAA Four-Diamond hotel on its own championship golf course. State-of-the-art business facilities meet the needs of those families combining business and vacation. Your kids will definitely enjoy the attractive outdoor pool during the summer. Extravagant evening buffets and Sunday brunch are popular with locals as well as guests. Nearby Park Meadows Mall offers upscale shopping. $$$$

Loews Giorgio. *4150 East Mississippi Avenue, Denver 80246; just off Colorado Boulevard, southeast of the Cherry Creek area; (303) 782–9300 or (800) 235–6397; www.loewshotel.com.* Looking for a convenient location away from downtown? Known to locals as the Darth

Vader building, this black-glass hotel offers family-friendly service in a luxury setting. With parents' approval, cookies and milk are delivered at bedtime, and the kids' bath kit includes no-tears shampoo. $$$–$$$$

Marriott Courtyard. *On the 16th Street Mall at Curtis, downtown; (303) 571–1114 or (800) 228–9290.* While this is a newer choice in downtown lodging, it's actually a historic landmark—the old Joslin's department store, built in 1886. Many rooms front the lively 16th Street Mall with large Chicago-style windows. All rooms have dataports in case you haven't left your work at home. King suite rooms provide a sofa sleeper for the kids in the living area. Staff members welcome families. They have games for your youngsters and can arrange babysitting if you wish. Starbucks and Rialto Café, a metropolitan bistro, are in the hotel. $$$ weeknights; $$ weekends.

The Victorian Holiday Chalet Hotel. *1820 East Colfax Avenue, Denver 80218; (303) 321–9975.* This family-friendly inn features ten guest rooms, three of which are suites with sitting alcoves. All have minikitchens and private baths; cribs are available. A complimentary continental-plus breakfast is served. $$–$$$

The Westin Tabor Center. *1672 Lawrence Street, Denver 80202; downtown; (303) 572–9100; www.westin.com.* If you request in advance, cribs and highchairs will be ready and waiting in your room upon arrival. Youngsters receive their own registration packets and either a sports bottle or tippy cup (depending upon the age of the child). The fourth floor beckons with an indoor/outdoor pool and health club. Referrals for licensed baby-sitting services are available through the concierge, and special children's menus offer such favorites as pizza, chicken fingers, and macaroni and cheese. Inquire about other kid-friendly features. $$$

Denver and Suburbs Annual Events

Ethnic, cultural, historic, culinary, or just for laughs—the Denver metropolitan area loves to celebrate. Almost every weekend year-round, you'll find a festival or special event suitable for the family. For exact dates and times, call (303) 892-1112 unless otherwise noted. Following is a sampling of yearly offerings.

JANUARY

National Western Stock Show. *Early to mid-January.* This three-week-long Old West experience, said to be the "world's premier stock show and one of the nation's largest," consists of rodeo performances, livestock competitions, auctions, a children's petting area, name entertainers, and food and western merchandise booths. This is your chance to rub elbows with cowboys, ranch hands, and farm kids with their 4-H exhibits. The rodeos are often sellouts, so make reservations early. $-$$

MARCH

St. Patrick's Day Parade. *Mid-March.* On the Saturday preceding St. Patrick's Day, Denver celebrates the "wearin' of the green" with its annual parade winding through the downtown streets. This is an especially festive occasion for all who are Irish, if only for one day. **Free**.

March Powwow. *Mid-March.* More than seventy tribes of Native Americans take part in this annual gathering. Arts and crafts booths, drumming competitions, and more than 700 musicians and dancers add to the excitement. $$

MAY

Cinco de Mayo. *Early May.* This is the state's largest event honoring those of Hispanic heritage. The main festival takes place in Denver's Civic Center. Booths offer crafts, art, and wonderful Mexican food; female dancers twirl in billowing red, orange, blue, and yellow dresses; and male performers in sleek black suits stamp their feet in time to lively mariachi music. Celebrating Mexico's victory over the invading French in 1862, Cinco de Mayo is now a national holiday in Mexico. **Free** admission.

Wells Fargo Culturefest. *Mid-May, (303) 871–4626; www.du.edu/humaninst/ cultfest.htm.* Held on the campus of the University of Denver, this celebration includes international food, music, and dance, with entertainers from Europe, Asia, Latin America, and Africa. This is a good opportunity for children to learn about other cultures. **Free** admission.

JUNE

Capitol Hill People's Fair. *Early June.* What began as a neighborhood block party expanded over the years to become a street fair. Now, more than twenty years later, it has become the largest annual arts and crafts fair in Colorado. Food booths, craft tables, strolling entertainers, and live music on several stages spread across the width and breadth of Denver's Civic Center. More than 700 volunteers work the fair, and the proceeds are divided among neighborhood nonprofit groups. **Free** admission.

Bethesda Dutch Festival. *Mid-June, (303) 639–9066.* This is a fun celebration for families. Costumed participants scrub the street with brooms and pails of water prior to the opening ceremonies. Other Dutch customs enacted here are wooden-shoe dancing and the playing of traditional Dutch music. You will see lots of colorful tulips and find Dutch food and products for sale. **Free** admission.

Denver International BuskerFest. *Late June.* Scattered throughout downtown Denver, buskers (street performers) from around the world entertain wide-eyed audiences. Sword-swallowing, juggling, balancing acts, mime, music, and magic—they are all here. **Free** admission; however, performers pass the hat after each performance. It's tradition.

JULY

Fourth of July Family Picnic. *July 4.* Four Mile Historic Park hosts a good old fashioned picnic. Bring your picnic hamper and blanket to celebrate in the style of the mid-1800s. Authentic live music by Denver's own 4th U.S. Artillery Regimental Band. $

Black Arts Festival. *July, (303) 331–1795.* This celebration extols African-American art, music, dance, food, and culture. You will find a replica of a traditional Nigerian village, a marketplace, and entertainment from around the world. **Free** admission.

OCTOBER

Harvest Festival. *Early October, (303) 795–3950.* This annual celebration, held at Littleton Historical Museum, features interpreters in period clothing, hayrides, music, and the sale of honey from the museum's beehives. Pumpkins may be picked and purchased from the patch. Tasty treats include hot cider and pumpkin pie. **Free** admission, $ for pumpkins.

The Great Pumpkin Harvest Festival. *Early October, (303) 399–1859.* At this festive fall celebration, held at Four Mile Historic Park, your family can choose just the right pumpkin to become this year's Halloween jack-o'-lantern, watch pumpkin-carving demonstrations, and, for a small fee, fashion their own scarecrow. There's live music, cider tasting, and warm cookies baked on an outdoor woodstove. Or how about a hayrack ride? **Free** admission.

DECEMBER

Parade of Lights. *Early December, (303) 892–1112.* This is an annual must for many families. Bring plenty of blankets, sit on the curb, and watch as hot-air balloons in the shapes of animals and cartoon characters, costumed figures representing favorite personalities from kids' TV shows, and clowns, clowns, and more clowns march by. Thousands of twinkling lights adorn floats. Santa's is the grand finale. **Free**.

World's Largest Christmas Lighting Display. *Early December to New Year's Day and then again during the National Western Stock Show from early to mid-January, (303) 892–1112.* More than 40,000 colored lights adorn Denver's City and County Building. Christmas carols and animated displays add to the festivities. **Free**.

Wildlights. *The month of December, (303) 892–1112.* There's something special about taking your kids to the zoo on a brisk winter night when most of the animals are sound asleep and the quiet menagerie comes alive with thousands of lights in the form of huge animals and beautiful Christmas trees. Make sure the entire family wears their warmest woollies, and plan to make several trips to the concession stand for hot cider. $

Blossoms of Light. *The month of December, (303) 331–4000.* Stroll through the Botanic Gardens amid twinkling lights in the form of giant flowers and leaping frogs. With Christmas carols floating across the frosty evening air, the outdoor gardens become a favorite holiday wonderland. Hot cider is available in the main building, so take your little ones inside occasionally to warm the tummies and toes. $

*S*tar Bright, Star Light . . . It was Christmas Eve 1914, and

on a quiet city street in downtown Denver, a young boy lay in his upstairs bedroom too ill to be carried downstairs to join family members around the Christmas tree. The lad's grandfather, D. D. Sturgeon, one of Denver's pioneer electricians, could not bear to see his grandson completely miss out on the festivities. Wanting to brighten the small boy's holidays, he took some ordinary light bulbs, dipped them in red and green paint, connected them to electrical wire, and proceeded to string the glowing baubles onto the branches of a pine tree outside his grandson's bedroom window within easy view of the boy's appreciative gaze. Thus a Denver tradition began.

From early December to late January, Denver's annual World's Largest Christmas Lighting Display adorns the neoclassical City and County Building with as many as 40,000 bulbs, innumerable floodlights, 17 miles of electrical wiring, and tons of evergreen boughs. Nightly, thousands of folks drive past to catch a glimpse of the glowing masterpiece. Thousands more brave the cold winter evenings to stroll Civic Center Park; pause before Santa, sleigh, and reindeer; and admire Mary, Joseph, and the Christ child in the nativity scene.

This extraordinary exhibit of Christmas lighting seems a fitting tribute to a little boy who, but for the ingenuity of his grandfather, would never have known the splendor of colored electric lights on a glistening outdoor pine tree. The display is lighted nightly from 6:00 to 10:00 P.M. during the Christmas season and then again during the National Western Stock Show, from early to mid-January. *Free.* For information call (303) 892-1112.

For More Information

Denver Metro Convention and Visitors Bureau, *1668 Larimer Street, Denver 80202; (303) 892–1112, (303)* *892–1505, or (800) 645–3446; www.denver.org. Visitor Guide* available.

Northeastern Colorado

The northeastern quadrant of the state is referred to as "Colorado's Final Frontier." Here you will find handcrafted hospitality provided by people who seem to have the time to listen and the heart to care. Besides a north-south ribbon of small cities, most of the countryside is made up of western-style towns, farms, cattle ranches, river valleys, and wide-open plains. Antelope, deer, prairie dog, coyote, raccoon, red fox, and rabbit roam the prairie lands.

Doris's Top Picks

in Northeastern Colorado

1. Colorado Railroad Museum, Golden
2. Loveland Public Sculpture, Loveland
3. Old Town/Kit Carson County Carousel, Burlington
4. Pearl Street Mall, Boulder
5. Rocky Mountain National Park, Estes Park
6. Rocky Mountain Pumpkin Ranch, Longmont
7. Roxborough State Park, Southwest Metropolitan Denver
8. Swetsville Zoo, Fort Collins
9. Sylvan Dale Guest Ranch, Loveland

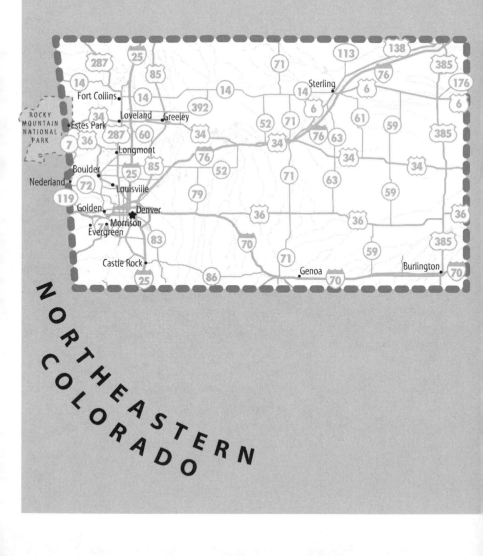

NORTHEASTERN
COLORADO

Castle Rock

The center of Colorado's fastest-growing county, Castle Rock is 28 miles south of Denver on I-25.

CASTLEWOOD CANYON STATE PARK (all ages)

State Highway 83, 6 miles south of Franktown (east of I-25 at Castle Rock); (303) 688-5242; www.dnr.state.co.us/parks/. Open every day of the year, weather permitting, sunrise to sunset. $ per car.

Castlewood Canyon—with turkey vultures drifting overhead, grazing pronghorn antelope, leaping leopard frogs, and tracks of bobcats and porcupines—offers nature and wildlife just thirty minutes from Denver. This popular hiking and picnicking day-use area also attracts technical rock climbers. One-mile-long Canyon View Nature Trail, leading to four overviews, is stroller and wheelchair accessible—a good choice for young children or "flatland" visitors. The park is 1,000 feet higher than Denver, so those—even children—not acclimated to the altitude may huff and puff with exertion. Hardier hikers choose trails into the colorful canyon, to a waterfall or the remains of Castlewood Dam, and along Cherry Creek. Keep your eyes open for prairie falcons and great blue herons flying overhead. Both nest in remote areas of the park.

A visitors center presents a fourteen-minute slide show and encourages children's curiosity with interactive displays. Check schedules for junior-naturalist programs or preschool storytime. Almost every Saturday there's a program or special event. Call for information and trail conditions during winter months.

DEVIL'S HEAD TRAIL & FIRE LOOKOUT TOWER (ages 6 and up)

From Castle Rock north 8 miles to Sedalia, southwest on State Highway 67 to junction with Rampart Range Road (at the Indian Creek Campground), and south approximately 7 miles. Campground, picnic sites, parking, and trailhead are 1 mile east of Rampart Range Road. **Free**.

Here's a hike with a special reward when you arrive. From parking lot to tower, this National Recreation Trail climbs more than 1,000 feet in less than 1½ miles. Whiners (adult or child) may become almost insufferable, but this is a classic Colorado family hike. As you enter a clearing, you find the last manned fire lookout tower in Pike National Forest awaiting your climb. Consider taking time for a snack and drink before ascending the 143 stairs to the lookout. During summer the ranger will show you around and even sell you a Forest Service T-shirt or cap. This may be the most scenic shopping you'll do in Colorado. The views stretch from Rocky Mountain National Park in the north to the Sangre de Cristos south of Pikes Peak, and west to the Continental Divide, spiked with the spires of the Collegiate Range. It's worth putting up with the whiners, big or little.

Devil's Head Folklore and Legends All that glitters just might be gold. In the 1870s an outlaw gang robbed a government train, making off with an estimated $60,000 in gold eagle coins. They buried the loot in the Devil's Head area, marked the spot with a knife stabbed into a tree, and left, a posse fast on their heels. It is said that the loot was never recovered. Could *you* be the one to find it? Keep your eyes open.

Rock hounds still search for topaz on Devil's Head slopes. In 1883 W. B. Smith discovered a rich deposit of the gems, some of the best found in the United States. The mother lode is yet to be found.

The first woman fire lookout, Helen Dow, served three summers at Devil's Head beginning in 1921. That first summer she reported sixteen fires.

Southwest Metropolitan Denver

CHATFIELD NATURE PRESERVE (all ages)

8500 Deer Creek Canyon Road, Littleton 80125 (southwest of C–470 on Wadsworth Boulevard); (303) 973–3705. Open daily year-round, 9:00 A.M. to 5:00 P.M. $, children under 6 **Free**.

A good place for pleasant walking, this 700-acre preserve maintains open grassland, a woodland river ecosystem, and ten acres of wetlands. There also are two nineteenth-century farms and a one-room schoolhouse, which functions as the visitors center. Kids will enjoy checking out the old-fashioned playground.

Along 2 miles of walking trails, self-guiding material helps you learn about plants. The survival garden has edible, medicinal, and poisonous plants. Stop in the wildlife blind overlooking the wetlands to observe birds. Deer, elk, and rabbits frequent the area.

The first Friday of each month is a **Free** day, and a **Free** guided tour is given at 11:00 A.M.

CHATFIELD STATE PARK (all ages)

South of C–470 on Wadsworth Boulevard (follow the signs to the state park entrance on the left); (303) 791–7275; www.dnr.state.co.us/parks/. Open daily 5:00 A.M. to 10:00 P.M. $ per car.

Another great place for family hiking! This state park is less crowded than most, yet there's lots to do and 5,600 acres to do it in. Trails lead you through grasslands, to ponds, along a reservoir, and through the woods. If you're quiet, you may spot lizards, frogs, toads, and turtles. There are good places to practice skipping rocks across the water.

Great blue herons nest within the park. Learn about them at an outdoor exhibit on the park's south side. At 4 feet tall with a 6-foot wingspan, they are a spectacular sight.

From Memorial Day through Labor Day, cool off at the swim beach. The chilly temperature of the reservoir doesn't seem to faze kids. There's a sandy beach, so bring your castle-building equipment. Floats are allowed in the water; lifeguards are on duty. The concession stand has reasonable prices, and there are rest rooms with showers and changing facilities. It's perfect! There is a separate entry fee for the swim beach: $1.00 per person.

If you still have energy after hiking and swimming, boat rentals and fishing await, and horseback riding is available within the park at Chatfield B & B Livery, (303) 933–3636.

ROXBOROUGH STATE PARK (all ages)

C–470 to the Santa Fe exit, south to Titan Road, which makes a sharp left turn, becoming Rampart Range Road. There are well-marked signs to the park; (303) 973–3959. Open daily. Summer hours generally 8:00 A.M. to 8:00 P.M.; winter hours vary monthly. Call ahead. $ per car.

History, geology, flora and fauna—it's all here, but many visitors come just to enjoy Roxborough's gentle looping hikes among stunning red-rock formations similar to those at the Garden of the Gods. On weekends there's often a docent with touch boxes on the patio at the visitors center. Inside, a fifteen-minute slide program gives an overview of the park. (Good family hint: Rest rooms here are open even if the visitors center is closed.)

A strong program of one-day workshops, lectures, guided hikes, and concerts includes many that are good for kids. Special toddler activities are offered every Tuesday morning, no advance registration—just show up.

Trailhead of the Colorado Trail

North of Roxborough State Park, at the mouth of Waterton Canyon, hikers find mile marker "0" for the Colorado Trail. Completed in 1987 after massive volunteer efforts, this is a continuous trail from Denver to Durango (in southwest Colorado) that is 461 miles long. Each summer hundreds set off to complete the entire trek; many others enjoy a few miles at a time. The first segment follows a Denver Water Board road to Strontia Springs Dam. While not a favorite section with hikers, the reward here is frequently spotting bighorn sheep. During travels in Colorado you will often be near segments of the trail. Take time to experience one of the state's great treasures.

Morrison

TINY TOWN (ages 1–8)

6249 South Turkey Creek Road, Morrison 80465; 5 miles west of the C–470 and U.S. Highway 285 interchange; (303) 697–6829; www.designcircuit.com/ eic/tiny.html. Open Memorial Day to Labor Day, 10:00 A.M. to 5:00 P.M. Open Saturday and Sunday only during May, September, and October. $, children 2 and younger **Free**.

This miniature, child-size village delights young visitors with its one hundred colorful buildings constructed to a one-sixth scale. You can play the game of "Who Lives Here" and let your youngsters choose homes for their grandmas and grandpas, aunties and uncles, or for imaginary families. The structures are big enough so that kids can peek in windows, and you can use them as backdrops for photos of your little ones. The Tiny Town Railway takes big and little passengers on a 1-mile journey around the early-twentieth-century town and up scenic Turkey Canyon. The railway station features a grown-up-size gift shop and snack bar.

MORRISON MUSEUM OF NATURAL HISTORY (ages 4 and up)

501 State Highway 8, Morrison 80465 (½ mile south of Morrison); (303) 697– 1873. Open Wednesday through Sunday noon to 4:00 P.M. $

This museum is housed in the Leland Cox cabin, built in 1945 as a replica of a stagecoach stop. It's located just a few miles from Dinosaur Ridge and is a good first stop. A twenty-minute video gives an orientation to the ridge. The collection includes bones of the original stegosaurus found on Dinosaur Ridge in 1877. There are hands-on exhibits where you can handle dinosaur bones, touch live reptiles native to this area, and learn what it's like to dig for fossils.

DINOSAUR RIDGE (ages 4 and up)

On West Alameda Parkway just west of C–470; (303) 697–3466. Visitors Center open daily year-round, 9:00 A.M. to 4:00 P.M. **Free**.

Dinosaurs once lived right here—about fifteen minutes from downtown—when Denver was an ocean. Dinosaur Ridge contains footprints and fossil remains of the giant creatures that roamed here 100 to 150 million years ago. Ocean waves are preserved in large sections of rock.

Parking is available at the Visitors Center on the east side of the ridge. Follow the 1-mile self-guided tour provided by Friends of Dinosaur Ridge, a nonprofit group. Sixteen interpretive signs describe important features. Guidebooks, giving more complete information for each stop, may be purchased. You'll be walking on the shoulder of a public road, so hang on to your children. It's easy to wander out onto the pavement.

One Saturday a month, from April through October, the road is closed to normal traffic for "Open Ridge Days," and a shuttle bus provides rides over the ridge. Tour guides are on board with lively explanations.

While some of the geological information is uninteresting to younger ones, everyone loves the giant dinosaur footprints. If you have dino fanatics in the family, you can arrange a guided tour by calling at least one week in advance. A minimum fee of $25.00 is charged for one to twelve students, or $35.00 for nonstudent groups. Groups of thirteen or more pay $3.00 per person.

If you have surefooted kids with you, climb up the wooden stairs on the east side of the ridge. They lead to the narrow Dakota Ridge Trail, which has magnificent views. Watch out for mountain bikers on the trail.

RED ROCKS PARK AND AMPHITHEATER (all ages)

12 miles west of downtown Denver, south of I–70 on State Highway 26; (303) 295–4444. **Free** *park admission, fees for events.*

You'll see lots of faces and forms in the unusual red-rock formations here. Although remarkable geology surrounds visitors, most come here for the music. The outdoor amphitheater, wedged between spurs of 300-million-year-old sandstone, has been the setting for popular summer concerts since it opened in 1941.

Try to visit on a nonconcert day. The amphitheater is a great place to bring a picnic. Enjoy the panoramic view of downtown Denver. Your kids will love standing on the stage and singing to you in the stands. The natural acoustics are phenomenal. They'll also love to run up and down the rows of seats. Don't follow them for too long, or you'll be sorry tomorrow.

Stop in at the Trading Post, a curio store in a Pueblo-style building. You'll find rest rooms here with entry on the outside of the building. (The rest rooms at the top of the amphitheater are sometimes locked.)

Evergreen

Located 30 miles west of Denver, Evergreen sits in pine-and-aspen forest at the base of 14,260-foot Mt. Evans. For generations prominent Denver families maintained mountain homes in this area. Today many residents live here year-round and commute to jobs in Denver.

EVERGREEN LAKE (all ages)

29614 Upper Bear Creek Road, Evergreen 80439; (303) 674–0532; www. evergreen.net/lakehouse. Open for ice-skating daily when the lake is safely frozen. Skating, $; rentals, $. Open for boating Memorial Day through Labor Day, weather permitting. $$

Spin, twirl, and glide along the frozen lake under sparkling blue Colorado skies and snow-blanketed mountain peaks. Our version of Currier and Ives, Evergreen Lake has been a winter tradition for many families for generations. When the chills set in, retreat to the log warming house for hot drinks and snacks. There's even an espresso bar. Lights make it possible to skate until 7:00 P.M., but temperatures drop sharply after sundown.

During the summer pedal or paddle using rental canoes and paddleboats, or spend some quiet time fishing. Since the lake serves as a water supply, swimming and wading are not permitted. A boardwalk through wetlands connects to a trail circling the lake and to a handicapped-accessible fishing pier. Picnic tables, a playground, and adjoining public golf course make this an outdoor stop for everyone.

HIWAN HOMESTEAD HISTORICAL MUSEUM (ages 4 and up)

4208 South Timbervale Drive, Evergreen 80439 (just off Meadow Drive); (303) 674–6262. Open year-round, Tuesday through Sunday; June through August, 11:00 A.M. to 5:00 P.M.; September through May, noon to 5:00 P.M. Free *tours.*

The seventeen-room log lodge illustrates summer mountain living from 1890 to 1930. Rooms are furnished in an eclectic blend of Old West, Native American artifacts, and period pieces. One of the two octago-

*E*vergreen Round-Trip I-70 to

the Evergreen Parkway is the fastest route from Denver to Evergreen. Make it a round-trip by following State Highway 74 along Bear Creek back to Morrison and U.S. Highway 285. The route passes through or near to numerous Jefferson County Open Space and Denver Mountain Parks that provide many opportunities for outdoor recreation or picnics.

nal towers has a Gothic-inspired chapel on the second floor. Numerous smaller buildings contain quilt and doll collections, carpentry and printing workshops, and cowboy gear. Some exhibits are hands-on. There's a real saddle to climb onto; perhaps you can try a little roping.

After-school programs feature historical crafts: whittling, papermaking, beadwork, and yarn dolls, among others.

Adjacent is Heritage Grove Park, a lovely shaded site for picnics and a popular spot for special events throughout the year.

For More Information

Evergreen Area Chamber of Commerce, P.O. Box 97, Evergreen
80437-0097; (303) 674–3412; www.evergreenchamber.org.

Golden

HOWDY, FOLKS. This large welcome sign that arches over Washington Avenue sets the tone in Golden. Once this region was the dividing line between Arapahoe and Utes—the meeting of plains and mountains. Today this thriving town is most famous as the home of Coors Brewery. But Golden also boasts museums, art galleries, a bustling downtown, and the Colorado School of Mines.

COLORADO RAILROAD MUSEUM (all ages)
17155 West 44th Avenue, Golden 80403; (303) 279–4591 or (800) 365–6263; www.crrm.org. Open daily, June through August, 9:00 A.M. to 6:00 P.M.; September through May, 9:00 A.M. to 5:00 P.M. Family rates available. $

If your family is into trains, plan to spend two or three hours here. More than 50,000 rare railroad photos, documents, and artifacts reside inside the replica of a circa-1880 train depot, while outside on the museum's twelve acres, more than fifty locomotives and other railroad memorabilia await. Your family can climb aboard many of the trains. And Santa comes by on the first weekend in December to hand out candy from the little red caboose. Several times a year an 1881 narrow-gauge steam locomotive is fired up, and visitors are offered free rides with museum admission. Take along a lunch or snacks to be enjoyed at one of the picnic tables, stay as long as you like, and be sure to bring your camera for some memorable happy snaps.

HERITAGE SQUARE (all ages)

Take exit 259 from I–70 and travel north on U.S. Highway 40 for 1 mile; (303) 279–2789; www.ingolden.com/attractions.html. Open Monday through Saturday 10:00 A.M. to 9:00 P.M. and Sunday noon to 9:00 P.M. Open times for entertainment facilities and summer hours vary; phone for exact times. Free *admission.*

If you haven't been to Heritage Square recently, you are in for a grand surprise. A more than one-half-million-dollar renovation of this Victorian-style shopping and entertainment center has resulted in a great place to take the family. You can shop for gift items, have an old-time portrait taken, and maneuver a paddleboat or bumper car. Younger children will delight in taking a spin on the colorful carousel and climbing aboard the miniature steam engine–powered train for a ride around the perimeter of the park. Older youngsters are sure to talk you into a game of laser tag, a ride on the Ferris wheel, and an exhilarating sweep down the alpine slide. When you're ready for a rest, popcorn, ice cream, and soft drink outlets come to the rescue, or consider having dinner at the Beer Hunter Restaurant.

HERITAGE SQUARE MUSIC HALL (ages 6 and up)

Located at Heritage Square; (303) 279–7800. Performances year-round (except first three weeks in January), Wednesday through Saturday evenings; Sunday matinee. Additional performances during Christmas holidays; phone for schedule. Dinner and show, $$$$; performance only, $$$.

If your family enjoys live theater, they are sure to love the performances at the Heritage Square Music Hall. Multitalented producer, director, and actor T. J. Mullin and his cast of merrymakers present outrageous comedy shows along with musical renditions ranging in nature from honky-tonk to nostalgic, old-time tunes—all family oriented and in good taste. Your kids will delight in hissing the villain and cheering for the hero and heroine. Special productions such as *Cinderella* are nearly always on the bill for children. Consider indulging in the all-you-can-eat buffet and show package. Or dine earlier and come for the performance only.

GENESEE BUFFALO HERD OVERLOOK (all ages)
West of Golden on I–70, exit 254; follow signs to overlook. **Free**.

As you climb into the foothills on I-70, the highway cuts through a Denver Mountain Park. Genesee is home to a herd of approximately forty bison. With 500 acres to freely roam, including their own tunnel under the interstate, I can't promise you'll always be able to spot these mighty American native beasts, but it's worth a try. Fall and winter, when they are hay-fed, provide the best opportunity to view them close to the highway. In the summer's heat check the shaded gullies north of I-70.

The park also keeps an elk herd of about the same size. They can usually be seen from the park road to the south toward the picnic grounds and shelter. By following Genesee Mountain Road and Genesee Drive, you can get back on I-70 at the Chief Hosa exit, 253.

Hint Heading west from Denver on I-70, especially if this is your first visit to the Colorado Rocky Mountains, be sure to note the view as you crest the hill at the Genesee exit. The award-winning overpass bridge perfectly frames a majestic scene sweeping to the Continental Divide. For eastbound travelers the bridge frames Denver and the Front Range.

GENESEE PARK BRAILLE TRAIL (all ages)
I–70 to exit 253, Chief Hosa; turn right onto Stapleton Drive and continue 1 mile to a gate across the road and a parking area. **Free**.

The Stapleton Braille Trail leads hikers along a 1-mile nature loop. Informative signs, printed and in Braille, enlighten as you follow the cleared, cabled path. Bask in the sun's warmth from the log bench on a south-facing slope. All visitors can enjoy this quiet stop. Bring a lunch; there is a picnic site with tables.

BUFFALO BILL MEMORIAL MUSEUM AND GRAVE (ages 4 and up)

987 Lookout Mountain Road, Golden 80401; (303) 526–0747; www.ingolden. com/attractions.html. Open daily May through October, 9:30 A.M. to 5:00 P.M.; November through April, open Tuesday through Sunday 9:00 A.M. to 4:00 P.M. No charge to view the gravesite. Museum: $, children 5 and younger **Free***.*

William F. Cody, better known as Buffalo Bill, is immortalized in this museum, located high atop Lookout Mountain, above the city of Golden. The assemblage, begun by Buffalo Bill's foster son, Johnny Baker, in 1921, showcases a comprehensive history of Cody's life, including old photographs, documents, and quality paintings. Also on display are Buffalo Bill's saddles and costumes from his Wild West Show and treasured gifts from his Native American friends. The latter include a ghost shirt, a hair shirt, Chief Iron Tail's headdress, and Chief Sitting Bull's bow and arrow. The museum also highlights the women of Buffalo Bill's Wild West Show.

LOOKOUT MOUNTAIN NATURE CENTER AND PRESERVE (all ages)

910 Colorow Road, Golden 80401; (303) 271–5925. From I–70 take exit 256 and follow the brown signs. Open year-round, Tuesday through Friday 10:00 A.M. to 4:00 P.M. and Saturday and Sunday 9:00 A.M. to 5:00 P.M. **Free***.*

Looking for something a little more active on Lookout Mountain? Head to the Nature Center and Preserve, a premier Jefferson County Open Space Park. Hike the nature trails, picnic under towering ponderosa pines, or participate in one of many naturalist-guided activities. Events—Weekend Wanderings, Toddler Times, It's a Wild World—are designed for specific age groups, parent/child or the entire family. Topics change with the season, so there is always something new and exciting.

Inside the nature center you'll find Discovery Corner, with interactive self-guided activity areas for the curious of all ages. Explorer theme packs to use while visiting the preserve may be rented for a small fee. If you find a book, game, or entire theme pack your child really relates to, new ones may be purchased. They're good ideas for gifts, too.

Enviroramas present the complex ecological system of the Ponderosa Pine Community. The facility exemplifies sustainable design, using environmentally responsible materials and promoting human health. Landscaping demonstrates fire-wise/low-water planning. Dedicated staff help visitors connect with nature's community.

Golden Walking, Hiking, and Biking Trails (all ages)

The city of Golden is blessed with numerous easy walking, hiking, and biking trails that are perfect for families with children of different ages. Here are a few. For more request the *Hiking and Biking Trails in Golden* and the *Golden Walk* brochures from the Golden Chamber of Commerce (303–279–3113).

The Clear Creek Trail runs west from Washington Avenue through a park and along the river. It has an easy grade with fine gravel and is ½ mile in length, one way.

The Tucker Gulch Trail begins at Vanover Park, located at Ford and Water Streets. This paved, 1¹⁄₁₀-mile (one way) trail leads through north Golden and ends at Norman D. Memorial Park.

The Golden Walk is actually a 1½-mile, self-guided walking tour of the city, with designated cultural and historical sites along the way. This fascinating excursion includes the Clear Creek Living History Park, the circa-1861 Territorial Capitol Building (now a restaurant), the 1867 Astor House Hotel Museum, the Foothills Art Center (**Free** admission), and the Geology Museum (**Free** admission).

GOLDEN GATE CANYON STATE PARK (all ages)

From Golden travel north on State Highway 93 for 1 mile, turn west on Golden Gate Canyon Road, and continue 13 miles to park entrance; (303) 582–3707; parks. state.co.us/Golden_Gate. Open daily year-round, weather permitting. Winter visitors are encouraged to call the park office for current conditions. $ per car.

In 1860 the road up Golden Gate Canyon was a toll road carrying fortune hunters to the gold fields near Black Hawk and Central City. Today, shorter routes lead to those old mining towns, while Golden Gate Canyon Road leads to outdoor adventure. Miles and miles of mountain trails keep hikers, mountain bikers, and horseback riders (bring your own horse, no stables) busy. From Panorama Point you can view more than 100 miles of the Continental Divide, a great backdrop for family pictures.

Stop in the visitors center for the interactive displays and audios or to put the ecosystem puzzle together. Just outside, a handicapped-accessible nature trail winds around a pond stocked with rainbow trout. This is an excellent spot for young children to practice their fishing skills. If they get lucky, you'll find picnic tables and grills nearby.

As the quiet solitude of winter settles on the park, opportunities abound for snowshoeing, ice fishing, skating, sledding, tubing, and cross-country skiing—even winter camping for really hardy souls.

Family Adventure Packs and Junior Ranger booklets lead families to new discoveries during their park visit. Show the completed booklets to a ranger for free certificates and badges. Interpretive programs are available throughout the summer.

Where to Eat

Table Mountain Inn. *1310 Washington Avenue, Golden 80401; (303) 277–9898. Open daily for breakfast, lunch, and dinner; weekend brunch.* Superb Southwestern cuisine draws locals here regularly. Generations of families often gather for the food, friendly service, and relaxed atmosphere. From burgers to a grilled portobello wrap, there's something for everyone. Favorites include the Southwestern Caesar salad and jalapeño corn muffins. "Wild" Friday-night dinner entrees highlight game dishes, but don't worry, the children's menu offers more typical kid fare. For dessert try the chocolate cherry tamale—creative, great flavors, and outstanding presentation. $$–$$$

Ice Cream Sitting side-by-side in downtown Golden are two shops serving locally made ice cream.

- **Cousin Jack's**, 1205½ Washington Avenue, piles cones high with Josh & John's ice cream.

- **Joyce's Subs**, 1207 Washington Avenue, offers many flavors from Lik's.

Where to Stay

The Golden Hotel. *800 11th Street, Golden 80401; (303) 279–0100.* This hotel has sixty-two rooms and a full-service restaurant. The junior and executive suites work nicely for families. The inn is adjacent to the bike and walking paths along Clear Creek, and two city parks are across the street. Nearby is the city's recreation center, with swimming pools and other sports facilities. $$–$$$

Table Mountain Inn. *1310 Washington Avenue, Golden 80401; (303) 277–9898; (800) 762–9898.* In the early 1990s this property underwent total renovation. The resulting Southwestern adobe–style exterior and decor add warmth and comfort to the thirty-two-room inn. Friendly staff gladly accommodate families with cribs and other special needs. There's no pool, but they provide passes to Golden's great recreation center with indoor pool. $$–$$$

Jefferson County Open Space Parks

Jefferson County Open Space Parks More than twenty-five years ago, citizens of Jefferson County elected to tax themselves to set aside and preserve lands within the county. Urban nature areas, rolling plains, wildlife habitats, craggy peaks, serene mountain meadows, historical sites, and trail corridors enrich the experiences of residents and visitors. Parks offer varied opportunities and facilities. Whether you hike, bike, cross-country ski, or just take in the view, these Open Spaces are a gift. Hiwan Homestead Historical Museum and Lookout Mountain Nature Center (both listed separately in this chapter) are good places to pick up maps and brochures for the Open Space Parks. For complete information call (303) 271-5925 or consult www.co.jefferson.co.us/dpt/openspac/. Here's just a partial sampling:

- **Alderfer/Three Sisters Park.** Dramatic rock outcroppings, trails, deer, and wildflowers.

- **Apex.** 661 acres with 8 miles of hiking trails near Lookout Mountain.

- **Crown Hill.** Handicapped-accessible trails lead around a fishing lake; hiking, biking, wildlife preserve, fitness circuit.

- **Elk Meadow Park.** Meadow and forest trails, good cross-country skiing, wildlife from squirrels to elk.

- **Lair o' the Bear Park.** 1½ miles of stream frontage with loop trails, handicapped-accessible fishing pier, picnic tables, and grills.

- **Matthew/Winters Park.** Popular with mountain bikers; shady picnic grove, historic town site and cemetery; connects to Red Rocks Park.

- **Mount Falcon Park.** Trails with magnificent views of the Front Range and Continental Divide; shelter, picnic tables, historical ruins.

- **Pine Valley Ranch.** Parts of area recently burned from a forest fire provide opportunity to see how nature regenerates. Shelters and gazebo survived the fire. River, hiking, biking, and fishing.

- **Reynolds Park.** Interpretive trail, hiking, overnight camping (by permit only) for hikers and equestrians.

- **White Ranch Park.** Trails, very popular with mountain bikers; picnic sites and shelter, designated cross-country ski trails, and overnight camping (by permit only) for hikers and equestrians.

For More Information

**Golden Chamber of Commerce/
Visitors Center,** *1010 Washington
Avenue, Golden 80401; (303) 279–3113*

*or (800) 590–3113;
www.goldencochamber.org.*

Lookout Mountain Loop Another great circle trip. Approach
Lookout Mountain on I-70. From exit 256 follow the signs to Lookout
Mountain Nature Center and/or Buffalo Bill's Museum and Grave. For
the return trip wind down the mountain on Lariat Loop Road. There are
great views of Denver and the prairie beyond. If the weather conditions
are right, passengers can observe hang gliders and parasailers. Drivers
need to proceed slowly and keep a close eye on the curvy, switchback road.
At the foot of the mountain, follow 19th Street into Golden for further
adventures, or turn right on U.S. Highway 6; it will intersect with I-70.

Boulder

"The little town nestled between the mountains and reality," the *Denver Post*
aptly describes its neighbor. "The People's Republic of Boulder" and "Berkeley
of the Rockies" are other lighthearted references to Boulder's ambience.

University of Colorado students and staff make up almost one-third of the
population. Several scientific institutions (National Center for Atmospheric
Research [NCAR], Ball Aerospace, National Institute of Standards) also draw
professionals to this well-educated community.

Hugging the Flatirons, so named because of their resemblance to old-
fashioned irons, Boulder's beautiful setting and sunny, mild, four-season climate encourage an outdoor lifestyle. Hiking, biking, skiing, skating, rock
climbing—Boulderites are rarely indoors.

Boulder's food, festivals, and fashion all reflect the ethnically diverse cultural life of a university town.

NATIONAL CENTER FOR ATMOSPHERIC RESEARCH (NCAR) (ages 6 and up)

*At the end of Table Mesa Drive in southwestern Boulder; (303) 497–1174;
www.ucar.edu. Open Monday through Friday 8:00 A.M. to 5:00 P.M. and Saturday, Sunday, and all holidays 9:00 A.M. to 4:00 P.M.* **Free**.

Perched high above Boulder against the Flatirons, Mesa Laboratory,
designed by famed architect I. M. Pei, is visible for miles. Here, scientists

study weather and climate, and exhibits explain their work. Much of the information is the highly technical type (read *boring*), but six interactive exhibits from the Exploratorium museum in San Francisco grab your attention. Learn how lightning works or how a tornado spins.

Free guided tours are given at noon Monday and Wednesday, September through mid-June, and Monday through Saturday during summer. Self-guided tours are always available. Within the building two art galleries highlight the work of local artists; the cafeteria and library are open to the public on weekdays.

Many visitors come to NCAR to hike. The Walter Orr Roberts Nature Trail, which crosses the site, provides signs with information about local weather phenomena. It's the only wheelchair-accessible nature trail in Boulder, and it works very well for strollers, too. Take some time to enjoy the spectacular setting, a good place for a picnic.

CHAUTAUQUA PARK (all ages)

900 Baseline Road, Boulder 80302; (303) 442–3282; www.chautauqua.com.

Boulder's first city park was acquired in 1898 as part of a national Chautauqua movement. Centers were established for education, culture, and recreation and named for Lake Chautauqua in New York, where the first site was established. Today, this popular twenty-six-acre park offers hiking trails, cultural events, and a historic dining spot.

HIKING

(303) 441–3408; www.colorado.edu. **Free**.

Extensive trails draw hikers of all abilities. Two circle hikes popular with families are the Chautuaqua Loops, each about 2 miles. But neither is a simple walk in a park, so don't be misled. Be sure your group is properly attired; remember the sunscreen and water. To sort out the best hike for your family, stop in the Rangers' Cottage for maps and advice. Plan on breathtaking scenery. You'll know you're not in Kansas, Dorothy.

Boulder Mountain Parks offer family-friendly guided hikes throughout the year. Check the Web site for a listing of these **Free** events.

CULTURAL EVENTS

(303) 442–3282; www.chautauqua.com.

Built in 1898, the Chautauqua Auditorium is now on the National Register of Historic Places. It's a favorite venue for performers and guest lecturers. Concerts are scheduled throughout the summer season. The Silent Film Festival offers the chance to show kids what going to the movies used to be like. The films are accompanied by live organ music.

 ## CHAUTAUQUA DINING HALL

(303) 440–3776. Open year-round. Breakfast and lunch, Wednesday through Saturday 8:00 A.M. to 2:00 P.M.; Sunday buffet brunch 8:00 A.M. to 2:00 P.M.; dinner, Wednesday through Sunday 5:00 to 9:00 P.M. Reservations accepted. $

Although this dining hall was built in 1898, the food is definitely up-to-date. Check it out after a hike or before an event.

UNIVERSITY OF COLORADO

(303) 492–1411.

It's never too early to take your kids to college. A simple walk across the campus may spark an interest—plant a seed that comes to life years down the road. Casual campus visits with youngsters develop a base of comparison and build personal knowledge that could be invaluable to later decision-making.

The University of Colorado (CU) campus could be a model for all college campuses: attractive architecture (rural Italian-style buildings of Colorado sandstone punctuated with red tile roofs) on a 600-acre tree-lined campus nestled against the mountains.

Founded in 1876, this university was under construction before Colorado became a state. Its history includes legislators riding on horseback between Denver and Boulder to secure funding in time for a critical vote. One faction wanted Boulder to be the site of Colorado's first university, while another group wanted a prison to be built here.

Old Main (still in use) constituted the entire university from 1876 to 1884. Today more than 25,000 students are enrolled. Famous former students include Supreme Court Justice Byron White, bandleader Glenn Miller, and actor Robert Redford.

On a walk across campus you'll discover great people-watching. Many trees in Norlin Quadrangle are more than one hundred years old. Basking turtles can be found at Varsity Pond; basking students are everywhere.

The university offers campus tours led by student ambassadors Monday through Saturday. It's best to make a reservation (303–492–7884).

Finding a parking space in the area can be trying, so head to Euclid Avenue AutoPark, just east of the University Memorial Center. Parking 7:00 A.M. to 5:00 P.M. is $1.00 per hour.

THE CU MUSEUM (ages 2 and up)
*In the Henderson Building on the University of Colorado campus; (303)
492–6892; www.colorado.edu/CUMUSEUM/. Open Monday through
Friday 9:00 A.M. to 5:00 P.M., Saturday 9:00 A.M. to 4:00 P.M., and
Sunday 10:00 A.M. to 4:00 P.M.* **Free**.

You can touch fossils here. This two-floor museum of natural history is low key, a delightful change from larger metro
facilities. Dinosaur Hall is a favorite with families. You can't
miss the spectacular triceratops head. Check out Discovery
Corner, an area specifically designed for children. Try on a giant
tortoise shell or deer antlers—lots of objects to touch here.

Ask about the museum's changing exhibits. Some are pretty
intriguing—past shows included Body Art (tattooing) and
Dinosaur Tracking.

 THE CU HERITAGE CENTER (ages 6 and up)
*In Old Main on the University of Colorado campus; (303) 492–6329;
www.cusys.edu (under alumni). Open Monday through Friday 10:00
A.M. to 4:00 P.M. and Saturday 10:00 A.M. to 2:00 P.M.* **Free**.

Old Main, completed in 1876 and renovated in 1982, is
home to The Heritage Center. This small museum chronicles
university life, highlighting special achievements of alumni and
faculty. It's more interesting than it sounds.

Highlights include "CU in Space," an exhibit featuring
space-travel artifacts from fifteen alumni astronauts. The Ath-
letics Gallery features proud reminders of CU's fine sports performances: trophies, photos, and autographed footballs along
with a display of athletic equipment from the past. The
mounted head of Ralphie, the Buffs' first mascot, is revered.

FISKE PLANETARIUM
*On Regent Drive on the University of Colorado campus (look for the geo-
desic dome); (303) 492–5002; www.colorado.edu/fiske/. The building
is open Monday through Friday 9:00 A.M. to 5:00 P.M. Shows for the
public on select Tuesday evenings, every Friday evening at 8:00 P.M., with
a laser show at 10:00 P.M., and Saturday at 2:00 P.M. $*

Cosmic Collisions, Galaxies at the End of the Universe, and
Mars Quest—just some of the star shows and live star talks that
are the main offerings here. Once a month laser light shows set
to rock or reggae music draw a crowd to special late-night per-

formances. Adjacent to the planetarium, Sommers-Bausch Observatory is open for **Free** observing sessions after most Friday-evening shows.

Browse the lobby, where you can touch a meteorite, split light into rainbows with prisms, and learn about magnetic force. "Toys in Space" is a nostalgic look at toys for exploring distant worlds.

COLORADO SCALE MODEL SOLAR SYSTEM

This self-guided walk starts in front of Fiske Planetarium, continuing north across Regent Drive and through the campus. On a scale of one to ten billion, the model planets illustrate the inconceivably vast distances in our solar system. Each step you take along the way represents 10 million kilometers; the *Voyager* spacecraft took ten years to go this same distance!

This model solar system is dedicated to the memory of University of Colorado alumnus Ellison S. Onizuka and his six crewmates of the space shuttle *Challenger.*

PEARL STREET MALL

Pearl Street from 11th to 15th Streets; (303) 449-3774. **Free**.

This is city living at its best. Eclectic shops and ethnic restaurants line this pedestrian mall. Street musicians, jugglers, and magicians entertain. Hundreds of seasonal flowers, intriguing sculptures, and the Rocky Mountain backdrop encourage visitors to relax on one of many benches. You won't find better people-watching! Always colorful, always fun; it's so very Boulder.

A favorite stop for kids is Into the Wind (303–449–5356). Colorful kites and banners attract customers immediately. This shop is filled with toys, games, and equipment that entire families love.

Peppercorn (303–449–5847) is a must-stop for all cooks. A feast for the eyes begins the moment you look in the window. This store literally overflows with food-related items. The extensive collection of cookbooks includes a children's section.

You may not want to take children in here. Touching is so tempting! The narrow aisles and volume crowds make it tough to roll a stroller around, but a playground is conveniently located right outside the door. So leave the little ones with the noncooking parent while you take twenty minutes to visit kitchen heaven.

BOULDER CREEK PATH (all ages)

16 miles of paved path from Boulder Canyon to 55th Street. **Free**.

Walkers, joggers, runners, cyclists, in-line skaters, those in strollers, and those in wheelchairs—they all love this path, which follows the creek. On bikes it's a convenient way to get around Boulder and avoid street traffic. Or it's a pleasant recreational ride that takes families to or near many appealing attractions. During warm weather you'll enjoy watching water-lovers in kayaks, canoes, and inner tubes.

Along the route near the Clarion Harvest House, stop at the Fish Observatory. Just off the path, stairs lead down to an almost hidden nook with four portholes looking into Boulder Creek. On a good day you can watch trout swim by. On a bad day the portholes are covered with scum and you won't see anything. But there are interesting signs that tell about what you *would* have seen!

COLLAGE CHILDREN'S MUSEUM (ages 2–9)

2065 30th Street, Boulder 80301; in Aspen Plaza; (303) 440–9894. Open Monday and Wednesday through Saturday 10:00 A.M. to 5:00 P.M. and Sunday 1:00 to 5:00 P.M. Special toddler hour on Friday, 9:00 to 10:00 A.M. $

Hands-on, interactive experiences geared toward the age-nine-and-under crowd await your kids at Collage. Exhibits change four times each year, so you never know exactly what you'll find—but it will be interactive, educational, and fun. A specific area for under-three toddlers includes easel painting, a sandbox, and building tools. There's a story hour every Wednesday at 3:30 P.M.

The admission fee is for the day. You can leave for lunch (or a nap?) and return. Collage is a great favorite with locals, so it's often crowded, especially when rare bad weather forces Boulderites indoors. Mondays are generally less crowded, and afternoons on any day are best. FYI: School groups come on Wednesday.

SCOTT CARPENTER PARK (all ages)

30th Street and Arapahoe Avenue; (303) 441–3427 (pool). Pool open Memorial Day through Labor Day. Open swim Monday through Friday 1:00 to 5:00 P.M., Saturday 1:00 to 6:00 P.M., and Sunday 1:00 to 5:00 P.M.; adult lap swim daily 11:00 A.M. to 1:00 P.M. Pool, $; park, **Free**.

Named for the Boulder astronaut, this park is a real haven for families. Conveniently located along Boulder Creek Path, it's a great destination for cyclists. During summer months the outdoor pool is the draw. There's a diving area, water slide, and separate toddler pool.

The playground has a rocket ship, in keeping with the astronaut theme.

BOULDER SKATEBOARD PARK (ages 8 and up)

In Scott Carpenter Park; (303) 441–4421. Open during the school year Monday through Friday 3:00 P.M. until dark and Saturday and Sunday 9:00 A.M. to 1:00 P.M. and 1:30 to 5:30 P.M. Summer hours daily, 10:00 A.M. to 2:00 P.M. and 3:00 to 7:00 P.M. $

Nirvana for the serious skateboarder and great fun for observers. The YMCA runs this park, a fenced-in area of ramps where teens and preteens strut their stuff on skateboards, in-line skates, and bikes. Parents will be happy to know that helmets, kneepads, and elbowpads are required. Each can be rented for $1.00 if you didn't bring your own.

CELESTIAL SEASONINGS (ages 5 and up)

4600 Sleepytime Drive, Boulder 80301; (303) 581–1202. Open Monday through Friday 9:00 A.M. to 6:00 P.M., with tours on the hour 10:00 A.M. to 3:00 P.M.; Saturday 9:00 A.M. to 5:00 P.M., with tours on the hour 10:00 A.M. to 3:00 P.M.; and Sunday 11:00 A.M. to 4:00 P.M., with tours on the hour 11:00 A.M. to 3:00 P.M. Free.

The largest herbal-tea company in the United States gives a great tour! In fact, it's rated as one of the top-ten factory tours in the country. You get to see, hear, taste, and smell. You'll remember your visit to the mint room long after you've left. Get your Free tickets for the tour as soon as you arrive. Be prepared for a wait during the summer and on school holidays. Browse the art gallery, investigate the outside herb garden, or sample tea. The gift shop tempts young and old. The company logo, Sleepytime Bear, embellishes merchandise from boxer shorts to pâté spreaders. There's a nice selection of children's items. An amazing array of Celestial Seasonings teas is sold at a hefty discount. You might want to stock up.

The Celestial Café, with indoor and outdoor dining areas, is just the spot to regroup. Nearby, wide grassy areas offer younger visitors room to run.

Please note that children under five are not allowed on the tour through the factory.

LEANIN' TREE MUSEUM OF WESTERN ART (ages 5 and up)
*6055 Longbow Drive, Boulder 80301; (303) 581–2100; www.leanintree.com.
Open Monday through Friday 8:00 A.M. to 4:00 P.M. and Saturday and Sunday
10:00 A.M. to 4:00 P.M.* **Free.**

Fans of Leanin' Tree greeting cards come to see where they are made
and discover a world-class art museum. Owner Ed Trumble started a
business in the 1940s by reproducing original artwork on greeting cards.
Through the years he amassed one of the country's largest private collections of contemporary western art. The free museum is tucked into
their corporate building, which combines offices, printing plant, and
distribution center.

Acrylics, oils, watercolors, and sculptures depict weathered cowboys,
Native Americans, wildlife, landscapes, and western humor. Easy-to-read
biographies of artists are mounted by their work. Your kids won't want
to spend all day here, but a quick walk-through gives them some experience with western art.

Savvy shoppers come to the gift shop with lists of birthdays and
anniversaries. All 2,500 Leanin' Tree greeting cards are available for purchase along with mugs, calendars, magnets, and posters.

Hop & Skip Park the car for the day and forget worrying about
traffic, directions, and finding a parking space at each destination. Two
shuttles make getting around Boulder easy and convenient. **HOP** loops
through central Boulder, including Pearl Street Mall, Crossroads shopping center, and the CU campus; look for the purple signs. **SKIP** runs
north/south on Broadway; find the green signs. Fare is 75 cents exact
change. For maps and information call HOP at (303) 447–8282 and
SKIP at (303) 299–6000.

Where to Eat

Boulder Dushanbe Teahouse. *1770
13th Street, Boulder 80302 (between Arapahoe Avenue and Canyon Boulevard);
(303) 442–4993. Open Monday through
Thursday 8:00 A.M. to 9:00 P.M. and Friday
through Sunday 8:00 A.M. to 10:00 P.M.*
This brightly colored teahouse was a
gift from Boulder's sister city,
Dushanbe, Tajikistan, in the former
Soviet Union. It arrived from Asia in

200 crates. The intricate designs, both painted and carved, will elicit oohs and aahs. Stop for a look, inside and out, even if you don't want refreshments.

The teahouse is operated by staff affiliated with the Naropa Institute, a local school started by Tibetan Buddhists. They serve international cuisine in addition to tea. $-$$

Cold Stone Creamery. *1964 13th Street, Boulder 80302; (303) 541–0668. Open Monday through Thursday noon to 10:00 P.M. and Friday through Sunday noon to 11:00 P.M.* You choose from a list of forty items (raspberries, candy bar pieces, caramel) to be hand-mixed with one or more of the sixteen flavors of freshly made ice cream for a custom treat. $

Dolan's. *2319 Arapahoe Road, Boulder 80303; (303) 444–8758. Dinner only, Monday through Saturday 5:00 to 10:00 P.M.* Lobster as low as $16 per serving. $-$$

Lucile's. *2124 14th Street, Boulder 80302; (303) 442–4743. Open daily for breakfast and lunch.* Beignets (New Orleans-style doughnuts) and chicory coffee are served here. This is where you'll find a taste of Louisiana—including praline waffles and Creole omelettes—right in the middle of Boulder. Be prepared for a wait on the weekends. A basket of toys on the stairs entertains toddlers. Although Lucile's doesn't have a children's menu, you can get half-orders. $-$$

Where to Stay

Homewood Suites Hotel. *4950 Baseline Road, Boulder 80303; (303) 499–9922.* Complimentary breakfast, fully equipped kitchens, fitness center. $-$$

Hotel Boulderado. *2115 13th Street, Boulder 80302; (303) 442–4344 or (800) 433–4344; www.boulderado.com.* Located in the heart of Boulder's lively downtown, this restored hotel provides contemporary comfort. Two-room suites give families plenty of space and privacy. Children under twelve stay **Free**. Walk to activities, restaurants, shopping, playgrounds, and shuttle buses. $$$$

Even if you don't stay here, stop in and admire the lobby's elegant stained-glass ceiling, the richly detailed woodwork, and the cantilevered staircase.

Quality Inn & Suites, Boulder Creek. *2020 Arapahoe Avenue, Boulder 80302; (303) 449–7550 or (888) 449–7550 (outside Colorado); www.qualityinn boulder.com.* This casual but upscale property offers a full range of services and amenities, including rooms with coffeemakers, microwave ovens, irons and ironing boards, refrigerators, and six deluxe suites with minikitchen areas. A sauna, Jacuzzi, LifeFitness workout room, and heated indoor swimming pool offer activities for the whole family. The inn is located a short walk from Boulder's famous Pearl Street Mall. Rates include a complimentary hot breakfast buffet and the use of all fitness facilities and the business center. $$-$$$

Silver Saddle Motel. *90 West Arapahoe Avenue, Boulder 80303; (303) 442–8022 or (800) 525–9509.* On the Boulder Creek trail at the mouth of Boulder Canyon, this motel offers simple comfort and convenience. Half the thirty-two units are vintage cabins with kitchenettes. The remaining motel suites have a little more space and come equipped with microwaves and small refrigerators. Bungalow 16, sleeping six to eight, is a good choice for large families. Children ages twelve and under stay 𝐅𝐫𝐞𝐞. A playground and the nearby creek with kayak course keep kids entertained. Fishing anyone? $$–$$$

For More Information

Boulder Convention and Visitors Bureau, *2440 Pearl Street, Boulder 80302; (303) 442–2911; www.boulder coloradousa.com.*

Nederland

ELDORA MOUNTAIN RESORT
21 miles west of Boulder. Take State Highway 119 to Nederland and follow signs to the ski area; (303) 440–8700; www.eldora.com. $$$$

The emphasis at Eldora is on skiing and snowboarding, not luxury lodging or fine dining. This area even has public bus transportation from Boulder. Little Hawk Family Zone offers families and learners of any age their own terrain. The Mountain Explorer package includes a lift ticket, ski rental, lunch, and a four-hour lesson ($$$$).

For the youngest skiers, Tykes Terrain Park features the Thunderbolt Mine, Fort Cannonball, and Indian Tepees—plenty of excitement to keep them interested. A conveyer lift, similar to the people movers in airports, gets beginners up the hill behind the children's center. Professional ski school classes start at age four, downhill or snowboard. *Half-pipe, gaps, tabletops,* and *transfers*—your preschooler may soon be talking a language you don't understand.

At the Nordic Center options include telemark, snowshoeing, cross-country skiing, and skate-skiing. Lessons, rentals, groomed tracks, and trails make trying something new easy and exciting.

Whichever activity you choose at Eldora, there are mountaintop and base lodges to keep you warm and nourished.

Louisville

 WOW! CHILDREN'S MUSEUM (ages 1–10)
1075 South Boulder Road, Suite 130, Louisville 80027; (303) 604–2424; www.wowmuseum.com. Open June through August, Monday through Friday 9:00 A.M. to 6:00 P.M. and Saturday 10:00 A.M. to 6:00 P.M.; September through May, Tuesday through Thursday 9:00 A.M. to 6:00 P.M., Friday 10:00 A.M. to 8:00 P.M., Saturday 10:00 A.M. to 6:00 P.M., and Sunday noon to 4:00 P.M. Children $$, adults and children under 15 months Free.

WOW stands for World of Wonder; this is a museum dedicated to children's discovery. A 22-foot pirate ship, rain forest, dance studio, theater, and playhouse entice youngsters to learn through play and activities. Special features include an after-school game room for children five and up, weekend face painting, and monthly Friday-night family programs.

Active, exploratory, and quiet experiences are designed for young children to develop gross and fine motor skills. To get the most out of a visit with your toddler, ask for the information sheet called *Visiting with Young Children*. Toddler-only events occur on Tuesday, 9:00 to 10:00 A.M.

Longmont

 ROCKY MOUNTAIN PUMPKIN RANCH (all ages)
9057 Ute Highway, Longmont 80503; (303) 684–0087; www.rockymtnpumpkin ranch.com. Open daily late September through October, 9:00 A.M. to 6:00 P.M.; phone for exact dates. Rides and some amusements operate on Saturday and Sunday only. Free *admission, but there is a small charge for pumpkins and amusements.*

When you're a kid, what could be more fun than picking out your own Halloween pumpkin at a genuine pumpkin patch? At the Rocky Mountain Pumpkin Ranch, some kids, toy wagons in tow, choose the first pumpkin they see, while others wander up and down the rows, determined to find just the right size and shape for their jack-o'-lantern-to-be. This event has evolved into a fall harvest festival with fresh produce, home-baked goods, Halloween items, homemade cider, sizzling bratwurst, fresh-roasted corn, and caramel apples. Kids can have their faces painted, take an antique car ride, visit Uncle Oscar's Hay Maze, walk through the petting corral, get a free apple from Wanda the Good Witch, and ride a pony.

BARR LAKE STATE PARK (all ages)

13401 Picadilly Road (I–25 north from Denver to I–76, northeast on I–76 to Bromley Lane, east to Picadilly Road, and south to park entrance); (303) 659–6005; www.dnr.state.co.us/parks/. Open daily 5:00 A.M. to 10:00 P.M. Visitors Center open Wednesday through Sunday 9:00 A.M. to 4:00 P.M. $ per car.

The forty-minute drive from town through flat, dusty farm country is not a high point with kids, but this state park offers pleasant, low-key family fun. The lake, surrounded by 2,600 acres of park, is the nesting site of bald eagles and more than 300 other species of birds. A boardwalk leads out to the gazebo, where you can do some bird-watching in relative comfort. Deer, red fox, rabbits, toads, turtles, and snakes also call this home. **Free** public programs include guided nature walks.

Fishing and boating are allowed on the northeast end of the lake. Since no motors are permitted, peace and quiet reign.

Kids like the Visitors Center with its many hands-on exhibits. There usually are some live animals on display (snakes, turtles, and toads are popular). Ask about using a **Free** Discovery Pack, full of kids' field guides, binoculars, bug boxes, and other objects that encourage youngsters to interact with nature. The staff can customize the pack for your child's special interest.

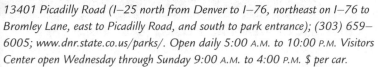

***S*weet as Sugar, and Twice as Sticky** If you are driving between Longmont and Lyons and it's time to let the kids out of the car, stop in at Madhava Mountain Gold Honey shop. Your youngsters can see busy bees at work making honey in a glass-sided hive. While there, pick up some HoneyStix in several flavors for snacking on later. Also for sale are honey, honey spreads, honey containers, beeswax candles, and gift packs. The shop, at 4689 Ute Highway, 1 mile east of Lyons, is open year-round, Monday through Friday 8:00 A.M. to 5:00 P.M.; also open Saturday 10:00 A.M. to 2:00 P.M., July through December 24; (303) 444-7999.

For More Information

Longmont Chamber of Commerce,
528 Main Street, Longmont 80501; (303) 776–5295; www.longmontchamber.org.

Greeley

HISTORIC CENTENNIAL VILLAGE (ages 4 and up)

1475 A Street, Greeley 80631; (970) 350–9220; www.ci.greeley.co.us. Open Memorial Day through Labor Day, Tuesday through Saturday 9:00 A.M. to 4:00 P.M.; mid-April through Memorial Day and Labor Day to October 28, open Tuesday through Saturday 10:00 A.M. to 3:00 P.M. $

The Historic Centennial Village provides visitors a glimpse of what it was like to live on Colorado's northeastern High Plains during the years from 1860 to 1920. The site's thirty restored structures include German, Swedish, and Hispanic homesteads. Your youngsters can crawl into an authentic Cheyenne tepee, view a one-room schoolhouse, go into the Union Pacific train depot to see an operational telegraph office, and enter a country church. Perhaps not of interest to children but respected and admired by adults are the homes' Victorian-era splendor and their Italianate, Queen Anne, and Colonial Revival architecture.

DENVER BRONCO TRAINING CAMP (all ages)

On the campus of the University of Northern Colorado. Open approximately six weeks during July and August. Call UNC's Athletic Department (970–351–2007) for exact dates and times for open practices and scrimmages. **Free**.

Summer means training camp for professional football teams, and in Greeley that means carloads of fans coming to watch their heroes. Serious autograph hounds arrive early and spend the morning waiting in line. Daily, during the noon break, several players participate in a signing session. You won't know who it will be, a ten-year veteran star or a first-year rookie. But then you never know when that rookie may be the next John Elway or Terrell Davis.

Fanatics don't miss a detail of each drill or practice play, while others open a lawn chair, watch a while, spot favorite players, and chat with friends. Strollers and wagons filled with toddlers, cold drinks, snacks, and toys are everywhere. It's all very casual, reminiscent of a big family reunion in the park.

Youngsters, age three to teens, play friendly pickup football games, encouraging observers to join in.

Concession stands sell food, drinks, and all manner of Bronco merchandise. Local and Denver newspapers publish practice schedules. Come on by.

CENTENNIAL PARK (all ages)

23rd Avenue and Reservoir Road, west of the University of Northern Colorado campus; (970) 330–2837. Pool open daily Memorial Day to Labor Day, 1:00 to 5:00 P.M. Admission to the park is **Free***, but there is a small charge for use of the pool.*

If you need to cool off after a morning at Bronco Training Camp, stop for a swim at Centennial Park. Plenty of green grass, picnic tables and shelter, tennis courts, ball fields, and a skate park make this a good family spot.

For More Information

Greeley Convention and Visitors Bureau, *902 7th Avenue, Greeley 80631; (970) 352–3567 or (800) 449–3866; www.greeleycvb.com.*

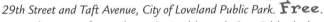

Loveland

Backed up against the foothills just 25 miles east of Rocky Mountain National Park, Loveland is the "Gateway to the Rockies." Don't be fooled by the quaint small-town look. Loveland is a cultural hot spot—a major center for art, especially bronze sculpture. Two important sculpture shows each August draw top-notch artists and art lovers from around the country. More than fifty well-known artists live here year-round, and many welcome visitors to their studios. Two foundries cast the work of local sculptors and international artists. Ask about scheduled tours—the bronze casting process is fascinating!

Loveland displays its art in easy-to-find public places. Watching for them as you drive through town can be fun for all ages. Circle past the firehouse, library, newspaper office, and baseball field.

BENSON PARK SCULPTURE GARDEN (all ages)

29th Street and Taft Avenue, City of Loveland Public Park. **Free***.*

A showcase for sculptural art, this park, just 3 blocks long with a lagoon at one end, is home to more than forty sculptures. Meander along the paths and marvel at the realism of the coiled boa and the great blue heron. *Unsteady Steadiness,* two boys riding double on their bike over uneven pavement, will make you smile. Kids love coming upon the alligator in the streambed and climbing on the turtles (all bronze!).

FOOTE LAGOON (all ages)
At the Civic Center, 700 East 4th Street. **Free**.

A walk around the lagoon and a romp in the playground make a great break from driving. Outside the library, a young boy pulls a wagon filled with little girls and books in *Overdue* by Jane DeDecker. You can almost hear the music from the quintet under a maple tree in George Lundeen's *Joy of Music*. The meaning of *Twist of Fate* will be a good conversation topic as you get back in the car.

Don't miss the opportunity to share quality art in Loveland's pleasant surroundings with your family.

SYLVAN DALE GUEST RANCH (all ages)
2939 North Country Road 31 D, Loveland 80538 (off State Highway 34, west of Loveland); (970) 667–3915; www.sylvandale.com. One-night to weeklong accommodations and ranch activities. Call for rates. $$$–$$$$

Nearly 50 percent of all guests at Sylvan Dale Guest Ranch are children. And it's easy to see why. This family-owned, family-run operation has been providing dude ranch accommodations, activities, and meals along with authentic western hospitality for more than fifty years. Horseback riding, cattle drives, overnight pack trips, and breakfast rides are only a few of the horse-related activities. Your family can swim together in the outdoor pool, go for a horse-drawn wagon ride, and go fishing in the river and lakes of the Sylvan Dale Valley. You can watch cattle being branded, play a set of tennis, and even help clean the barn, if you are so inclined. No sitting in circles, cutting and pasting for kids at this ranch. No siree, "pahdner." Depending on their ages, the little buckaroos can help groom the horses and soap the saddles, take off on accompanied nature hikes and scavenger hunts, float on inner tubes on the pasture ponds, pan for gold, or take a farm tour. This is where memories are made.

For More Information

Loveland Chamber of Commerce,
5400 Stone Creek Circle, Suite 200, Loveland 80538; (970) 667–6311; www.loveland.org.

Won't You Be My Valentine? The city of Loveland earns its

moniker, "The Sweetheart City."

In 1946 the Loveland Postmaster and his wife decided to share the romantic name of their town with the whole world, and the Valentine Remailing Program was born. Volunteers hand-stamp a special four-line rhyme, new each year, on all valentines mailed from Loveland. The Loveland Post Office creates a special cancellation mark for the holiday. An average 300,000 valentines are remailed from this small town every February to destinations in fifty states and 104 countries.

How can you add this special touch to your valentine? Before February 9, preaddress and stamp your valentine. Enclose it in a larger first-class envelope and mail to:

Postmaster
ATTN: Valentines
USPS
Loveland, CO 80538–9998

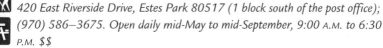

Estes Park

Adjacent to Rocky Mountain National Park and just 65 miles northwest of Denver, this town of 9,000 residents has been a Colorado favorite for more than one hundred years. Its tree-lined streets are accented with Victorian-style lampposts, flower boxes, and sidewalk benches. More than 200 shops and thirty restaurants tempt browsers and diners with an amazing variety of goods and edibles. An attractive Riverwalk offers families a place to stroll off the main street. Nearby Rocky Mountain National Park offers hands-on experiences with nature. Fun with the family comes easily in this mountain valley.

 AERIAL TRAMWAY (all ages)
420 East Riverside Drive, Estes Park 80517 (1 block south of the post office); (970) 586–3675. Open daily mid-May to mid-September, 9:00 A.M. to 6:30 P.M. $$

If you don't have much time but you'd like a mountain experience, this attraction is for you. A gondola whisks you up the mountain in less than five minutes, affording panoramic views of Longs Peak, the Continental Divide, and the town below. There are picnic tables at the top and a snack bar in case you didn't pack your lunch. Easy hiking trails appeal to families.

Remember, though, this is a commercial operation. I suggest that you also drive into Rocky Mountain National Park and stop for a hike in pristine wilderness, away from machinery and fast food.

COLORADO BICYCLE ADVENTURES (all ages)

184 East Elkhorn Avenue, P.O. Box 1301, Estes Park 80517; (970) 586–4241 or (800) 607–8765; www.coloradobicycling.com. Shop and rentals open Monday through Friday 9:00 A.M. to 7:00 P.M. and Saturday and Sunday 9:00 A.M. to 8:00 P.M. Tours begin at 8:00 and 9:00 A.M., and 1:00 P.M. $$$$, includes bike rental.

You will find downhill tours for nearly all ages here. Bike seats, tandems, tagalongs, or trailers are available for the younger crowd. Three-hour trips on paved roads wind through grand scenery, while friendly guides keep you focused on fun. You might want to try their number-one family tour, the Cinnamon Roll Ride. This 10-mile downhill adventure takes you through a gorgeous canyon where bighorn sheep frequently graze on the steep slopes. The tour stops at the general store for a cinnamon roll—with buttercream icing.

COLORADO WILDERNESS SPORTS, INC. (ages 4 and up)

358 East Elkhorn Avenue, P.O. Box 4079, Estes Park 80517; (970) 586–6548 or (800) 504–6642; www.estesparkmountainshop.com. Open daily year-round, Memorial Day to Labor Day, 8:00 A.M. to 9:00 P.M.; winter closing hours vary. $$–$$$$

Family adventure is this outfit's middle name. In the store you'll find quality outdoor gear and clothing and knowledgeable salespeople. But even better, they also offer family adventures in climbing, rafting, and fly-fishing.

What your kids are apt to love most here is the indoor climbing wall. Keep this place in mind on a rainy afternoon. "Never-Evers" to "Thrill Seekers" are welcome. The fully trained staff assists in making your climbing adventure safe and rewarding. As sponsors of an afternoon program with the Estes Park schools, they have had lots of experience working with youth. Learn the basics and try three climbs for just $10, adult or child.

Miniclinics to full days, ladies only, large groups or just your family, indoors or out, there is a climbing program for everyone from ages four to ninety-four.

KID'S ADVENTURE PROGRAM (ages 7–14)

During the summer, Monday through Saturday 9:00 A.M. to 3:00 P.M. Reservations at least one day in advance required. $$$$

Warning: It will be hard to top this one! A hike, tramway ride, orienteering, outdoor ropes course, mountaintop lunch, ecology, and indoor climbing make for an active day. Each participant is provided with a pack containing map, compass, poncho, water bottle, climbing harness, helmet, gear, and other necessities. Bring a lunch, or a box lunch can be supplied for a small additional fee. All instructors (no more than six students to one instructor) are extensively trained, and most have classroom teaching experience.

After riding the Aerial Tramway to Prospect Mountain, the kids will participate in activities that include using map and compass skills to hike to the summit, plant and animal identification, knots, rock climbing, and rappelling. After lunch your adventurous ones return to the indoor gym for high-tech climbing practice. Excitement and confidence radiate as kids demonstrate new proficiencies for parents at the end of the day.

FLY-FISHING (ages 10 and up)

Just outside Colorado Wilderness Sports's back door, the Big Thompson River beckons. In a two-hour lesson you'll experience the basics of casting, fly presentation, and reading the water. If you rent your gear from the store, you can keep it for the rest of the day to practice. This program is a very popular way for grandparents to introduce grandchildren to the sport. Full- and half-day sessions are available. $$$$

STANLEY HOTEL (ages 5 and up)

333 Wonderview Avenue, P.O. Box 1767, Estes Park 80517; (970) 586–3371 or (800) 976–1377; www.stanleyhotel.com. $–$$

Built in 1909 by F. O. Stanley, inventor of the Stanley Steamer, this hotel offers your family a glimpse of what life was like for Estes Park tourists almost one hundred years ago. Its more recent claim to fame was as the inspiration for Stephen King's book *The Shining*. The made-for-television miniseries was filmed here. Stroll through the lobby and public rooms of this 133-room hotel. Visit its small museum on the lower level. Tours of the hotel are available at 11:00 A.M. and 2:00 P.M. through a nonprofit organization that operates the museum ($).

TROUT HAVEN (all ages)

 810 Moraine Avenue, Estes Park 80517 (1½ miles west of downtown on U.S. Highway 36); (970) 586–5525; www.trouthaven.com. Open daily late April through September, 8:00 A.M. until sunset. $

You can take kids fishing in lakes and streams all around the Estes Valley, but if you want to be sure that they catch something, head to Trout Haven. No license is required, and you pay only for what you catch (60 cents an inch). Bait, poles, and help are provided. They'll even do the yucky part—clean and pack your trout on ice. Or arrange to have it prepared and served to you. The cafe serves breakfast, lunch, and dinner.

ESTES PARK CENTER, YMCA OF THE ROCKIES (all ages)

 2515 Tunnel Road, Estes Park 80511-2550; (970) 586–3341; www. ymcarockies.org. Open year-round. Rates vary widely due to numerous accommodation, meal, and activity choices. $–$$$$

 Mention "YMCA," and most people think of swimming classes, a workout room, and perhaps a day-care facility. The YMCA of the Rockies's Estes Park Center, however, is a year-round low-key resort catering to conference groups and individual families. Here you can ride horses; hike, bike, and fish; play miniature golf, tennis, basketball, volleyball, and softball; swim in the indoor pool; and roller skate at the indoor rink. Cross-country skiing is right outside your door during the winter. And there is a craft shop, a small library, and a museum. Guests have access to dining facilities, including all-you-can-eat buffets, and accommodations range from lodge rooms to two- to four-bedroom cabins. Several of the latter will sleep up to ten people. Some families have made the center a gathering place for several generations. What a great place this would be for a family reunion!

ENOS A. MILLS CABIN (all ages)

 6760 State Highway 7, Estes Park 80517 (8 miles south of Estes Park); (970) 586–4706. Open Memorial Day through Labor Day, Tuesday through Sunday 11:00 A.M. to 4:00 P.M. Winter hours by appointment only. **Free** *(donation box).*

 Enos Mills is the man to thank for Rocky Mountain National Park. An early conservationist and dedicated educator, he lobbied the government to establish this area as a national park and was successful in 1915.

This one-room cabin served as his home base for twenty years. Inside you'll see photos taken by Mills, his journals, and letters written to him with some impressive signatures—Helen Keller, Theodore Roosevelt, and John Muir, for example.

While all of that can be boring to younger children, the area outside the cabin is just right for them. Three short nature trails beckon with handmade signs identifying trees, rocks, and flowers. Weathered tables hold collections of rocks and natural treasures waiting to be touched. Look for two llamas behind the small gift shop. A bench in the peaceful glen encourages young and old to experience what Mills called "the gentle influence of nature." It's all very homey and noncommercial.

Mills's daughter, Enda Mills Kiley (970–586–1016), now in her seventies, often shows visitors around. It's a real treat to meet her.

 HORSEBACK RIDING

For many vacationers it just wouldn't be a trip "out west" without swinging into a saddle and taking in the view from atop a horse. Whether it's pony rides for toddlers or overnight pack trips, area stables can accommodate your family's adventure.

HI COUNTRY STABLES (all ages)

Hi Country Stables has two locations within the park: Glacier Creek Stables, (970) 586–3244, and Moraine Park Stables, (970) 586–2327; www.sombreroranches.com.

Hi Country Stables operates the only stables within Rocky Mountain National Park, and it has had this concession for forty years. You can call ahead (even months ahead) to reserve a ride. Your two- to eight-hour ride begins in the heart of the park.

Real cowpokes ride even if the sun isn't shining—ponchos are provided for the "mist." They'll take riders as young as one year old. Children under six ride double with an adult. $$$$

SK LTD. (all ages)

Many area residents recommend this outfit for a good family experience. It has ponies for your younger cowhands, is authorized to ride within Rocky Mountain National Park and Roosevelt National Forest, and also has two locations. Reservations are recommended. $$$$

- **Cowpoke Corner Corral.** *On State Highway 66, 3 miles from downtown; (970) 586–5890. One-hour to half-day rides with flexible departure times.*

- **National Park Village Stables.** *On U.S. Highway 34 at the Fall River Entrance to Rocky Mountain National Park; (970) 586–5269. Two-hour rides depart on the hour beginning at 8:00 A.M.; partial-day rides vary in departure time; full-day rides begin at 8:00 A.M.*

THE LIVERY AT ASPEN LODGE (ages 8 and up)

6120 State Highway 7, Estes Park 80517 (8 miles south of Estes Park); (970) 586–8133 or (800) 332–6867; www.aspenlodge.com. Open year-round; June through August, every day; September through May, Tuesday through Sunday. Mid-October through May, advance reservations required by 10:00 A.M. day of ride. Walking rides minimum age 8. Hay wagon and sleigh rides all ages. $$$–$$$$

Want to ride on a clear, crisp winter day? The Livery at Aspen Lodge remains open year-round when weather and trail conditions are safe. For experienced riders, the three-day summer pack trip over the Continental Divide guarantees a memorable vacation.

Summer hay wagon rides through a field of longhorn cattle followed by a cowboy dinner delights families of all ages. Winter brings out the sleigh, warm woolen blankets, and Belgian draft horses complete with bells. A warm fire and dinner in the lodge await your return.

LAKE ESTES MARINA (all ages)

1770 Big Thompson Avenue, P.O. Box 1379, Estes Park 80517 (½ mile east of town on U.S. Highway 34); (970) 586–2011. Boat rentals $–$$$; bike rentals $–$$.

Lake Estes Marina and adjoining Stanley Park are good places to stop when your kids need to work off steam. Take a boat out for an hour. Choose a canoe, sailboat, or three- to five-passenger paddleboat. If you've brought along the whole troop, you might need the nine-passenger pontoon. They've got life jackets for all sizes. The wakeless speed limit ensures a gentle boating experience—and better fishing. Bait, tackle, and fishing licenses are available at the marina store. Your children will also enjoy the beach and wading area. Sand toys are provided.

The pirate ship playground offers more activity. Although it's designed primarily for ages six and up, there are some toddler-size swings. Or rent a bike and take to the paths. Child carriers, tagalongs, and tandem cycles allow families to ride together. For the ultimate group ride, rent a surrey cycle.

Other Estes Valley Recreation and Park District facilities near the marina include an indoor pool, tennis courts, a skateboard park, and two golf courses. Phone the park district at (970) 586-8191 for more information.

LAZY B RANCH CHUCKWAGON SUPPERS
1915 Dry Gulch Road, Estes Park 80517; (970) 586–5371 or (800) 228–2116. Open early June until Labor Day, nightly Tuesday through Sunday; call for varying schedule during May and September. $$

Here's that sort of hokey western experience that your kids will talk about for years. A hearty chuck wagon supper is served at 7:00 P.M. followed by the Lazy B Wranglers Live Stage Show. Western gift shops are open before and after. You'll be indoors, so even if it rains you'll enjoy the evening.

COWBOY SING-ALONG (all ages)
Downtown in Bond Park; (800) 44–ESTES (800–443–7837). Mid-June through August, Thursday through Monday at 7:30 P.M. **Free**.

Wander over to Bond Park after dinner for a good old-fashioned sing-along, western style. Sit around the campfire. Everybody's welcome and encouraged to participate.

Where to Eat

Baldpate Inn. *4900 South State Highway 7, Estes Park 80517; (970) 586–6151. Open late May through September for lunch and dinner.* This rustic lodge got its name from the novel/movie *Seven Keys to Baldpate,* which also inspired its famous key collection. It's the largest such collection in the world, and your family will have a good time perusing it and reading the labels. You can even add a key of your own. One family with two preteens was overheard locating the key Mom and Dad had donated before the kids were born. What fun!

But how about the food? It's outstanding—an all-you-can-eat buffet of salads, breads, and homemade soups that's available all day long. The array is continuously refreshed, so it's always inviting. This is a good place to know about when everyone is suddenly hungry at 3:00 in the afternoon. A huge deck with porch swings and rockers overlooks some of America's best scenery. Did I mention the homemade pie? $

Ed's Cantina. *363–366 East Elkhorn Avenue, Estes Park 80517; (970) 586–2919. Open for breakfast, lunch, and dinner.* Burgers and sandwiches, along with Mexican specialties, make up most of the menu. Nothing fancy, just good food at reasonable prices. And it's easy to find Ed's, "The Hottest Place in Town," right on the main street. $

Mama Rose's. *338 East Elkhorn Avenue, Estes Park 80517, on the Riverwalk in Barlow Plaza, downtown; (970) 586–3330. Open year-round for dinner; open Memorial Day through Labor Day for breakfast buffet also. Buon Appetito!* Mama Rose's looks like Grandma's old Victorian home. Her welcoming front porch overlooks the river. All food items are homemade with an Italian flair. Children's pasta dinners include salad and garlic bread. Bring hungry diners. $–$$

Penelope's. *229 West Elkhorn Avenue, Estes Park 80517; (970) 586–2277. Open for lunch and dinner; closing hour varies with season.* "The Hometown Place with the World Wide Reputation." Locals know Penelope's as the place for the best burger in Estes Park: 100 percent fresh ground beef, never frozen, and cooked when you order. Crispy fries come from potatoes cut on the premises. An old-fashioned malt is the perfect beverage. Soup, sandwiches, and vegetarian choices are also offered. There's no waitstaff here. You order, eat, and get back to the great outdoors in minimum time (and expense!). $

Poppy's Pizza & Grill. *On the Riverwalk in Barlow Plaza, downtown; (970) 586–8282. Open daily year-round, at 11:00 A.M.* Kids will love Poppy's pizza, and so will you. Poppy's offers lots of choices: five different sauces and toppings from traditional to smoked trout. There's a soup-and-salad bar and lots of sandwiches, including burgers, on the menu for that rare no-pizza person. Save room for homemade desserts. $

Sweet Basilico. *401 East Elkhorn Avenue, Estes Park 80517; (970) 586–3899. Open for lunch and dinner.* Pizza, pasta, and sandwiches in a funky, friendly setting. There's cozy indoor dining year-round in this former gas station and summertime dining on the rooftop patio. Hearty portions of exceptionally tasty food make Sweet Basilico popular with the local crowd. Don't be discouraged by the limited parking in front. Try the public lot by the library 1 block west. $

Where to Stay

As the gateway to Rocky Mountain National Park, Estes Park is a popular summertime destination. Visitors from around the world come to experience the beauty of RMNP. Many families return year after year for their vacations. In some cases, it's become a tradition. While the area is full of hotels, motels, condos, cabins, and inns, the accommodations fill quickly. Lodging owners encourage everyone to plan ahead and reserve early. Make your summer plans by February to ensure a wide range of choices.

With more than 175 lodging facilities, finding the right match for your needs can be time consuming. The Estes Park Visitors Center (800–443–7837) provides a free lodging referral service and can pair you with the perfect property. If you do find yourself in the area without reservations in summer, stop in at the visitors center. The staff keeps up-to-date on vacancies, and they will save you a lot of time, effort, and frustration.

Aspen Lodge. *6120 State Highway 7, Estes Park 80517 (8 miles south of Estes Park); (970) 586–8133 or (800) 332–6867; www.aspenlodge.com.* This dude ranch features a broad selection of summer activities beyond horseback riding. Located next to Rocky Mountain National Park, possibilities abound for hikes, tours, mountain biking, fly-fishing, canoeing, and kayaking. Three-, four-, and seven-day family vacation packages include children's programs for ages three to twelve and teen adventures. $$$$

Winter guests have just as many choices: guided snowshoe hikes, cross-country ski lessons, ice skating, hockey, broomball, sledding, tubing, and sleigh rides. Read beside the fire, or gather your family around a board game while it snows outside your cabin. Lodge rooms also available. Nightly lodging rates Labor Day to Memorial Day; separate activity fees. $$$–$$$$

Boulder Brook. *1900 Fall River Road, Estes Park 80517 (2 miles west of downtown on U.S. Highway 34); (970) 586–0910 or (800) 238–0910.* Fall River tumbles past Boulder Brook with a soothing sound. This top-of-the-line inn sits between Estes Park and Rocky Mountain National Park. Facilities combine the best of motel lodging with the favorite amenities of a cabin. Each large suite includes daily housekeeping service and a full or partial kitchen. Beautifully maintained grounds include a picnic area, and there's fishing right outside your door.

While many couples choose Boulder Brook for getaway weekends, the staff welcomes families and accommodates those with children in a section away from the romantic spa suites, so all guests are comfortable and happy. $$–$$$$

The Stanley Hotel. *333 Wonderview Avenue, P.O. Box 1767, Estes Park 80517; (970) 586–3371 or (800) 976–1377; www.stanleyhotel.com.* The Stanley Hotel is a fine example of elegant Georgian architecture, both inside and out. Children will enjoy the playground, tennis courts, and heated outdoor swimming pool (open summers only). The hotel's dining room is rather pricey, but less expensive restaurants and snack shops are close by. $$–$$$$

Wildwood Inn. *2801 Fall River Road, Estes Park 80517; (970) 586–7804 or (800) 400–7804; www.esteswildwoodinn. com.* Fully equipped kitchens and large condo suites (up to 1,650 square feet), some with hot tubs, are the draw here. There's lots of area to run; the property borders Rocky Mountain National Park. A playground and picnic area complete with grill make family travel easier. If you have a large family, this is the place for you. $–$$$$

For More Information

Estes Park Chamber Resort Association, *500 Big Thompson Avenue, Estes Park 80517; (970) 586–0144; www.estes parkresort.com.*

Rocky Mountain National Park

Spectacular scenery, snow-capped peaks, rugged wilderness, and wildlife draw three million visitors a year to Rocky Mountain National Park. No matter how long you stay (the average summer visit in Estes Park is three nights), it won't be long enough to do everything. So sample a variety of activities, and plan to return, perhaps in another season.

The park is open year-round. Trail Ridge and Old Fall River Roads are seasonal. The Park Service strives to clear Trail Ridge by Memorial Day and keep it open until late October. Old Fall River's season is even shorter.

Park entrance fees are valid for seven consecutive days, $$$ per car. Annual passes ($$$$) and the national Golden Eagle Pass ($$$$) are also honored. For more information log onto www.estes-park.com/rmnp.

Park Visit Checklist

- **Take a hike**—even ½ mile makes a difference in what you see.

- **Participate in a ranger-led event, hike, or program**—learning is part of the experience.

- **Drive high**—drive above timberline into the tundra, a unique landscape.

- **Stop near water**—whether it's the quiet solitude of a backcountry lake or the roar of a waterfall. Reflect on the importance and impact of this vital natural resource.

- **Observe wildlife**—enjoy the inhabitants of the park in their natural environment.

BEAVER MEADOWS VISITOR CENTER/PARK HEADQUARTERS (all ages)

At the east entrance to the park on U.S. Highway 36; (970) 586–1206; www. nps.gov/romo. Open daily year-round; summer, 8:00 A.M. to 9:00 P.M.; fall through spring, 8:00 A.M. to 5:00 P.M. **Free**.

For most visitors this is the first stop for orientation to the park. Pick up a copy of *High Country Headlines*, a seasonal park newspaper for schedules of events. *Fountain of Life*, a somewhat dated film heavy on the environmental message, runs every half hour from 8:30 A.M. to 4:30 P.M. Park personnel are available to answer questions and help plan your visit. Evening programs are presented nightly during the summer.

Need maps, guidebooks, posters, or postcards? The Rocky Mountain Nature Association operates a bookstore within the visitors center. Check out the series of inexpensive (less than $3.00), informative booklets on specific park locations published by the association.

FALL RIVER VISITORS CENTER (all ages)

3450 Fall River Road, Estes Park 80517 (on U.S. Highway 34); (970) 586–1415. Open daily year-round; summer, 8:00 A.M. to 5:00 P.M.; hours vary fall through spring. **Free**.

LILY LAKE VISITOR CENTER (all ages)

7 miles south of Estes Park on State Highway 7. Open daily May through September, 9:00 A.M. to 4:30 P.M. **Free**.

Exhibits at this center help you plan a walk, an adventure, or a nature experience. Displays about wildlife, wildflowers, and bird-watching educate campers, backpackers, and photographers. A well-stocked bookstore deserves browsing, especially on a damp afternoon when there's a warming fire in the big stone fireplace.

 ### MORAINE PARK MUSEUM AND NATURE TRAIL (all ages)

South of U.S. Highway 36 on Bear Lake Road; (970) 586–1206. Open daily May through September, 9:00 A.M. to 5:00 P.M. **Free**.

This restored lodge with log fireplace mantels and wooden rockers reminds visitors of the park's early days, but the exhibits created by the Denver Museum of Nature and Science are very "today." After learning about glaciation, spend time on the second-story glassed-in porch where the moraine lies before you. Were you caught in an afternoon thunderstorm? The weather and climate displays explain rapidly changing conditions.

An art gallery and bookstore are on the lower level.

Looping behind the center is a ⁶⁄₁₀-mile nature trail that even little legs can manage. See how many plants and animals the family can identify, and enjoy the great views.

ALPINE VISITOR CENTER (all ages)

Atop Fall River Pass on Trail Ridge Road. Open daily June through September, 9:00 A.M. to 5:00 P.M. **Free**.

At 11,796 feet, the aptly named Alpine Visitor Center is the highest facility in the park. A stop here feels like you're on top of the world, and the views are spectacular. There could be snow in July or balmy sunshine in September; it's always a surprise. Parking facilities are often crowded, but it's still worth a stop.

***B*ooks Especially for Kids** The Denver Museum of Nature and Science publishes a series of well-done nature books for children. Titles include *Above the Treeline* and *In the Forest* by Ann Cooper and *Field Guide for Kids* by Elizabeth Biesiot. If your children have watched the pikas scampering about on rocks, they are sure to want *The Pika's Tail* by Sally Plumb, published by the Grand Teton Association. These make great souvenirs instead of one more T-shirt.

TRAIL RIDGE STORE (all ages)
Next to the Alpine Visitor Center; (970) 586–9319. Open daily June through September, 9:00 A.M. to 5:00 P.M.

The only souvenir shop within the park sells much more than T-shirts and postcards. Select from handmade Native American crafts, jewelry, or original art. Outdoor enthusiasts find quality packs, boots, and clothing. There are plenty of items for young buyers, too. (How are you going to feel about that drum 10 miles down the road?) A snack bar satisfies hungry shoppers.

JUNIOR RANGER PROGRAM (ages 6–10)
Ask for a Junior Ranger Log Book at any of the visitors centers. Use it as your family explores the park. Keep a checklist of wildlife spotted, learn conservation and mountain safety, and attend a ranger-led program. When you've completed the requirements, show your book to a ranger to have the certificate signed, and receive your official Junior Ranger badge. **Free**.

TRAIL RIDGE ROAD
One of America's most scenic roads, Trail Ridge carries travelers across the Continental Divide from Estes Park to Grand Lake. The 48-mile trip includes 11 miles that run high above the timberline through alpine tundra, a world of fragile and fascinating beauty. From beaver meadows and mountaintops to river valleys, you'll view a world much as it was

when Native Americans followed this route long ago. Numerous pull-outs, viewpoints, and trailheads dot the way, so it's easy to get out of your car. Feel the power of the wind, examine tiny tundra flowers, or watch the eagles in soaring flight.

Reasons for Rules

Throughout the park you'll see warnings not to feed the wildlife. Many people think that applies just within the park boundaries, but there are very good reasons not to feed wildlife in *any* location. You put animals at risk with improper diet and a loss of ability to survive on their own. You put yourself at risk to injury and disease. That cute chipmunk you're tempting with peanuts may be carrying rabies or fleas infected with bubonic plague. Watch from a distance. Do not come in contact with wild animals even if they appear to be tame. Do your part by letting them *remain* wild.

OLD FALL RIVER ROAD

Construction on this road began in 1913, two years before the area was designated a national park. Seven years later the first motor route across the park was completed. Nine miles in length, the one-way, mostly gravel roadway leaves Endovalley near the Fall River Entrance Station and joins Trail Ridge Road at the Alpine Visitor Center. From there you can continue to the west side of the park or complete a loop back to Estes Park. Because of the narrow roadbed and sharp hairpin turns, vehicles more than 25 feet long and pulled trailers are prohibited, but four-wheel drive is not required.

Along your journey you'll pass through three distinctive ecosystems: the Montane, Subalpine, and Alpine Tundra. Geography, geology, botany, and ecology aren't just textbook subjects here. Witness evidence of glaciers, avalanches, wind, and man. Chasm Falls, a popular stop, tumbles 25 feet into a whirlpool a short walk from the road.

FAMILY HIKING

Park personnel report that most visitors ask, "Where can we take a hike?" With more than 300 miles of trails, there's an option for every age and ability, from boardwalk nature walks to the arduous Longs Peak climb. Whether you have less than an hour or several days, there is a trail just right for your family. Out of the car you can listen for birds and other animals, smell the ponderosa pine, and see nature unfold. Kids' natural curiosity will lead to discovery along forest, meadow, rocky slopes, or tundra trails. Brochures and detailed guidebooks are available for purchase at visitors centers. Ask rangers, local residents, and other visitors about their favorite destinations, or choose one of these. (Distances are one way except where noted.) **Free**.

SPRAGUE LAKE

This ½-mile nature trail, which is stroller and wheelchair accessible, circles the lake. Bug enthusiasts will love the variety of insects to study. Riding stables and picnic tables are nearby.

ALBERTA FALLS

Almost everyone loves waterfalls. This one is just $6/10$ mile from Glacier Gorge Junction. Listen for the sound of the falls long before you see it. Aspens along the trail make this a great autumn hike. Hardier hikers can continue to Mills Lake ($1 9/10$ miles farther) or the Loch ($2 1/10$ additional miles from the falls).

BEAR LAKE AREA

This is one of the most popular areas of the park. Try to visit here very early or late in the day or, even better, in the off-season. At the peak of the summer, when the parking lot fills, free shuttle buses access the area.

The $6/10$-mile walk around the lake is fairly level, a good choice for a mixed-ability group. You are almost guaranteed to see chipmunks along the way. Remember to observe, not feed or touch.

A chain of lakes above Bear Lake lures hikers farther up the trail: Nymph Lake, ½ mile; Dream, $1 1/10$ miles; Emerald, $1 8/10$ miles. Climbing upward, the vistas are ever changing and rewarding. Go as far as your group is comfortable, but remember: The only way back to the car is on foot.

*B*e Prepared Mountain weather changes rapidly and frequently. For good reason, there's a mountain range here named "Never Summer." Always have jackets with you for every member of the family. Don't leave them in the car when you leave for a hike. Coats with hoods are a good choice since most body heat is lost through the head. Stuff pockets with fleece headbands and stretchy gloves for protection without a lot of additional bulk. By being prepared you'll enjoy your adventure even when conditions fluctuate.

LILY LAKE

Along the ¾-mile walk around Lily Lake, you're sure to spot summer wildflowers. The trail and fishing are handicapped accessible. Longs Peak, the highest mountain in the park at 14,255 feet, towers majestically to the south.

WILD BASIN AREA

In the park's southeastern corner, this trail leads to waterfalls, cascades, and lakes. At ³⁄₁₀ mile you'll find Copeland Falls, hardly worthy of its name. The more interesting Calypso Cascades are 1½ miles farther. A bridge provides views of the rushing creek below. The trail gets steeper if you tackle an additional ⁸⁄₁₀ mile to Ouzel Falls, a watery plunge definitely worthy of its name.

Water Ouzel Ouzel Falls is named after a fascinating bird found in the park. About the size of a robin, the gray bird named water ouzel or dipper dives underwater to catch aquatic insects. Watch as it bobs up and down from a midstream rock.

This area is a popular winter location for cross-country skiing and snowshoeing.

GEM LAKE

For a hike with a different view, try the Gem Lake trail. Outcroppings of rounded rock in weird formations are a kid's delight. Lumpy Ridge is a favorite with technical rock climbers; just watching can be dramatic. The nearly 2-mile route of moderate difficulty takes you past Twin Owls and Paul Bunyan's Boot (check out the hole in the sole). Make a game of naming formations along the way to divert tired hikers.

SPECIAL PROGRAMS

Ask for a printed schedule of programs at visitors centers. Some require advance reservations. **Free** *to $$$$.*

Hikes, slide shows, workshops, or campfires will enrich your experience at Rocky Mountain National Park. Some are for families; others, for children only. Watch your kids absorb knowledge from new adventures while they have a great time. Try Rocky after Dark, a nighttime guided hike; learn about beavers in Rocky's Engineers; or take a three-hour class for kids called Come Bug a Ranger or Nature Sketchbooks.

HIKING WITH RANGERS

From one-hour nature hikes that unravel mysteries and sharpen your senses to strenuous four-hour treks along the Continental Divide, ranger-led hikes are a great way to see the park beyond the roadway. You'll find out about native wildlife, forces that formed the park, and humans' impact. Or take one of the photography walks and learn techniques for better outdoor photos. Free.

CAMPFIRE TALKS

At campgrounds and the Beaver Meadows Visitor Center; daily during the summer. Free.

Experience the age-old ritual of gathering around a fire, sharing information, telling tall tales, and singing. Campfire themes differ, so you can go every night without a repeat. Remember to dress warmly. No matter how hot it was during the day, evening temperatures can chill.

If the kids are too tired and cranky to attend an evening campfire program, there's an alternative at Moraine Park. Bring a mug—the hot beverages are provided—for a morning chat (9:00 A.M.) with a ranger around a campfire.

CAMPING

Campgrounds in the park are often filled during the summer. Reservations for Moraine Park and Glacier Basin (800–365–2267) may be made three months in advance; cost is $16 per site per night. Aspenglen, Longs Peak (tents only), and Timber Creek sites are available on a first-come, first-served basis and may be filled before noon; cost is $12 per site per night. There are no showers or RV connections in any park campground.

Permits ($15) are required for all backcountry camping; reservations are accepted starting March 1 each year. The Backcountry Office (970–586–1242) near the Beaver Meadows Visitor Center is open during the summer, 7:00 A.M. to 7:00 P.M.

Fort Collins

Agriculture meets academia in this town of 100,000 residents. While farms and ranches surround Fort Collins, and nearby mountains gently roll into plains, the city itself is home to Colorado State University. Here, small-town friendliness mingles with the cultural advantages of a college town. Add to this the beauty of the Poudre River Valley and a backdrop of majestic mountains, and you have an outstanding blend of Old West/New West.

Main Street U.S.A. You might think you're on Main Street U.S.A. in Disneyland—and with good reason. Disneyland's quintessential hometown street was actually based on this very place, and the Magic Kingdom's Main Street Fire Station is an exact model of Fort Collins's 1882 city hall/firehouse.

SWETSVILLE ZOO (ages 2 and up)

4801 East Harmony Road, Fort Collins 80525 (off I–25, southeast of Fort Collins); (970) 484–9509; www.ftcollins.com/attractions.htm. Open year-round, dawn to dusk. Donations are appreciated, but admission is **Free**.

This "zoo" is like none other, and it's a great place for kids. It all began when owner Bill Swets decided to make a dinosaur out of some old rusty nuts, bolts, shovels, and plough shins he had lying around his farm. It took about five weeks, but when he was finished, there stood in his front yard a 900-pound tyrannosaurus rex that came all the way up to the eaves on the Swets's farmhouse. And now there's Harry the Hitchhiker and his companion, Penny the Dimetrodon, Dino the Brontosaurus, and scores of other sculptures, including flowers, windmills, animals, and more dinosaurs, all made from farm machinery, car parts, and scrap metal.

Bring lunch and stay as long as you please. Picnic tables are provided.

Kids love exploring this whimsical menagerie to see what sort of creature they can find next. Don't miss the wealthy old Chinese dragon named Kyle the Kyleeasaurus and the ferocious fighter Polly the Polacanthus.

DISCOVERY CENTER (all ages)

703 East Prospect Road, Fort Collins 80525; (970) 472–3990; www.CSMATE. ColoState.edu/DCSM. Open Tuesday through Saturday 10:00 A.M. to 5:00 P.M. and Sunday noon to 5:00 P.M. $, children under 4 **Free***.*

Have fun together while you learn about gravity, pulleys, sound waves, and electricity at the only museum in Colorado devoted entirely to science. Started more than ten years ago by volunteers, Discovery Center now has more than ninety exhibits, from aerodynamics to zoology, which are all interactive. Located in a former school building, the center provides plenty of room for your kids to spread out on their journey of discovery. Build with pipes and joints, use levers, make arcs and sparks. Learn how a fax works, and use a videophone. A full program of classes and workshops for ages three and up is offered.

OLD TOWN (all ages)

Downtown Fort Collins. **Free***.*

Shady trees, brick sidewalks, and one-hundred-year-old buildings present a bit of nostalgia while the shops, galleries, and restaurants are definitely "now." Take a self-guided historic walking tour, or just browse on your own.

CHILDREN'S MERCANTILE COMPANY

111 North College Avenue, Fort Collins 80524 (in Old Town); (970) 484–9946 or (888) 326–8465. Open Monday through Saturday 9:30 A.M. to 8:00 P.M. and Sunday 11:00 A.M. to 6:00 P.M.

Quality and quantity! One look in the window, and you won't be able to bypass this toy store.

CITY PARK (all ages)

1500 West Mulberry Street, Fort Collins 80521; (970) 221–6640. **Free***.*

Picnic tables, a large playground, grassy running room, an outdoor swimming pool, and a miniature train make this a pleasant all-day excursion. The small lake has a handicapped-accessible fishing pier and paddleboats to rent.

MINIATURE TRAIN

1599 City Park Drive, Fort Collins 80521; (970) 416–2990. Open daily June through August, 10:00 A.M. to 6:00 P.M.; varying hours on weekends only in late May and September. $, one parent may accompany each child under 2 for **Free***.*

The park's miniature train has been entertaining Fort Collins's families since the 1950s.

SWIMMING POOL

(970) 484–7665. Open June through Labor Day, Sunday through Friday 12:30 to 5:30 P.M. and Saturday 10:30 A.M. to 5:30 P.M. $

PADDLEBOATS

Open June through Labor Day, Sunday through Friday 12:30 to 6:30 P.M. and Saturday 10:30 A.M. to 6:30 P.M. $ *per half-hour rental.*

FORT COLLINS MUNICIPAL RAILWAY (all ages)

P.O. Box 635, Fort Collins 80522; (970) 482–8246. Open weekends and holidays, May through September (weather permitting), noon to 5:00 P.M. Runs from City Park to downtown. $

Ride back in time on the only original restored city streetcar in the western United States. Car 21 and 1½ miles of track were renovated by the volunteers who operate and maintain this line.

ENVIRONMENTAL LEARNING CENTER (all ages)

3745 East Prospect Road, Fort Collins 80522; 1 mile east of Timberline; (970) 491–1661. Visitor Center open daily mid-May through August; weekends only September through April, 10:00 A.M. to 5:00 P.M. Trails open daily, sunrise to sunset. **Free**.

Colorado State University operates this environmental education center along the Poudre River. You'll see four major ecological habitats as you explore 2½ miles of trails. The Visitor Center houses interpretive displays and a gift shop.

The Rocky Mountain Raptor Program is located here, so you'll be sure to see eagles and other birds of prey. Be sure to notice the nesting and feeding towers for osprey along the river.

ANHEUSER-BUSCH TOUR CENTER (all ages)

I–25 north to Mountain Vista Drive, exit 271; (970) 490–4691. Open daily June through August, 9:30 A.M. to 5:00 P.M., and in September, 10:00 A.M. to 4:00 P.M.; October through May, Thursday through Monday 10:00 A.M. to 4:00 P.M. **Free**.

Bring your family to visit the famous Budweiser Clydesdales in their Rocky Mountain home. The Fort Collins Brewery serves as a training center where the horses learn to pull a wagon before they join an eight-hitch team.

The magnificent horses, weighing more than 2,000 pounds each, are often outside in the morning and late afternoon. Otherwise, walk over to their home, Clydesdale Hamlet. This grand, gleaming building is no ordinary stable. As you walk along the stalls, consider that each horse consumes fifty to sixty pounds of hay, twenty to twenty-five quarts of feed, and up to thirty gallons of water every day. Take time to watch the twenty-five-minute video and peruse the exhibits interesting to both children and adults. Compare the size of an average horseshoe to one of the Clydesdales' shoes—quite a difference.

Be sure to say hello to Suds, the Dalmatian mascot, who resides in his own fancy digs near Clydesdale Hamlet.

On the first Saturday of each month, you can get even closer to the Clydesdales. On Budweiser Clydesdale Camera Day, from 1:00 to 3:00 P.M. a trainer escorts one of the horses onto the grounds outside the visitors center. Bring a camera to immortalize your family standing next to a gentle giant. Touching is allowed! In case of bad weather, the photo session takes place inside.

Anheuser-Busch welcomes visitors even if they choose not to take the brewery tour.

THE FARM (all ages)

600 North Sherwood Street, Fort Collins 80525 (at Lee Martinez Park); (970) 221–6665. Open mid-April through August, Tuesday through Saturday 10:00 A.M. to 5:30 P.M. and Sunday noon to 5:30 P.M. Open September through mid-April, Wednesday through Saturday 10:00 A.M. to 4:30 P.M. and Sunday noon to 4:30 P.M. Dates and hours vary by season for the museum, Silo Store, pony rides, and trail rides. Call ahead. **Free**.

Chickens, pigs, goats, sheep, cows, ponies, and horses—they're all here, along with pony rides for kids twelve and under. (Parents lead ponies around the arena.) Purchase packets of feed to entice the animals closer to the fence. You are allowed to reach through and pet them.

At this quality museum depicting farm life over the last one hundred years, grandparents enjoy showing their families how things used to be. See if you can identify the mystery tool. The Silo Store sells arts and crafts with a farm theme.

HORSETOOTH RESERVOIR AND LORY STATE PARK (all ages)

South on Taft Hill Road to 38E west. Follow the signs to the reservoir, about ten minutes from town. Open daily year-round. $ per car.

Horsetooth Reservoir is a real treasure in landlocked Colorado. Besides being popular with water-skiers, it has a swim beach and covered picnic tables, perfect respites on a hot summer's day. At Horsetooth Yacht Club near the beach, you can purchase lunch or dinner.

Lory State Park borders the reservoir with 2,400 acres of grassy open meadows, ponderosa pine forests, sandstone hogbacks, and unique rock outcroppings. A variety of trails attracts hikers, bikers, joggers, and horseback riders. In winter months, cross-country skiing, sledding, and tubing are the draw. No snowmobiling is allowed.

THE DOUBLE DIAMOND STABLE
710 Lodgepole Drive, Fort Collins 80525, in Lory State Park; (970) 224–4200. Open Memorial Day through Labor Day, Thursday through Tuesday. Two-hour rides at 9:00 A.M., one-hour rides at noon, 2:00, and 4:00 P.M. Saturday-night barbecue. $$$–$$$$

Trail rides, hayrides, and cookouts just twenty minutes from downtown Fort Collins.

PAWNEE NATIONAL GRASSLANDS AND PAWNEE BUTTES (ages 5 and up)

East of Fort Collins, north of Fort Morgan. County Road 129 north from State Highway 14 at New Raymer; (970) 498–2770. Access to within 1½ miles of West Butte is via dirt and gravel roads. Not recommended in inclement weather. Free.

The Pawnee National Grasslands cover 193,060 acres of short-grass prairie ecosystems alive with wildlife habitats and archaeological resources. Here you are apt to see pronghorn antelope, mule deer, coyotes, foxes, badgers, snakes, and prairie dogs. Birdlife includes the golden eagle, hawks, the burrowing owl, and the lark bunting, Colorado's state bird. More than 400 species of plants thrive in the grasslands. Depending on the season, you will see an abundance of wildflowers, including the pink, yellow, and red blossoms of prickly pear cactus, sunflowers, and coneflowers. Walkers and hikers are welcome, but motorized vehicles must stay on routes marked by numbered posts to prevent erosion and unintentional trespass onto private land.

The Pawnee Buttes rise 250 feet above the prairie surface, approximately 11 miles northeast of the small town of Keota. A dirt road provides access to the trailhead and overlook, and a 1½-mile trail takes you to the base of the western butte. The eastern butte is nearby but can't be accessed without crossing private land. Because hawks and other birds of prey use the buttes for nesting, the north overlook and the cliffs near the buttes are closed to the public March through June. With binoculars it is possible to observe birds searching for field mice or even to see young birds in the nests, but it is important to stay at least 300 yards away from the nests. Climbing on the buttes is not recommended due to the crumbling sandstone. Watch for antelope and birds, and watch out for rattlesnakes.

Disc Golf

It's been called the sport of the future, and Fort Collins is one of the hot spots for it.

Played much like traditional golf, but using discs (Frisbees) instead of balls and clubs, disc golf can be enjoyed by everyone. It doesn't require special skills to begin, and the initial equipment investment is less than $10 and easily transported.

Bill Wright, owner of Wright Life, a downtown Fort Collins sporting-goods store, has been a driving force in the development of this activity soon to be included in the World Games. To learn about disc golf and to purchase or rent discs, stop in to see him at Wright Life, 200 Linden Street (970–484–6932). Then head out for some great family fun. A round of disc golf takes one and a half to two hours.

Wright Life has maps of the four *Free* courses:

- **Bolt Junior High,** on the grounds of a junior high school. This course is the easiest since it was designed for schoolkids.

- **Colorado State University Campus Course,** near the Student Center.

- **Edora Park,** 1420 East Stuart Street. This park also has a playground, fitness course, BMX track, trails, and the EPIC recreation center (disc golf course map available here) with indoor pool and ice arena.

- **Grateful Disc Course,** behind the University Park Holiday Inn, 425 West Prospect Road.

Many Colorado ski areas have disc golf courses for summer use. The one atop Aspen Mountain has great views. Look for more than two dozen other courses throughout the state during your travels.

Where to Eat

Bisetti's. *120 South College Avenue, Fort Collins 80524 (downtown); (970) 493–0086. Open daily for dinner; Monday through Friday for lunch.* Year after year the locals vote this the best Italian food in Fort Collins. Family-owned and located in Old Town since 1980, the restaurant serves hearty, traditional pasta. $-$$

Egg and I. *2809 South College Avenue, Fort Collins 80525; (970) 223–5271. Open daily for breakfast and lunch.* This is the place to go for one of the best breakfasts in town, according to local residents. $

Sundance Steakhouse and Country Club. *2716 East Mulberry Street, Fort Collins 80524; (970) 484–1600. Open nightly, except Monday, for dinner and entertainment.* Forget your idea of a cosmopolitan country club; real local cowboys eat here. There's a collection of old "retired" boots on one wall. If you choose, you can even learn to line dance here. The country-western entertainment won't be for everyone, but the steaks are the best. Perhaps you'd like to try some bison. $$$

Treats in Town
Homemade ice cream calls your name at two emporiums in the Fort Collins Old Town area. Try either one for a memorable treat. Better yet, try them both!

- **Kilwin's Chocolates and Ice Cream.** *114 South College Avenue; (970) 221–9444.* Choosing is difficult—there are thirty-two flavors. Toasted Coconut or Fort Collins Mud? Try a free sample of fudge. You won't be able to leave without a purchase. They make it on the premises. The hand-dipped caramel apples also are irresistible. And then there's Kilwin's chocolates—creams, truffles, caramels, oh, my!

- **Walrus Ice Cream.** *125 West Mountain Avenue (½ block west of College Avenue); (970) 482–5919.* Here's where you'll get the "best ice cream in Fort Collins," at least according to the local vote. The sign advises, ALL THINGS IN MODERATION—EXCEPT ICE CREAM. Be prepared for delicious dips and a sense of humor. The list of flavors often includes one to catch your eye. On one particular day, the special was Spicy Orange Spam. Try it, if you dare.

  Check out their wall-size bulletin board to find out what's happening around town.

Where to Stay

Best Western Kiva Inn. *1638 East Mulberry Street, Fort Collins 80524; (970) 484–2444.* **Free** continental breakfast; exercise room, outdoor swimming pool, guest laundry, in-room microwave ovens. $-$$$

The Helmshire Inn. *1204 South College Street, Fort Collins 80524; (970) 493–4683.* Minikitchens, nonsmoking inn. $$–$$$

Motel 6. *3900 East Mulberry Street, Fort Collins 80524; (970) 482–6466.* Outdoor swimming pool; **Free** HBO and ESPN; kids under 12 stay **Free**. $–$$

Sterling

The town of Sterling, 125 miles northeast of Denver on I-76, is a laid-back community of friendly people and intriguing attractions.

CITY OF LIVING TREES

Sterling is sometimes referred to as the "City of Living Trees" due to the fascinating works of former resident Brad Rhea, a gifted artist who became a one-man beautification project for the town. Early in his career, this highly acclaimed sculptor took dead trees, stripped off their bark, and carved wondrous sculptures from them. Although Rhea has long since become a renowned sculptor of marble and now lives in the nearby town of Merino, his work still draws thousands of visitors to Sterling to seek out his tree art. Take a walk around town to see who in your family can spot the next carving. Keep score to determine who has found the most at the end of your trek. In the process you will discover a herd of five giraffes carved from a single tree in Columbine Park. See if you can find the clown, a mermaid, and an actor with the masks of comedy and tragedy. Thankfully, several of the sculptures are housed inside public buildings to avoid the destructive effects of the elements. A map of the sculpture locations is available at the visitors center across from the Overland Trail Museum on U.S. Highway 6.

OVERLAND TRAIL MUSEUM (ages 2 and up)

Located on U.S. Highway 6, east of Sterling; (970) 522–3895; www.sterlingcolo. com. Open April through October, Monday through Saturday 9:00 A.M. to 5:00 P.M. and Sunday and holidays 1:00 P.M. to 5:00 P.M.; November through March, Tuesday through Saturday 10:00 A.M. to 4:00 P.M. **Free**.

Built in the form of an old fort, this museum displays artifacts from the days when pioneers traveled the Overland Trail from Kansas City to Denver. From 1862 to 1868, this branch of the trail, which led along the South Platte River, was the most heavily traveled road in the entire country. The museum grounds reveal a Concord stagecoach, a covered wagon, old farm machinery, and a shaded, well-equipped picnic area. You can enter the old country store, a blacksmith shop, a country church, and the one-room Stoney Buttes Schoolhouse. During the summer your children can attend short classes held in the old school.

The indoor exhibits showcase items that once belonged to the westward-bound pioneers and to the Native Americans who inhabited the area for many generations. You will find antique dolls, sunbonnets, bottles, and period wedding dresses. Native American artifacts include buckskin clothing, arrowheads, and stone metates, used to grind corn. Bring along a lunch, and after touring the museum, sit under a shade tree and suggest that each member of your family tell what he or she liked best about the museum and why. Then make a game of imagining what the people were like who once owned these items and lived, studied, and worshipped in these buildings.

 NORTH STERLING RESERVOIR STATE PARK (all ages)
13 miles north of Sterling; (970) 522–3657; www.dnr.state.co.us/parks/.

 This is a boaters' paradise on the high plains, with coves and lake fingers to explore with expansive views of buttes and bluffs. Three campgrounds, a sandy swim beach, visitors center with interpretive summer programs, picnic sites, and fishing and wildlife viewing lure visitors to this northeastern Colorado park.

Where to Eat

Country Kitchen. *In the Ramada Inn, I–76 and U.S. Highway 6; (970) 522–2625.* Children's menu. $

Shake, Rattle & Roll Diner. *1107 West Main Street, Sterling 80751; (970) 526–1700.* Open every day; hours vary. $

Where to Stay

Sterling Motor Lodge. *731 North 3rd Street, Sterling 80751; (970) 522–2740 or (800) 762–2740.* Kitchenettes and rollaways available. $–$$

Super 8 Motel. *12883 Highway 61, (970) 522–0300.* Swimming pool. $–$$

Ramada Inn. *I–76 and U.S. Highway 6; (970) 522–2625 or (800) 835–7275.* Tropical courtyard with indoor swimming pool, sauna, whirlpool, and games. Special packages for family escapes. $$–$$$

For More Information

City of Sterling, *421 North 4th Street, Sterling 80751; (970) 522–9700; www.sterlingcolo.com.*

Logan County Chamber of Commerce, *109 North Front Street, Sterling 80751; (970) 522–5070.*

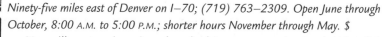

Genoa

GENOA WONDER VIEW TOWER AND MUSEUM

Ninety-five miles east of Denver on I–70; (719) 763–2309. Open June through October, 8:00 A.M. to 5:00 P.M.; shorter hours November through May. $

You will spot a gigantic red-and-white tower on the north side of the highway at Genoa. Welcome to the Genoa Wonder View Tower and Museum. It is said that Ripley, of "Believe It or Not" fame, proved that six states could be seen from the top of this tower.

Inside the twenty-room museum you will find an unbelievable assortment of priceless items alongside those of total gimcrackery. Old bottles, jars, and inkwells; 300 different kinds of barbed-wire fence strands; more than 1,000 paintings rendered more than fifty years ago by Raven Wing, a Sioux princess; a buffalo hairball (!); a stuffed, two-headed calf; a pair of woolly mammoth tusks; washboards; antique guns; fish fossils; and more than 20,000 Native American artifacts haphazardly line the floors, hang on walls, and reside in dusty showcases.

The museum is the pride and joy of Jerry Chubbuck, who has been its owner and curator since 1974. According to Chubbuck, "If it ain't here, it don't exist." After wandering through this museum, you just might agree.

Chubbuck has antiques and inexpensive curios for sale. The buildings are unheated, so although they bring a welcome relief from the heat of summer, they are bone-chillingly cold in winter. Bundle up if you plan to come by during fall, winter, or early spring. It's best to call ahead during the off-season to make sure someone is around to let you in.

Burlington

Located off I–70 in extreme eastern Colorado, almost to the Kansas border, the small town of Burlington provides an opportunity to experience turn-of-the-twentieth-century life in the heart of the Eastern Plains.

OLD TOWN (all ages)

420 South 14th Street, Burlington 80807; (719) 346–7382 or (800) 288–
1334. Open daily year-round, 9:00 A.M. to 6:00 P.M. Extended hours Memorial
Day through Labor Day. $

Old Town is a six-and-one-half-acre complex of twenty fully restored historical buildings filled with artifacts from the area. The entire facility is wheelchair and stroller accessible. Here you will see a schoolhouse built in 1911 for the children of homesteaders, a "soddie" made of thick slabs of buffalo grass because there were few trees or rocks for house building, and a drugstore that sold everything from hot water bottles to milk of magnesia toothpaste. Your children will want to see the playhouse filled with a unique collection of dolls, one of which was made from bread dough.

Stop in at the Longhorn Saloon to purchase peanuts, popcorn, and beverages. During the summertime see can-can girls dance on tabletops and roughhousing cowboys settle arguments with their shootin' irons. (Phone ahead for performance times.) Peek into the jail, sample old-fashioned candy in the general store, and order a root beer float while listening to the jukebox at the soda fountain. In the Emporium you will find handmade crafts such as barbed-wire wreaths, pottery, wheat weaving, wood carvings, and carousel figures.

 KIT CARSON COUNTY CAROUSEL (all ages)

Open daily Memorial Day to Labor Day, 1:00 to 8:00 P.M. The 25-cent admission
fee includes a twenty-minute tour and a memorable four-minute ride.

When you have finished touring Old Town, wait out front of the Emporium for a horse-drawn wagon ride aboard the Old Town Express to the Kit Carson County Carousel. This treasure was built in 1905, number six of only seventy-four manufactured by the Philadelphia Toboggan Company. Now designated as both a National Historic Site and a National Landmark (one of only thirteen in Colorado), it is the only antique carousel in the United States still maintaining its original paint on both the animals and the scenery panels.

Forty-six intricately hand-carved horses, lions, giraffes, deer, zebras, and a camel "march" (the animals are stationary and do not move up and down) to festive melodies played by a restored circa-1912 Wurlitzer Monster Military Band Organ, a one-hundred-key instrument measuring almost 7 feet high and 10 feet wide and with musical output equal to a twelve- to fifteen-piece band. Your kids will long remember riding on this carousel. Bring plenty of film.

Where to Stay

Super 8 Motel. *2100 Fay Street, Burlington 80807; (719) 346–5627.* $

Travelodge. *450 South Lincoln Street, Burlington 80807; (719) 346–5555.* $–$$

For More Information

State Welcome Center at Burlington, *just off I–70; (719) 346–5554.*

Northeastern Colorado Annual Events

MAY

Kinetic Conveyance Race. *Boulder, the first Saturday in May; (303) 713–8000.* "Wacky" best describes this Boulder springtime celebration. Witness human-powered machines struggle through deep water and across muddy beaches. Themes and costumes are definitely creative. $$

Bolder Boulder. *Boulder, late May; (303) 442–1044.* This high-altitude championship competition is considered to be one of the nation's top footraces. You can watch as runners from around the world compete in the 10-kilometer race through the city streets. Runners $$$$, observers **Free**.

JUNE

Greeley Independence Stampede. *Greeley, mid-June to July 4; (970) 356–2855; www.greeleystampede.org.* This celebration has grown from a small rodeo to become one of the top twenty PRCA rodeos in the world. Performances from country music stars, flapjack feeds, chili cook-offs, barbecues, carnival rides, trail rides, and a Fourth of July parade and fireworks make this a family-friendly event. $$–$$$$

Renaissance Festival. *Larkspur (I–25 south from Denver to the Larkspur exit), eight weekends in June and July; (303) 688–6010; www.coloradorenaissance.com.* King and queen, lords and ladies, strolling minstrels, jousting knights—you're back in the sixteenth century. More than 200 costumed artisans sell handcrafted goods. Continuous entertainment and tempting food booths. $$$

Wool Market. *Estes Park, mid-June; (970) 586–6104.* Celebrate wool! Live animals (sheep, llamas, alpacas) and lots of demonstrations make this festival interesting for kids. 𝐅𝐫𝐞𝐞 admission.

JULY

Rooftop Rodeo. *Estes Park, mid-July; (970) 586–6104.* This rodeo is a favorite not only with audiences but with the cowboy athletes as well. Six nights of PRCA rodeo, wild horse racing, and "Mutton Bustin." It's all kicked off with a festive parade. $$

Buffalo Bill Days. *Golden, late July; (303) 279–3113.* You will see lots of Buffalo Bill look-alikes at this festival put on in his honor. Activities include a Wild West Show, a burro race, craft and food booths, and a parade. 𝐅𝐫𝐞𝐞 admission.

SEPTEMBER

Longs Peak Scottish-Irish Festival. *Estes Park, early September; (970) 586–6308.* You've heard of the "wearin' of the green." Well, during these festivities, Estes Park celebrates the "wearin' of the plaid" as the traditions of both Scotland and Ireland bring forth bagpipe band concerts, Celtic competitions, and a parade. 𝐅𝐫𝐞𝐞 admission to some events; others, $–$$$.

Potato Day at Centennial Village. *Greeley, mid-September; (970) 350–9220.* Held at the living-history museum of Centennial Village, Potato Day is a jolly event. You can take part in a variety of old-fashioned family activities, watch a blacksmith at work, explore Buffalo Joe Flier's one-room cabin, and dine on baked potatoes with all the trimmings. $

OCTOBER

The Pumpkin Festival and Corn Maze at Chatfield Nature Preserve. *Held at the Denver Botanic Gardens' suburban Chatfield Nature Preserve, early September through October; (303) 973–3705.* This celebration of fall offers a you-pick pumpkin patch, hayrides, and food and craft booths. A new five-acre maze cut among cornstalks provides a giant puzzle for kids to amble through. You won't be able to keep your toddlers from exploring the smaller version, designed just for them. $

Rocky Mountain Pumpkin Ranch Harvest Festival. *Longmont, late September through October; (303) 684–0087.* Bring the kids and let them pick out their own Halloween pumpkin amid the gaiety of a fall farm fest. Games, activities, food, a hay maze, pony rides, and farm animals add to the merriment. **Free** admission, $ for activities.

Old Town "Ghost Town." *Burlington, late October; (800) 288–1334.* Old Town becomes a ghost town for an evening of trick-or-treating in a safe and controlled environment. Kids go from building to building to pick up their Halloween snacks and play games for small prizes upstairs in the barn. The lower level of the barn becomes a "haunted house" for those brave enough to enter. There is no charge for this "spooktacular" event, except for a 25-cent admission fee to the haunted house.

Southeastern Colorado

History and tradition run deep in southeastern Colorado, and more than a trace of the Spanish explorers, fur traders, mountain men, Native Americans, and pioneers that long ago crisscrossed this land remains today. Cultures as diverse as the landscapes enhance this region of the state.

Doris's Top Picks
in Southeastern Colorado

1. Bent's Old Fort, La Junta
2. Cave of the Winds, Manitou Springs
3. Cripple Creek & Victor Narrow Gauge Railroad, Cripple Creek
4. Florissant Fossil Beds National Monument, Florissant
5. Flying W Ranch, Colorado Springs
6. The Manitou Cliff Dwellings Museum, Manitou Springs
7. North Cheyenne Cañon Park, Colorado Springs
8. Olympic Training Center, Colorado Springs
9. Santa's Workshop and North Pole, Cascade

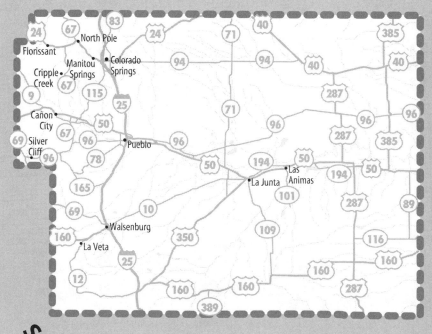

SOUTHEASTERN COLORADO

Colorado Springs

Colorado Springs bustles as the state's second-largest city. A terrific vacation destination, it has one of the highest concentrations of natural and commercial attractions in the state.

This is Pikes Peak country, and enough activities lie in its shadow to keep a family busy for weeks. Christened "The Long One" by Ute Indians who once hunted in the area, the 14,110-foot mountain became known to white settlers through the efforts of explorer Zebulon Pike in 1806.

"America the Beautiful" In 1893 a young schoolteacher named Katharine Lee Bates joined several other schoolmarms aboard a mule-drawn prairie wagon in an effort to reach the top of the mountain. A sign across the rear of the wagon—PIKES PEAK OR BUST—revealed their determination. Once at the summit, Bates, overcome by the spectacular panoramic view, penned the poem that eventually became the lyrics to the song "America the Beautiful."

UNITED STATES AIR FORCE ACADEMY (all ages)

Located north of Colorado Springs; I–25 to exit 156B; (719) 333–7749. Visitors Center open daily 9:00 A.M. to 5:00 P.M.; summer until 6:00 P.M. **Free**.

The United States Air Force Academy is Colorado's most frequently visited man-made attraction. The Academy Visitors Center features exhibits detailing life as a U.S. Air Force cadet, a 250-seat theater, a cafeteria, a gift shop, academy merchandise, and a nature trail leading to the Cadet Chapel. All proceeds from sales at the Visitors Center go to support collegiate and intramural cadet sports. You are welcome to visit the Protestant, Catholic, and Jewish sanctuaries in the chapel and take a self-guided driving tour to view the extensive wildlife sanctuary.

FALCON SUMMER SPORTS CAMPS (ages 8–18)

June. These camps are extremely popular, and enrollment is taken on a first-come, first-served basis. Reservations are accepted after January 1 of the year the camp is held; (719) 472–1895 or (719) 333–2116; www.airforcesports.com. $$$$

The U.S. Air Force Academy–offered Falcon Summer Sports Camps are designed to challenge and improve existing skill levels and abilities. The camps feature academy intercollegiate head coaches as instructors. Topics include baseball, basketball, football, hockey, golf, soccer, lacrosse, tennis, wrestling, track and field, cross-country, volleyball, self-defense, swimming, diving, gymnastics, strength/power/speed training, and cheerleading/dance. Boarders live in the cadet dorms, eat in the cadet dining rooms, and use the academy's outstanding athletic facilities. Commuter campers attend on a daytime basis but still lunch in the dining halls, use the academy's athletic facilities, and participate in the same classes as the live-in attendees.

WESTERN MUSEUM OF MINING AND INDUSTRY (ages 4 and up)

1025 North Gate Road, Colorado Springs 80921; (719) 488–0880. I–25 exit 156, east of the United States Air Force Academy. Open year-round, Monday through Saturday 9:00 A.M. to 4:00 P.M.; summer also open Sunday 1:00 to 4:00 P.M. Escorted tours available at 10:00 A.M. and 1:00 P.M. $–$$

At this museum visitors learn by experience. Your youngsters can pan for gold and try their hand at the process of "single jacking" as they see how the miners timbered, drilled, blasted, mucked, and moved ore from the mines. Guides direct tours through a life-size underground mine reconstruction. Unique to this museum is the actual operation of restored multiton steam engines, drills, hoists, and other mining machines. Begin your tour by viewing "Mining in the West," a lively, eighteen-minute multiprojector slide presentation showing what life was like in the early camps. Find out how the miners and their families survived the rigors of a miner's life. Exhibits, including an 1890s New Mexican silver bar studded with pesos and Morgan dollars, are on display in the main lobby. Inquire about special exhibitions and events held throughout the year. The museum's twenty-seven-acre site and picnic area are great places to have lunch and let the kids run off excess energy.

GARDEN OF THE GODS (all ages)

1805 North 30th Street, Colorado Springs 80904; (719) 634–6666. Open daily May through October, 5:00 A.M. to 11:00 P.M.; November through April, 7:00 A.M. to 9:00 P.M. **Free**.

Located within the Colorado Springs city limits, this 1,300-acre park is a Registered National Natural Landmark containing magnificent rock formations more than a million years old. Sculpted by time and erosion, they bear names befitting their various shapes, such as Kissing Camels, Cathedral Spires, and Sleeping Giant. Mainly level cement paths lead among the towering, rusty-red sandstone monoliths. The 1-mile Central Garden Trail, in the heart of the park at the base of the highest formations, is wheelchair and stroller accessible. Depending on the season, you are apt to see cottontail rabbits, chipmunks, rock squirrels, hawks, white-throated swifts, swallows, and black-billed magpies. Watch carefully and you might even see a mule deer or bighorn sheep.

GARDEN OF THE GODS VISITORS CENTER (all ages)
Garden of the Gods east entrance; (719) 634–6666; www.gardenofgods. com. Open daily June through August, 8:00 A.M. to 8:00 P.M.; September through May, 9:00 A.M. to 5:00 P.M. **Free** *admission. Multimedia show, $.*

Before entering the Garden of the Gods, stop first at the Visitors Center to view a fast-paced twelve-minute multimedia show in order to answer the question your kids are sure to ask: "How did those rocks get there?" The center's state-of-the-art interactive exhibits and touch-screen CD-ROMs will intrigue your children as they reveal the geology, ecology, cultural history, and American Indian heritage involved in the making of this one-of-a-kind park. The center features nature talks, a large deck for photographing the area, a gift shop, a cafe, rest rooms, and free maps.

 ### GARDEN OF THE GODS TRADING POST
Past Balancing Rock, southwest end of the park; (719) 685–9045 or (800) 874–4515; www.co-trading-post.com. Open daily June through August, 8:00 A.M. to 8:00 P.M.; September through May, 9:00 A.M. to 5:30 P.M. Cafe open summer only. **Free** *admission.*

Built in 1900 by local artist and Indian trader Charles E. Strausenback, the Garden of the Gods Trading Post is designed in the adobe style of the Pueblo Indians. It is now Colorado's largest trading post. From the usual T-shirts and trinkets to prized kachina dolls; valuable Santa Clara, Acoma, and Jemez Pueblo pottery; and original paintings by legendary Navajo artist R. C. Gorman, thousands of gift items parade across the shelves, line the walls, and fill the many chambers.

ROCK LEDGE RANCH HISTORIC SITE (all ages)

1401 Recreation Way, Colorado Springs 80904; near the Garden of the Gods Visitors Center; (719) 578–6777; www.springsgov.com. Open June through Labor Day, Wednesday through Sunday 10:00 A.M. to 5:00 P.M.; Labor Day to Christmas, some weekends and for special events. $

Visit this living-history museum in the heart of Garden of the Gods. You'll find an 1868 homestead, an 1890s working farm and blacksmith shop, and the 1907 Orchard House. Interpreters in period clothing bring the history of the area to life. Popular special events include military reenactments and the annual holiday traditions celebration.

A Taste from the Past While visiting Rock Ledge Ranch, stop in the General Store. Cool off with a frosty bottle of sarsaparilla soda, a refreshing taste Grandpa might have enjoyed. Or choose from a variety of flavored candy sticks. Historical reproductions, books, and unique gifts reflect an earlier era.

ACADEMY RIDING STABLES (ages 8 and up)

4 El Paso Boulevard, Colorado Springs 80904 (near south entrance to Garden of the Gods); (719) 633–5667 or (888) 700–0410; www.arsriding.com. Open daily 8:00 A.M. to 5:00 P.M., weather permitting. $$$–$$$$

The Academy Riding Stables provides guided horseback tours through the Garden of the Gods Park. Whether your family members are experienced equestrians or novices, the stables' personnel will select a horse that is just right for each individual. Wranglers will identify the various rock formations as you ride along and, with your camera, even snap a family photo or two for you. One-, two-, and three-hour rides are offered. Participants must weigh less than 250 pounds and be at least eight years old.

FLYING W RANCH (ages 2 and up)

3330 Chuckwagon Road, Colorado Springs 80919; (719) 598–4000; www. flyingw.com. Open daily Memorial Day through September; chuck wagon suppers served outdoors. (Heated shelter available in case of inclement weather.) Friday and Saturday evening, October until Christmas and March to Memorial Day, dinners and shows in the Steak House. Reservations are required. $–$$$

Your kids will be happy to know that they don't have to "sit still and be quiet" at this eatery, where chuck wagon suppers are served outdoors at wooden tables and benches. If they drop a biscuit on the ground, they can just go get another one, because this is an all-you-can-eat feast of barbecued beef, baked potatoes, Flying W baked beans, chunky apple-sauce, hot biscuits, old-fashioned spice cake, coffee, and lemonade.

During the summer months begin the evening by wandering through the Old Western town to watch the blacksmith at work, visit the under-ground kiva, and observe Indian women as they weave rugs in ancient Native American patterns.

If you have a toddler in tow, seek out Irene's Homestead for a stick horse for your little cowpoke. Kids delight in exploring the tepee and rid-ing the miniature train through the interior of an old mine and around the village area.

Following dinner, the Flying W Wranglers present an hour-long stage show of wholesome, family-style entertainment, including skits and old-time country tunes accompanied by guitars, fiddles, drums, and piano. During the summer it's best to arrive by 5:00 P.M. to allow plenty of time to play before dinner. They are often booked two weeks or more in advance, so make your reservations early.

Western Day-Tripper Plan a western theme day. Start at Academy Stables with a breakfast ride in the Garden of the Gods. Bring your camera; the morning light on the rock formations is perfect for outstanding photos. In the afternoon visit the Pro Rodeo Hall of Fame and American Cowboy Museum. On their patio try your hand at ropin'. Return to Garden of the Gods for a chuck wagon dinner and western show at Flying W Ranch.

PRO RODEO HALL OF FAME AND AMERICAN COWBOY MUSEUM (ages 4 and up)

101 Pro Rodeo Drive, Colorado Springs 80919 (I–25 at exit 147); (719) 528–4764. Open daily 9:00 A.M. to 5:00 P.M. $$, children 5 and younger Free.

This museum pays tribute to the only competitive sport that evolved from a working lifestyle. Two multimedia presentations address the his-tory of the rodeo, from its haphazard origins in Deer Trail, Colorado, in 1869, to its present status as a major spectator sport. More than ninety exhibits—showcasing saddles, chaps, ropes, boots, clothing, trophies, and artifacts—trace the progress of rodeo over the years. Be sure to check out the entertaining anecdotes about the lives and experiences of the men and women who have made rodeo a world-class event. Outside, children enjoy meeting the retired rodeo stock, which includes a live rodeo bull, a bucking bronco, and a longhorn steer. And you may have a difficult time dragging them out of the gift shop, with its more than 1,000 different rodeo and western gift items.

SKY SOX BASEBALL (all ages)

4385 Tutt Boulevard, Colorado Springs 80922; (719) 591–7699; www.skysox.com. Mid-April through early September. $–$$

The Sky Sox, a Colorado Rockies Triple A team, play in Colorado Springs. Watch future major league players or, sometimes, today's stars on rehab assignment. Players are accessible for autographs before and after each game.

COLORADO SPRINGS FINE ART CENTER

30 West Dale Street, Colorado Springs 80903; (719) 634–5581. Open year-round, Tuesday through Saturday 9:00 A.M. to 5:00 P.M. and Sunday 1:00 to 5:00 P.M. $, **Free** *on Saturday.*

Kids (and many adults) can hardly resist the urge to reach out and touch sculpture. In the Tactile Gallery it's encouraged. Explore works in wood, stone, and bronze through the sense of touch. Other galleries include a fine Native American and Hispanic collection, "The West and Charlie Russell," and a sculpture garden courtyard complete with totem poles. The changing shows frequently include themes interesting to children. Watch for Family Days such as Funky Jewelry Making for children and parents.

AMERICAN NUMISMATIC MUSEUM (ages 5 and up)

818 North Cascade Avenue, Colorado Springs 80903; (719) 632–2646; www.money.org/musintern.html. Open year-round, Monday through Friday 9:00 A.M. to 4:00 P.M. and Saturday 10:00 A.M. to 4:00 P.M. **Free**.

Gold, silver, coins, medals, and a $100,000 bill—see them all when you make this quick stop just around the corner from the Colorado Springs Fine Art Center. It's a spot for everyone who has ever collected a jar of pennies or arranged nickels by mint date. Displays include history of coinage from 700 B.C. to the present, Olympic commemorative sets, Colorado's Gold Rush Era, an engraver's workshop, and presidential memorabilia. Kids are surprisingly interested. They get to pick one coin from the treasure chest as they leave.

OLYMPIC TRAINING CENTER (all ages)

One Olympic Plaza, Colorado Springs 80909 (corner of Union Boulevard and Boulder Street); (719) 578–4618; www.olympic-usa.org. Open daily year-round; call (888) 659–8687 for tour schedule. **Free**.

Striving to perfect their sport, thousands of athletes train at the Olympic Training Center yearly. In the Visitor Center view a fifteen-minute orientation film and browse the U.S. Olympic Hall of Fame. A guided one-hour walking tour stops at numerous training facilities: the flume (a swimming treadmill), gymnasiums for fourteen sports, weight training, sports medicine and science, aquatic center, and shooting ranges. Sites seen on the tour vary due to training schedules. You might see Olympic volleyball medalists or the German wrestling team—every visit is different.

Opportunities for photos abound along the Irwin Belk Olympic Path, where forty-five Olympic and Pan American Games sports are depicted in colorful two-dimensional sculptures. From the rooftop terrace, the Olympic flame display stands before panoramic views of Pikes Peak. Purchases from the U.S. Olympic Spirit Stores directly support American athletes. Here, you are likely to find the perfect souvenir among the wide selection of unique merchandise.

In addition to being the headquarters of the United States Olympic Committee, Colorado Springs is home to twenty-three national sports federations. Check the local newspaper to see if there are competitions taking place while you're in town. It's an opportunity to see world-class athletes in peak condition.

MEMORIAL PARK (all ages)

1605 East Pikes Peak Avenue, Colorado Springs 80909; (719) 385–5940, skating rink (719) 578–6883, pool (719) 578–6634; www.colorado-springs.com/parksrec/. Open year-round; some facilities seasonal. **Free** *admission.*

Need some play time? Just east of downtown, Memorial Park offers what you're looking for and more. Choose from three playgrounds, including Pollywog (designed for disabled individuals), miles of trails and bikeways, a swim beach, boat rentals (paddle, row, sail, or canoe), indoor ice-skating, and pool.

VELODROME (ages 4 and up)

250 South Union Boulevard, Colorado Springs 80910 (in Memorial Park, off Union Boulevard); (719) 634–8356. Open daily year-round, weather permitting. Some competitive events $, otherwise **Free**.

Speed, skill, stamina—the thirty-three-degree banked track at the 7-Eleven Velodrome is one of the top three cycling facilities in the world. If the gates are open, you're welcome to stop in and see champions, juniors and adults, train. Records are set at this site that has hosted World Championships and U.S. Olympic trials.

Road, track, and mountain bikers all altitude-train in the Colorado Springs area. In the early morning you may see packs of riders setting off through town.

CHILDREN'S MUSEUM OF COLORADO SPRINGS (all ages)

In the Citadel Mall, upper level, next to JCPenney; (719) 574–0077. Open Wednesday through Saturday 10:00 A.M. to 5:00 P.M. Adults and children $, babies under 12 months **Free**.

Crawl through a model of the human heart in the Health and Wellness Center, or watch yourself on a television monitor as you perform at Let's Pretend. There are plenty of "do things" at this stop in a shopping mall. Exhibits change several times a year to keep local kids interested. Toddlers have their own room to explore. Frequently on Sunday, special programs are included in the price of admission.

GHOST TOWN (ages 3 and up)

400 South 21st Street, Colorado Springs 80904; (719) 634–0696; www.pikes-peak.com. Open Memorial Day through Labor Day, Monday through Saturday 9:00 A.M. to 6:00 P.M. and Sunday 11:00 A.M. to 6:00 P.M. The rest of the year, open Monday through Saturday 10:00 A.M. to 5:00 P.M. and Sunday noon to 5:00 P.M. $, children 5 and younger **Free**.

To capture a bit of the Old West, stop by this museum. Here a wooden sidewalk leads guests to a blacksmith shop, general store,

Pikes Peak Ice Cream Pick This outstanding Colorado Springs hometown business will satisfy your ice-cream cravings.

■ **Colorado City Creamery.** *2602 West Colorado Avenue, Colorado Springs 80904 (in Old Colorado City); (719) 634–1411.* Fresh dairy cream with 14 percent butterfat guarantees a rich, smooth ice cream. Pick a flavor and create your own treat at the sundae bar. For a sound from yesteryear, drop a quarter in the forty-four-note electric piano called a pianino. The shop is small and the line can be down the block, but the ice cream is great.

saloon, jail, livery, Victorian home, and several Main Street shops where animated characters tell about life in this turn-of-the-twentieth-century town. Your kids can play old-time arcade machines with silent movies, try their luck in the shooting gallery, and pay a visit to the gypsy fortune-teller. Several antique vehicles, including a 1903 Cadillac and the 1867 Wells Fargo Express Concord stagecoach that once carried the railroad payroll between Denver and Cheyenne, Wyoming, are on the street.

SIMPICH DOLLS (ages 3 and up)

2413 West Colorado Avenue, Colorado Springs 80904; (719) 636–3272 or (800) 881–3879; www.simpich.com. Open year-round, Monday through Saturday 10:00 A.M. to 5:00 P.M. **Free.**

Watch skilled artists delicately paint individual doll faces, while craftspeople form the bodies, hand-stitch clothing, dress, and detail each creation. In a historic building in Old Colorado City, visitors are welcome to view the construction of these storybook, Christmas, and historical character dolls. Of course there is a salesroom—bring your Christmas list.

BEAR CREEK NATURE CENTER (all ages)

245 Bear Creek Road, Colorado Springs 80906; (719) 520–6387. Open year-round, Tuesday through Saturday 9:00 A.M. to 4:00 P.M. **Free.**

This nature center is a friendly, low-key gem. Touch drawers and interactive displays teach about Colorado Life Zones. More than 180 birds have been identified in the park. Using their binoculars, naturalists will help you identify the Cooper's hawk drifting on wind currents. Along the short Songbird Trail, which is stroller and wheelchair accessible, signs identify commonly seen species. A bench allows quiet observation at a large feeder. Listen carefully to hear a variety of birdsongs.

NORTH CHEYENNE CAÑON PARK (all ages)

2120 North Cheyenne Cañon Road, Colorado Springs 80906; (719) 578–6146. Open year-round, weather permitting. **Free.**

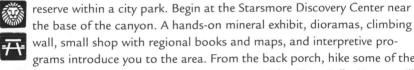
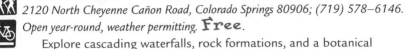

Explore cascading waterfalls, rock formations, and a botanical reserve within a city park. Begin at the Starsmore Discovery Center near the base of the canyon. A hands-on mineral exhibit, dioramas, climbing wall, small shop with regional books and maps, and interpretive programs introduce you to the area. From the back porch, hike some of the 56 miles of trails or drive up the canyon to Helen Hunt Falls. Here you'll find a small visitors center and, for hearty hikers, a steep trail to Silver Cascade Falls.

Old Colorado City

Old Colorado City For five days in 1859, Colorado City served as the first Territorial Capital of Colorado. Today you'll find a National Historic District with the log cabin "capitol," parks, unique shopping, dining, lodging, and a great ice-cream vendor.

SEVEN FALLS (ages 4 and up)

2850 South Cheyenne Cañon Road, Colorado Springs 80906; (719) 632–0765. Open daily year-round, summer, 8:30 A.M. to 9:30 P.M.; winter, 9:00 A.M. to 4:15 P.M. $–$$

Park your car in the parking lot and walk a short distance along a stream to a clear mountain pool inhabited by rainbow, brook, and golden trout. Here seven separate falls splash, crash, and tumble 181 feet down a sheer granite canyon wall. A 224-step staircase runs perpendicular to the waterfall. At the top a mile-long, forested nature trail is frequented by Abert squirrels, chipmunks, white-tailed deer, and hummingbirds. For families with children unable to climb the many steps, the Mountain Express Elevator transports visitors to the Eagle's Nest platform for a bird's-eye view of all seven falls.

Beautiful during daylight hours, the falls become a spectacular fantasyland at night when enhanced by colored lights. This is when Native American performers present interpretive dances. Visiting children are permitted to participate.

For more than fifty years, Seven Falls has admitted guests free of charge for special night lighting displays during a ten-day period at Christmastime. The proceeds from donations are used to provide toys for less-fortunate children.

CHEYENNE MOUNTAIN ZOO (all ages)

4250 Cheyenne Mountain Zoo Road, Colorado Springs 80906; (719) 633–9925; www.cmzoo.org. Open daily year-round, Memorial Day weekend through Labor Day, 9:00 A.M. to 5:00 P.M. The rest of the year, 9:00 A.M. to 4:00 P.M. $–$$

The slogan at this zoo is "The Zoo with a View." And indeed it is. With a base elevation of 6,800 feet, it is said to be the only "mountain zoo" in the United States. The exhibit areas are actually carved out of the lower slopes of a 9,400-foot mountain. Set beneath jagged rock cliffs and amid groves of oak, pine, spruce, and aspen, the 700-acre complex houses more than 500 wild and wonderful animals.

Because of the zoo's hillside location, your children can come face-to-face with towering giraffes and hand-feed

"I've Never Seen Anything like It!"

Why does everyone hit the brakes and stare like a tourist? The late sculptor Starr Kempf's front yard is home to silvery futuristic sculptures, taller than surrounding trees—quite a visual treat. Some parts move in the breeze. Look for this bizarre display near the entry to North Cheyenne Cañon Park. Practice saying, "I've never seen anything like it." And watch your driving.

them the special "animal crackers" available for purchase. Kids able to tackle the slightly rugged terrain can walk to the zoo's highest point; otherwise they can ride a tram to the top. Here you will find picnic grounds, a snack bar, a nature trail, a carousel (seasonal), and an area where children can feed and touch the animals.

Admission includes entry to the Will Rogers Shrine of the Sun, a granite tower with spectacular views of the Front Range of the Rocky Mountains.

WORLD FIGURE SKATING MUSEUM AND HALL OF FAME (ages 3 and up)

20 1st Street, Colorado Springs 80906 (off Lake Avenue near the Broadmoor Hotel); (719) 635–5200. Open year-round, Monday through Friday 10:00 A.M. to 4:00 P.M.; also open Saturday May through October and the first Saturday monthly November through April. $, children under 6 Free.

Sit Spin, Lutz jump, Triple-toe-loop—figure skating entertains millions of spectators every year. Here you'll find a tribute to the sport's greatest stars, glittering costumes, Olympic medals, videos of historic performances, and intriguing exhibits. Skates made from animal bone and leather straps from the eighth century, toddler ice walkers, and Japanese skates with cloth toe thongs demonstrate the evolution of equipment. Works by Currier and Ives, Norman Rockwell, and Andy Warhol appear in the largest collection of skating art in the world. A stop here could put dreams in the minds of young skaters.

WORLD ARENA (ages 3 and up)
3185 Venetucci Boulevard, Colorado Springs 80906; (719) 477–2150; www. worldarena.com. Open daily year-round for public skating sessions; times vary. Rentals available. $

This ice arena, home to training camps for the U.S. Olympic Training Center and professional and collegiate hockey teams, opens daily for public skating. You can also watch future champions in practice sessions. A great way to cool off on a hot summer afternoon.

Olympic Theme Day-Tripper Make a vacation day an Olympic event. Stop by the World Arena to see Olympic-hopeful figure skaters during a morning training session. Visit the nearby World Figure Skating Museum and Hall of Fame. Tour the U.S. Olympic Training Center and see athletes in action. While you're there, check the schedule for evening games, events, or competitions. Perhaps there's racing at the Velodrome in Memorial Park. Get in the act with some afternoon ice time at the World Arena.

 MAY NATURAL HISTORY MUSEUM OF THE TROPICS (ages 4 and up)
710 Rock Creek Canyon, Colorado Springs 80926 (9 miles southwest of Colorado Springs on State Highway 115); (719) 576–0450 or (800) 666–3841; www. maymuseum-camp-rvpark.com. Open daily May through September, 8:00 A.M. to 6:00 P.M. $, children 5 and younger **Free**.

Most kids are fascinated by bugs, even if it's just for the fun of wrinkling up noses and letting out a squeal or two. That could be the reason this museum is such a hit with children. The only museum in North America entirely devoted to the display and study of giant tropical insects, it attracts students from preschool to college age to see more than 8,000 of the world's largest, rarest, most poisonous, and most beautiful insects and related jungle creatures. The irreplaceable collection represents a lifetime of work by current curator John May and his father, the late James May. It is said that if someone were to begin collecting now, with $1 million dollars and fifty years of time at his or her disposal, it is unlikely that that individual would be able to even come close to duplicating May's collection.

At the museum's entrance stands a designed-to-scale, exact replica of a *Dynastes hercules,* the world's largest beetle. This gigantic 25-foot-long, 15-foot-high sculpture is only a hint of what is to come, and it is sure to entice your youngsters to want to see more.

MUSEUM OF SPACE EXPLORATION (ages 4 and up)
Admission to the May Natural History Museum of the Tropics includes entry to the adjacent Museum of Space Exploration. Hours are the same for both museums.

This collection depicts man's first attempts at flight up to the present space program. Included are hundreds of official National Aeronautics and Space Administration (NASA) photographs and models of early aircraft, World War II planes, and spacecraft. Visitors can view official NASA films of the first moon landing, the shuttle program, and the exploration of the solar system.

 CHALLENGE UNLIMITED (ages 8 and up)
204 South 24th Street, Colorado Springs 80904; (719) 633–6399 or (800) 798–5954; www.bikithikit.com. Open mid-May to mid-October. $$$$

This easy 20-mile ride down Pikes Peak via the Pikes Peak Highway provides individuals an exciting journey through five distinct vegetation and animal-life zones. Although this adventure takes place on Pikes Peak, it begins at the Challenge Unlimited office, where, depending on the ride you plan to participate in, you will be treated to a breakfast or a snack. During this time you will have the opportunity to meet the guides and your fellow bikers. Your family will then be driven to the 14,110-foot summit and issued twenty-one-speed mountain bikes, helmets, all-weather clothing, and souvenir water bottles. Experienced guides with training in first aid and emergency medical techniques will accompany you down the mountain. One van will travel in front of the group and another will follow behind. Periodic stops will allow you to take photos, learn about the area, and rest. Along the route you will stop for either a picnic lunch or a snack, again depending on your choice of ride.

Where to Eat

Conway's Red Top. *Four locations: 1520 South Nevada Avenue, Colorado Springs 80906; (719) 633–2444; 390 North Circle Drive, Colorado Springs 80909; (719) 630–1566; 3589 North Carefree Circle, Colorado Springs 80917; (719) 596–6444; 1228 East Fillmore, Colorado Springs 80907; (719) 329–1445. Open* daily for lunch and dinner. Hungry for a burger? Conway's has been chosen one of the "Top 5 Best Hamburgers in America." The Conway family—with ten kids and lots of energy—has been serving up giant hamburgers since 1962. Grandma Esther's recipes for soups, stews, and chili are still faithfully followed. The milk shakes are the real thing—thick and frosty. When you see the size of the burger, you'll know why buns are baked especially for Conway's. $

Giuseppe's Old Depot Restaurant. *10 South Sierra Madre, Colorado Springs 80903; (719) 635–3111; www.giuseppes-depot.com. Daily lunch and dinner, served continuously from 11:00 A.M.* Located in a century-old former railroad depot, Giuseppe's serves an extensive Italian and American menu—stone-oven pizzas, calzones, pasta, sandwiches, and steaks. Try the Italian meatball sandwich. The Baggage Cart salad bar overflows with sixty-five items. Note that Giuseppe's serves all afternoon, so you don't have to settle for fast food when you're hungry at 3:00 P.M. $–$$

Where to Stay

Dale Downtown Motel. *620 West Colorado Avenue, Colorado Springs 80904; (719) 636–3721.* This family-oriented budget motel is close to restaurants and attractions. It has a heated pool, cable TV, and family units with kitchenettes. Cribs and rollaway beds are available. A two-room family unit that will sleep four runs $–$$.

For More Information

Colorado Springs Convention and Visitors Bureau, *515 South Cascade Avenue, Colorado Springs 80903; (800) 888–4748; www.coloradosprings-travel.com.*

Pikes Peak Country Attractions Association, *354 Manitou Avenue, Manitou Springs 80829; (719) 685–5894 or (800) 525–2250; www.pikes-peak.com.* Check the Web site for on-line coupons.

Manitou Springs

Geographically adjacent to the northwest section of Colorado Springs but totally different in lifestyle and tempo, Manitou Springs thrives as a laid-back artisan community. The Ute and Arapahoe Indians considered this area to be a sanctuary where they could gather in peace to worship the god Manitou.

GOOD OLD SUMMERTIME ICE-CREAM SOCIAL
Soda Springs Park, Manitou Springs; (719) 685–5089 or (800) 642–2567. Annually in mid-July, 5:00 to 8:00 P.M.
Along with ample supplies of ice cream from a local dairy, this annual affair brings a popular homemade ice-cream contest. Prizes are

awarded in a variety of categories, including "best vanilla ice cream," "most creative ice cream," and "best ice cream made with Manitou Springs mineral water." Musical entertainment is provided. Generous servings of ice cream are available for $1.00.

MIRAMONT CASTLE (ages 4 and up)

9 Capitol Hill Avenue, Manitou Springs 80829; (719) 685–1011; www.pikespeak.com/castle/. Open Memorial Day through Labor Day, Tuesday through Sunday 10:00 A.M. to 5:00 P.M.; after Labor Day through Christmas, Tuesday through Sunday 11:00 A.M. to 4:00 P.M.; after Christmas to Memorial Day, Tuesday through Thursday noon to 3:00 P.M. $

Built in 1895 by Jean Baptiste Francolon, a Catholic priest from France, the grandiose castle is a composite of nine architectural styles—Queen Anne, Romanesque, English Tudor, Fleming, Domestic Elizabethan, Venetian Ogee, Byzantine, Moorish, and Chateau—all beautifully blended together. Exquisite antiques will require that little ones not touch, but your children are likely to be intrigued by a sojourn through the magnificent castle to see a ceiling sheathed in gold, a 200-ton sandstone fireplace, and an elaborate 400-square-foot bedroom that once belonged to the priest's mother, Marie Francolon.

After a tour through the mansion's many rooms, reward your well-behaved youngsters with a stop at the castle's Museum of Miniatures and Model Railroad Museum, followed by a snack in the Queen's Parlor Tearoom.

From late November until Christmas Day, Miramont Castle is decorated in grand Victorian style. A tour through this opulent masterpiece during the holidays is a lovely way to celebrate the season.

THE MANITOU CLIFF DWELLINGS MUSEUM (ages 5 and up)

West of Manitou Springs, on U.S. Highway 24, Manitou Springs 80829; (719) 685–5242; www.cliffdwellingsmuseum.com. Open daily June through August, 9:00 A.M. to 8:00 P.M.; September through May, 9:00 A.M. to 5:00 P.M., weather permitting. $–$$, children 6 and younger **Free**

Nineteenth-century architecture, stately Victorian bed-and-breakfasts, art galleries, and craft shops line Manitou Springs's narrow, curving streets, while just outside of town are former accommodations and artwork of a different sort. The Manitou Cliff Dwellings Museum allows visitors to experience a culture created by the Ancient Pueblo People (formerly called the Anasazi) during the peak of their civilization, from A.D. 1100 to 1300.

The Springs of Manitou

Nine of Manitou Springs's twenty-six constantly flowing mineral springs have been completely restored and are safe for drinking. The water from each tastes a little different, depending upon the exact mineral content. Chemists claim that carbonic acid is responsible for the water's bubbles. Indian legend states that the spirit of the great god Manitou breathed into the waters their sparkly effervescence. The Indians brought their sick and aged to drink from the health-giving waters, leaving behind offerings of blankets, bows, moccasins, and knives, which they threw into the water or hung on trees.

The current residents of Manitou Springs continue to advocate the healthful benefits of drinking the spring water. Many townspeople can be seen filling jugs and bottles at the pipes leading from the springs. They drink the water as it is or mix it with fruit juice. Your children will no doubt insist on trying the mineral-laden water. Be prepared, though, for a negative reaction to the taste.

Although the structures were relocated here from McElmo Canyon in southwestern Colorado, the reasons for moving them are well founded. At the time the museum was established, in 1904, looters and "pot hunters" were vandalizing these structures, and it was in the interest of preserving them for future generations that they were transplanted to this location. The Federal Antiquities Act, which makes it a federal offense to destroy or remove artifacts, was not enacted until 1906.

Your children can pretend to be explorers and archaeologists on your self-guided tour through the forty rooms, which include a lookout tower, sleeping quarters, and a kiva—a sunken, circular, dome-covered structure once used for ceremonial purposes. One three-story dwelling housed nine families in its tiny rooms that average 6-by-8 feet wide and 5½ feet high. The upstairs chambers are reached by ladders.

The main building at the museum, modeled after the pueblos of the Southwest, houses examples of the Ancient Pueblo People's pottery, baskets, jewelry, tools, burial urns, and weapons. The gift shops feature Indian-made jewelry, pottery, and crafts. Native American dancing is performed during June, July, and August.

CAVE OF THE WINDS (ages 7 and up)

North of U.S. Highway 24, on Serpentine Drive; P.O. Box 826, Manitou Springs 80829; (719) 685–5444; www.caveofthewinds.com. Open daily May through Sunday of Labor Day weekend, 9:00 A.M. to 9:00 P.M. (last tour begins at 8:00

P.M.); Labor Day through April, 10:00 A.M. to 5:00 P.M. (last tour at 4:30 P.M.). During summer high season, advance reservations are recommended. $$–$$$, children 5 and younger Free.

Your children won't soon forget an adventurous journey into these mysterious caves. With Mom, Dad, or grandparents close at hand, youngsters will experience the thrill of being in a cave deep within the Rocky Mountains. They will discover colorfully displayed stalactites and stalagmites in an underground created by nature over millions of years.

On the Discovery Tour, the most popular, guides lead visitors along a well-lighted path past breathtakingly beautiful formations and secretive nooks and crannies that turn-of-the-twentieth-century explorers suspected were the homes of gnomes and trolls. This tour lasts approximately forty-five minutes.

The one-and-a-half-hour Lantern Tour takes you along pitch-black passageways, illuminated only by your candlelit lanterns. As you venture through the darkness, the lantern light causes fascinating configurations to come alive among the crevices and shadows and dance against the rock walls. This tour is best suited for children age eight or older, although younger ones are not denied admittance.

LASER CANYON LIGHT SHOW (ages 4 and up)

Adjacent to Cave of the Winds; (719) 685–5446. Open nightly May through Labor Day; showtime at 9:00 P.M. $–$$, children 5 and younger Free.

In Williams Canyon, next door to the Cave of the Winds, the Laser Canyon Light Show explodes with color. During this spectacular presentation, you and your children sit perched on bleachers 500 feet above the canyon floor, mesmerized by brilliant images and animated figures that dance across the cliffs fifteen stories high and ½ mile wide. Set to music ranging from Mozart to U2, the swirling, careening renderings include soaring eagles with 300-foot wingspans.

Where to Eat

Queen's Parlor Tearoom. *9 Capitol Hill Avenue, Manitou Springs 80829, in the Miramont Castle; (719) 685–1011. Open during the summer months only, 11:00 A.M. to 4:00 P.M., this peaceful tearoom* serves dainty assorted sandwiches, homemade soups, salads, scones, cheesecake, and old-fashioned ice-cream sodas. $

Where to Stay

Frontier's Rest Bed & Breakfast.
*341 Ruxton Avenue, Manitou Springs
80829; (719) 685–0588.* This is a wonderful place for families to stay while in this region. Ideally located within easy walking distance to many area attractions, the inn has four guest rooms, all with private baths. The Settler room, with a queen-size bed plus a queen-size trundle bed, is particularly convenient for families. Kids love the adjacent Trailblazer, a narrow, two-bedded attic hideaway with a sloped ceiling. This chamber works well with the Settler as a two-bedroom, two-bathroom unit. Innkeeper Jeanne Vrobel's hearty breakfasts, never-empty cookie jar, and delectable evening desserts are sure to be a hit with children and parents alike. $$–$$$

Spring Cottage and Spring Cottage, Too. *113 Pawnee Avenue, Manitou Springs 80829; (719) 685–9395; www. springcottage.com.* This inn consists of two lovely dollhouselike cottages. The larger of the two accommodates a family of seven, with two white-iron double beds in the front bedroom and two youth beds and a single in the back bedroom. A crib and a portable crib are available, if needed. Two couches and a white wicker rocker enhance the living room, and the kitchen features a wooden table and chair set, a cooking stove, and a refrigerator. Children have a yard, with a sandbox and tire swing, to play in. A full breakfast is served in your cottage. $$–$$$

Up (and Down) the Pike

Historically, Pikes Peak has stood as a challenge to many over the years. Zebulon Pike, for whom the mountain was named, not only failed to reach the top but found the prospect so awesome that he declared, "I believe no human being could have ascended to its pinnacle." In 1820 Edwin James did just that, but it was Zalmon G. Simmons (of Simmons Mattress Company fame and fortune) who, after riding to the top on the back of a mule in the early 1880s and proclaiming the beauty to be astounding but the journey dreadful, set about to make the mountain accessible by rail.

PIKES PEAK COG RAILWAY (all ages)

515 Ruxton Avenue, Manitou Springs 80829; (719) 685–5401; www.cograilway. com. Open mid-April through mid-November; phone for exact hours. Reservations are strongly recommended. $$$–$$$$

The first locomotives to reach the summit of Pikes Peak were steam operated. These were replaced by diesel engines in the 1940s. Since 1965, Swiss-made railcars, constructed exclusively for the Pikes Peak Cog Railway, have transported millions of riders along the 9-mile track.

The train chugs out of the Manitou Springs station and through aspen glens and steep canyons filled with wildflowers and cascading streams. Arrival at the summit reveals expansive vistas of the Continental Divide and the Great Plains. Traveling at just 8 miles per hour, the locomotive provides photographers ample time to capture the magnificent panoramas.

After nearly an hour-long ride, your children can stretch their legs at the Summit House, get a snack at the concession stand, and browse the curio shop before embarking on the return trip down the mountain.

Hiking Hints Before you set out on a hike, let someone know where you are going and when you expect to return.

The U.S. Forest Service advocates that all hikers carry the ten essentials: map, compass, flashlight, sunglasses, extra food and water, extra clothing, matches, candle, knife, and first-aid kit. And at Colorado's high altitude, sunscreen is a must.

PIKES PEAK HIGHWAY (all ages)

South of U.S. Highway 24 at Cascade; (719) 385–7325 or (800) 318–9505; www.pikespeakcolorado.com. Open year-round, weather permitting; May through September, 7:00 A.M. to 7:00 P.M.; October through April, 9:00 A.M. to 3:00 P.M. Cost $10 per person older than 16, maximum $35 per car, pass valid two consecutive days.

"Pikes Peak or Bust." It's an American tradition to want to stand atop Colorado's best-known mountain. Pikes Peak Highway makes that a greater possibility than in Zebulon Pike's day. While the drive is still not for the faint of heart—many miles are gravel with no center stripe or crash barriers—the family sedan will get you to the top. The round-trip can be done in less than two hours, but a better choice is to take a full or at least a half day to enjoy activities on the mountain. Crystal Reservoir gift shop, just after mile marker 6, offers boat rentals, fishing, hiking, some interpretive exhibits, snacks, grills and a picnic area, and souvenirs. You'll find Halfway Picnic Ground at the midpoint of your ascent.

Geography and vegetation change frequently as you ascend almost 8,000 feet. Just below timberline, stop at Glen Cove Inn, where you can grab a burger or some barbecue. In the restored log lodge, coffee drinkers revel—a cup of hot java for only a nickel! The rock formations here are favorites of climbers. Note the effect of wind and weather on the gnarled, twisted bristlecone pines. Among Earth's oldest living things, they can be more than 1,000 years old.

Watch for yellow-bellied marmots in the tundra areas below 12,000 feet. This cousin to the woodchuck hibernates for seven to nine months each year. Building up body fat during the summer requires lots of munching on grasses and wildflowers. If you hear his loud, shrill call, you'll understand the nickname "whistle pig." Devil's Playground earned its name because of the way lightning skips from rock to rock here. If the weather is threatening, stay in your car. Approaching curves, with no view of the road ahead, you feel as if you're driving into the heavens.

It's camera time at the summit—family snowball fights in July, clouds swirling in the valley below, shiny red cars of the Cog Railway. If you're panting and gasping for oxygen at the peak, think about the yearly marathon racers who run up—and back down. Winners have raced in less than three hours and twenty minutes. Check out the souvenir selection in Summit House. How about a "Real Men Don't Need Guard Rails" T-shirt for the trip back down the mountain?

Wonder Woman We remember Zebulon Pike (although he never made it to the top), but hardly anyone has heard of Julia Archibald Holmes. She is credited as the first woman to reach the top of Pikes Peak in 1858. At age twenty, with an adventurous spirit, she left her home in Lawrence, Kansas, and walked with a wagon train to the Colorado Territory. That walk must have been great conditioning for the climb to the summit. In a letter to her mother she reported, "Nearly everyone tried to discourage me from attempting it, but I believed I should succeed . . ."

PIKES PEAK ALPINE SCHOOL (ages 3 and up)

Location: Behind Glen Cove Inn on Pikes Peak Highway. Mailing address: 823 East Monument Avenue, Colorado Springs 80903; (719) 630–3934 or (800) 358–6867; www.pikes-peak.com/alpine. Open at Glen Cove, June through August, 10:30 A.M. to 5:30 P.M. $$$

When you stop at Glen Cove Inn and your kids watch rock climbers on the crags behind the inn, don't be surprised if they want to give it a try. Guides from Pikes Peak Alpine School provide equipment (climbing shoes and harnesses for even preschoolers) and instruction for an introductory experience. What a great place to try your skill at climbing. More difficult routes are available for those with experience.

Classes and guided rock climbing are also conducted year-round in Garden of the Gods and seasonally in North Cheyenne Canyon. Snowshoeing, skiing, mountaineering, and avalanche clinics are offered during the winter.

Popcorn Stop "Family fun is what it's all about," says Mike Myers, owner and proprietor of the **Pikes Peak Gourmet Popcorn** factory and store, at Pikes Peak Highway and U.S. Highway 24 in Cascade (8025 West Highway 24, Cascade 80809; www.members.aol.com/ppgpop), approximately 5 miles west of Manitou Springs. From home milk delivery by horse-drawn wagon in 1925 to filling orders via the Internet, the Myers family has been in the business of pleasing customers for more than seventy years.

This is the sort of place kids beg to stop at, and parents and grandparents don't find it hard to take, either. The first thing that hits you as you enter the door is the wonderful aroma of just about every flavor of popcorn imaginable. For starters there are almond-pecan crunch, cherry cordial, butter rum, mountain raspberry, Irish cream—you get the idea—packed in attractive decorator tins of several sizes and every description. Or how about an unusual basket, crafted of corncobs and packed with half-gallon bags of any flavor popcorn you choose? If you are visiting this area as someone's house guest, a tin or basket filled with popcorn would be a delightful gift for your host or hostess. You will be happy to know that you also can purchase smaller quantities in plastic bags, enabling you to satisfy everyone, just in case your youngsters can't agree on a flavor.

Pikes Peak Gourmet Popcorn is open daily January through mid-May, 10:00 A.M. to 6:00 P.M.; mid-May through December, 10:00 A.M. to 5:00 P.M. Open dates are approximate, depending on weather. Best to phone. Free samples are always available. Call (719) 684–9174 or (800) 684–1155 for more information.

North Pole

SANTA'S WORKSHOP AND NORTH POLE (ages 2–10)
550 Pikes Peak Highway, Cascade 80809; (719) 684–9432. Open June through August, daily 9:30 A.M. to 6:00 P.M.; September through December 24, Friday through Tuesday 10:00 A.M. to 5:00 P.M. Admission price includes shows and unlimited rides. $$$

In 1940 an eight-year-old girl was asked by one of Walt Disney's artists what Santa Claus's home and village looked like. Blessed with a vivid imagination, the child shared her vision of Santa Claus land. Thus Santa's Workshop and North Pole was created.

Santa's village is a fantasyland that is sure to please your little ones. Here they will find Santa's reindeer, llamas, deer, rabbits, chickens, and ducks. They can watch Elmer the Elf's magic show, swing through the sky on Santa's space shuttle, and climb aboard the carousel, the Ferris wheel, the miniature train, and nearly twenty more rides. You can all shop in gingerbread-style houses with pointy roofs and mail your postcards here so that the cancellation will read "North Pole."

Ah, but the best part of a visit to Santa's Workshop and North Pole is when your youngsters enter Mr. and Mrs. Claus's little cottage to sit on Santa's lap and, no matter if it happens to be July or December, whisper into his ear the hopes and dreams for Christmases to come. You can snap a photo of the occasion for next year's Christmas card or have Santa take a picture automatically while he listens to your youngster's requests.

Cripple Creek

From Woodland Park head west on U.S. Highway 24. At Divide, turn south onto State Highway 67 to go to Cripple Creek.

In 1890 "Crazy Bob" Womack discovered the largest gold deposit in the history of the world in Poverty Gulch, near Cripple Creek. Until then Womack's dubious claim to fame had been his ability to lean down from his horse at a full gallop and snatch a whiskey bottle with his teeth. Alas, "Crazy Bob" got tipsy one time too many and, during one such occasion, sold his claim—eventually worth $600 million—for a measly $300. He died penniless.

By the late 1800s Cripple Creek boasted a population of nearly 50,000 people. Archives record churches of all denominations, 150 saloons and gambling halls, and "almost constant sunshine and no tramps, everybody prosperous."

Many celebrities have roots in Cripple Creek. Groucho Marx delivered groceries here. The Wright brothers won an auto race from Cripple Creek to Colorado Springs. Boxer Jack Dempsey labored in the mines by day and boxed by night, and cowboy actor Tom Mix worked as a bouncer in a Bennett Avenue saloon.

Though no longer as wild and woolly as it was during the Gold Rush days, Cripple Creek is still plenty lively due to legal small-stakes gambling and several

Wild West–type attractions. Families will find inexpensive dining establishments, reasonably priced lodging, and numerous family-oriented activities.

 ## MOLLIE KATHLEEN GOLD MINE (ages 4 and up)

On the north end of Cripple Creek; P.O. Box 339, Cripple Creek 80813; (719) 689–2466; www.goldminetours.com. Open daily May through mid-October, 9:00 A.M. to 5:00 P.M. Sometimes open during winter months (depending on weather). $–$$$

To learn what life was like for the hard-rock miners of old, plan to take a tour of the Mollie Kathleen Gold Mine. Legend states that while on a family outing in 1892, Mollie Kathleen Gointner discovered the gold outcropping that eventually led to a successful mining operation that lasted from 1892 to 1961. Don't let the touristy exterior discourage you. The tour is an exceptionally good one, led by gentlemen guides who have been associated with gold mining most of their lives.

The tour lasts about forty minutes. During that time you will board a miner's cage called a "skip" and descend a shaft 1,000 feet into the earth. You will see mining equipment and working areas and learn what stopes, winzes, crosscuts, and drifts are and what they had to do with gold mining. You will see gold veins and a display of various gold ores found in Colorado, and you and your kids will each receive a souvenir ore specimen that contains actual gold.

This tour is easily navigated by children and grandparents. There are no steps, climbing, or rough ground involved.

CRIPPLE CREEK & VICTOR NARROW GAUGE RAILROAD (all ages)

North end of Bennett Avenue; P.O. Box 459, Cripple Creek 80813; (719) 689–2640; www.ccvngrailroad.webjump.com. Open daily Memorial Day through mid-October; trains depart every forty-five minutes beginning at 10:00 A.M. $–$$

As the engineer blows the whistle, clouds of steam escape from the engine's stack, and the train chugs out of the Cripple Creek station for a 4-mile round-trip journey back in time. The country's only steam locomotive that crosses a historic gold camp district, the fully restored fifteen-ton iron horse of the 0-4-0 type—representative of the early-day steam engines—transports passengers over a trestle and past head frames, ore dumps, "Crazy Bob" Womack's abandoned cabin, Poverty Gulch, and mine site after mine site to the ghost town of Anaconda. A narrator provides an informative and educational spiel, highlighting points of interest along the way. The train stops several times so that photographers can obtain some memorable shots, and when the engineer blows the train whistle at Echo Valley, passengers strain their ears to determine how many times the sound reverberates across the land. This trip is especially beautiful during fall, when aspen leaves of brilliant yellow and burnt ocher remind viewers that there still is "gold in them thar hills."

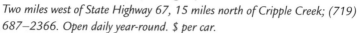

MUELLER STATE PARK (all ages)

Two miles west of State Highway 67, 15 miles north of Cripple Creek; (719) 687–2366. Open daily year-round. $ per car.

Forests and meadows with miles of trails, modern camping facilities, fishing, and abundant wildlife create an ideal state park. Bighorn sheep are abundant. Note the scars on the lower trunks of aspen trees—signs of elk gnawing during the winter when snow covers the natural grasses. Black bears, bobcats, and an occasional mountain lion are spotted in remote areas of the park. Because of the large number of aspen, fall is a golden time to visit.

Some of the more than 90 miles of trails are hiking only, but most are multiuse—hiking/biking or hiking/horse. Difficulty ranges from a relaxed walk along the self-guided Wapiti Nature Trail to all-day treks. During the summer rangers lead hikes, activities, and amphitheater presentations. Kids can participate in a Junior Ranger program, and there's a small playground in the ninety-site campground.

More than 50 miles of marked cross-country ski and snowshoeing trails make this a popular winter day-trip from Colorado Springs. Sledding and tubing are permitted when there is enough snow to prevent resource damage. When conditions allow, frozen ponds are cleared for skating.

Where to Stay

Gold King Mountain Inn. *P.O. Box 1329, Cripple Creek 80813; (719) 689–2600 or (800) 445–3607.* Located in a quiet area, ¼ mile out of town, this hotel offers free shuttle service to attractions and complimentary continental breakfasts consisting of fresh fruit, cereals, milk, juice, and baked goods. Roll-away beds are available. $$

Victor Hotel. *4th Street and Victor Avenue, P.O. Box 185, Victor 80860;* *(719) 689–3553.* Located 6 miles from Cripple Creek, this renovated historic structure has served as a bank, offices for the Western Union Telegraph Company, and the infirmary for Dr. H. G. Thomas, father of author and broadcaster Lowell Thomas. Children will enjoy riding in the antique "birdcage" elevator, original to the building. Rates include a complimentary continental breakfast. $–$$$

For More Information

Cripple Creek Chamber of Commerce, P.O. Box 650, Cripple Creek 80813; (719) 689–2169.

Cripple Creek Welcome Center, P.O. Box 430, Cripple Creek 80813; (719) 689–3315 or (877) 858–4653; www. cripple-creek.co.us/.

Footloose and Fancy-Free As you meander Cripple Creek's

narrow streets, listen for a hearty hee-haw or two and watch for a herd of donkeys, the town's mascots, which are looked upon as pets by the locals. They are protected by city ordinance but are owned by the Two Mile Club, a community booster club not unlike a chamber of commerce. Allowed to roam at will during the summer months and taken to pasture during the winter, the furry critters can be found just about anywhere in town and as far as 6 miles away in the former mining town of Victor. They are said to be descendants of the burros that at one time helped work the mines. Of course, children should use care when approaching the donkeys, but with parental supervision they can feed them "Donkey Treats," available for purchase in local shops.

Florissant

FLORISSANT FOSSIL BEDS NATIONAL MONUMENT (all ages)
U.S. Highway 24, 8 miles west of Divide; P.O. Box 185, Florissant 80816; (719) 748–3253; www.nps.gov/flfo. Open daily year-round, June through August, 8:00 A.M. to 7:00 P.M.; September through May, 8:00 A.M. to 4:30 P.M. $

Home to an abundance of wildlife, including deer, antelope, cougars, black bears, elk, bighorn sheep, porcupines, golden eagles, and mountain bluebirds, the Florissant Fossil Beds National Monument preserves some of the finest fossil deposits of the Oligocene epoch found anywhere in the world. Today, the paper-thin, light-gray, fossil-bearing shales occur in only a few areas at the monument, so the best places to see the fossils are in the exhibits at the visitors center and on two interpretive trails.

Since the Florissant Fossil Beds were discovered in 1873, numerous paleontologists have come to this mountainous environment to collect specimens that now reside in more than twenty museums, including Harvard University's Museum of Comparative Zoology, the Smithsonian Museum of Natural History, the Denver Museum of Natural History, and the British Museum in London.

Many special programs well suited for families take place at the monument during summer and fall. You can take a "Hike with a Ranger" to some of the less-visited areas of the park. Bring a lunch, water, and sunscreen. You can learn about "Native People and Pioneers" during a two-hour session, including a slide presentation at the Fowler Education Center and a tour of the Hornbeck Homestead. And if you don't mind getting your feet wet, you can accompany your youngsters on the "Junior Ranger Stream Studies," where children in kindergarten through sixth grade earn a Junior Ranger Certificate. For this one, bring a lunch, water, sunscreen, and shoes suitable for wading into the stream. During autumn on designated days, you can participate on a "Wapiti [elk] Watch." This is bugling season for the elk, and during the early evening your group will take an easy hike to see and listen to a herd of these fine animals. Bring warm clothing and a flashlight. (The National Park Service reminds children that the elk bugle only when it is very, very quiet.) There is no charge for these programs, but reservations are strongly recommended. Call for times and dates.

 ## PETRIFIED FOREST LOOP

The Florissant Fossil Beds National Monument is a marvelous place for picnicking and hiking. There are 12 miles of good hiking trails. Perhaps of special interest to your children would be the self-guided Petrified Forest Loop, a 1-mile trail through ponderosa pine forest to the "Big Stump," a giant sequoia measuring 12 feet tall and 74 feet in circumference. This tree is thought to have stood 200 to 250 feet tall 700 years ago when it was buried in volcanic mud flows. Your children are sure to ask why there are broken saw blades in the top of the stump, and you can explain to them how a failed attempt to cut the stump in quarters and send it to Chicago for the Columbian Exposition was conducted in 1893. Also of interest to children are the numerous animals that frequent the area: ground squirrels, coyotes, elk, and antelope. Watch for the very special Abert squirrel, a pointy-eared little critter that depends on the ponderosa pine for its survival. This trail and the ½-mile Walk through Time route are stroller and wheelchair accessible.

 ## HORNBECK HOMESTEAD

While at the Florissant Fossil Beds National Monument, you'll want to take your children through the old Hornbeck Homestead, located at the north end of the park and open during summer months only. Here they can wander through widow Adeline Hornbeck's home and across the land where she raised four children, grew potatoes and garden vegetables, and cut twenty tons of hay. You can tour the main house, the bunkhouse, the carriage shed, the barn, and the root cellar. Plan to bring a lunch and go back in time a hundred years.

Pueblo

The city of Pueblo, located south of Colorado Springs at the juncture of I-25 and U.S. Highway 50, is a major center of activity in southeastern Colorado. The remaining destinations in this chapter will be accessible from Pueblo, first to the east, then to the west, and finally to the south.

EL PUEBLO MUSEUM (ages 2 and up)

325 West 1st Street, Pueblo 81003; (719) 583–0453. Call for hours. $

At this museum, kids can climb aboard a saddle, crawl into a full-size tepee to snuggle into furry animal hides, and see artifacts from frontier life prior to 1870.

GREENWAY AND NATURE CENTER OF PUEBLO (ages 2 and up)

In Rock Canyon on the Arkansas River, 1 mile west of Pueblo; 5200 Nature Center Road, Pueblo 81003; (719) 549–2414. **Free**.

You will find a profusion of outdoor family activities here. For starters you can rent bikes at the visitors center to ride the paved, 21-mile River Trails System. The bike path adjoins state lands and the Pueblo Reservoir with 16 additional miles of trail to the west. To the east, another trail extends to the city center and as far as the University of Southern Colorado. Most of the trails nicely accommodate strollers and wheelchairs.

At the Cottonwood Nature Shop you will find nature-oriented items, including bird feeders, books, music, and T-shirts. Other amenities at the Greenway and Nature Center include a playground, a fine picnic area, and a fishing deck.

RAPTOR CENTER (ages 2 and up)

Don't miss stopping in at the nature center's Raptor Center (719-549-2327), a rehabilitation facility for injured birds. You are likely to see eagles, falcons, and several kinds of owls. Those that can be healed are released back into the wild. Others that are too disabled to fend for themselves are housed here permanently. The naturalists are good with children and will be happy to answer their questions (and yours). **Free**.

BUELL CHILDREN'S MUSEUM (all ages)

210 North Santa Fe Avenue, Pueblo 81003; (719) 583–6214; www.sdc-arts. org. Open year-round (except for major holidays), Tuesday through Saturday 11:00 A.M. to 4:00 P.M. $

Located in downtown Pueblo, the two-level, 12,000-square-foot Buell Children's Museum offers exciting and innovative "hands-on" exhibits, programs, and technology focusing on science, history, and the arts. Programs in the colorful Magic Carpet Theatre change regularly, bringing musicians, storytellers, and plays, as well as prerecorded presentations. Kids can even put on their own play, learning about lighting, sound, scenery, and costuming through the use of the theater's cutting-edge technology equipment.

Plan not to rush this stop. Take time to let your youngsters create their own splash of color inside King Kong's Kaleidoscope; make their own masterpiece with boxes, paper, ribbon, wax, and lots of wiggly, gooey material in the Artrageous studio; and watch in wonderment in the Reilly Family Gallery, where a 10-foot kinetic sculpture channels colorful balls around vortexes until, for a brief moment, they drop to the base only to be swooped up for another descent.

Children under the age of four have their own Buell Baby Barn, where wee ones nurture their motor skills while playing in a winsome barnyard setting. When energy levels drop and the hungries take over, amble on over to the Kid Rock Cafe for snacks and beverages.

PUEBLO ZOO (all ages)

In Pueblo City Park, Pueblo Boulevard and Goodnight Avenue; (719) 561–9664; www.pueblozoo.org. Open year-round; winter, 9:00 A.M. to 4:00 P.M. Monday through Saturday and noon to 4:00 p.m. Sunday; summer, 10:00 A.M. to 5:00 P.M. Monday through Saturday and noon to 5:00 P.M. Sunday. $, children under 3 **Free**.

The Pueblo Zoo is the only Zoo Historic District in the country. It is small in area, so you can easily see all the animals, 110 different species, in a half day. And it's easily accessible for strollers and wheelchairs. The black-footed penguin exhibit is a "must see." Also called "jackass" penguins, the birds can be heard braying. The state's only underwater penguin-viewing area lets you watch their antics.

The Discovery Room welcomes families to touch, explore, and learn more about the animal kingdom with living coral tanks, microscopes, insects, and a "What Is It?" table.

PUEBLO CITY PARK (all ages)

Pueblo Boulevard and Goodnight Avenue; (719) 566–1745; www.pueblo.org/ visitorsguide/parks.htm. Park open year-round; pool and rides open June through mid-August. Train, kiddie rides, and carousel 25 cents each; City Park **Free**.

In addition to the zoo, City Park has two fishing lakes, an outdoor swimming pool, playground, and lots of room for sports and letting off steam. Young family members will want to ride all eight of the kiddie rides and the miniature train.

Carousel lovers from around the country come to ride a restored 1911 gem. There are fewer than 200 hand-carved wooden carousels still in existence. This community treasure is on the National Register of Historic Places.

For More Information

Pueblo Visitor Information Center, *302 North Santa Fe Avenue,*

Pueblo 81003; (719) 542–1704 or (800) 233–3446; www.pueblochamber.org.

La Junta

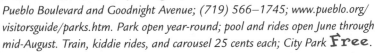

Take U.S. Highway 50 east from Pueblo to La Junta. The name means "the junction," and a lot of other roads converge here as well.

BENT'S OLD FORT (ages 4 and up)

State Highway 194, 8 miles northeast of La Junta; 35110 Highway 194 East, La Junta 81050; (719) 383–5010; www.nps.gov/beol. Open daily June through August, 8:00 A.M. to 5:30 P.M.; September through May, 9:00 A.M. to 4:00 P.M. **Free** *during winter months. During summer $, children 5 and younger* **Free**.

On the high plains of southeastern Colorado stands Bent's Old Fort, a masterful reconstruction based on drawings and descriptions from the diaries of early travelers. Originally built in 1828 by brothers Charles and William Bent and Ceran St. Vrain, the massive adobe structure was the only place on the Santa Fe Trail between Boonville, Missouri, and Santa Fe, New Mexico, where travelers could rest their livestock, repair their wagons, and replenish their supplies. Bent's Old Fort became a major trading post where goods manufactured in the East were traded for those of Mexican and Native American origin. Mountain men and fur traders also bartered for needed items here. Cloth, hardware, glass, tobacco, coffee, and firearms were exchanged for Navajo blankets, beaver pelts, buffalo hides, horses, and mules. Kit Carson was hired by William Bent in 1841, at $1.00 per day, to help hunt for the 1,000 pounds of meat needed daily at the fort.

Today's visitors to Bent's Old Fort can take a ranger-led tour of the premises or wander at will, imagining what life was like here in the 1800s. Enter the kitchen to see where Charlotte Green, the fort cook, managed to bake bread and prepare meals under primitive conditions. Go into the blacksmith shop to see the smithy at work. Consider the plight of Susan Magoffin as you stand in the chamber where the nineteen-year-old spent ten days in 1846 after suffering a miscarriage. Her meticulously kept diary made it possible for historians to accurately re-create life at the fort.

Annual Events at Bent's Old Fort

On the Fourth of July, docents, as they do on other special days, wear period dress and act out the roles of former residents and visitors, all the while fielding questions and keeping their answers strictly to the time period they are portraying. Children excitedly gather in the courtyard for the piñata breaking, which results in much scurrying for the spilled candy.

In late July this National Historic Site comes alive when volunteers and staff reenact the fort's trading days during the annual Santa Fe Trail Encampment.

In mid-August, Kid's Quarters allows children to spend a half day at the fort learning games, skills, chores, and activities of the 1840s. This day camp helps youngsters ages seven through eleven better understand the lives of children in earlier times.

For two days in early December, your family is welcome to join in as the park's staff and volunteers celebrate Christmas in nineteenth-century frontier style.

KOSHARE INDIAN MUSEUM

115 West 18th Street, P.O. Box 580, La Junta 81050 (on the Otero Junior College Campus); (719) 384–4411 or (800) 693–5482; www.koshare.org. Open daily year-round, Monday and Wednesday 10:00 A.M. to 9:00 P.M.; Tuesday and Thursday through Sunday 10:00 A.M. to 5:00 P.M. Extended hours on show nights. $

A tribute to Native American heritage, western art, dedicated leadership, and American youth stands proudly on the southeastern plains. Since 1933 the Koshares have used proceeds from their dance performances to acquire American Indian art and artifacts. Gifts from artists who respect the Koshare mission enrich the collection. An evaluation team from the American Association of Museums declared this to be "one of the finest collections of American Indian artifacts in the world." Pieces from this collection have been borrowed for display by the Smithsonian Institute.

When you stop to see the pottery, baskets, jewelry, and early Taos paintings, you're likely also to see young men practicing dance steps or patiently completing bead or quill work for their costumes.

On the first Sunday of each month, a **Free** day, the museum hosts visiting artists who demonstrate their techniques and sell their wares. At the Kiva Trading Post shoppers find a selection of authentic Native American art and a comprehensive book section.

KOSHARE INDIAN DANCES

At the kiva next to the museum. Weekends June and July (check for additional performances), 8:00 P.M.; winter ceremonials between Christmas Eve and New Year's Eve; times vary. $

The pulsating beat of the traditional Taos drum and the haunting call of an Indian flute set the stage for the colorful Koshare dancers. Swirling fringe, feathers, and quills of the

Who Are the Koshare Indian Dancers? James Francis "Buck" Burshears's dream to incorporate respect and understanding of Native American cultures within the Boy Scout program has become a legend. Since 1933, numerous boys in the La Junta area have spent their teenage years not only camping and hiking but also studying the lore, legends, and lives of Plains and Southwestern Indians. Dancers must be active in a Scout Troop or Exploring Post and meet all Boy Scout of America (BSA) advancement requirements. More than 575 have achieved the rank of Eagle Scout—the highest honor a Scout can earn.

As he learns the songs and dances, each Scout researches, designs, and makes his own dance costume using authentic materials. The troop gives more than fifty performances a year in their kiva and around the United States. Presidents and world leaders have enjoyed the Koshares' precise footwork, intricate regalia, and inspiring devotion to a dream.

Fancy Dancer; black-and-white stripes of the Koshare Clown; or dramatic agility of the fire hoop dancer—all will entertain children and adults. This will be a long-remembered performance.

Where to Stay

Holiday Inn Express. *27994 U.S. Highway 50, La Junta 81050; (719) 384–2900 or (800) 465–4329. This hotel has an indoor pool and spa and serves a complimentary, all-you-can-eat* continental-plus breakfast of cereals, fresh fruit, milk, juice, and baked goods. Guest rooms have refrigerators. $–$$

For More Information

La Junta Chamber of Commerce, *110 Santa Fe Avenue, La Junta 81050;* *(719) 384–7411; www.lajuntacochamber.com.*

Las Animas

At the intersection of U.S. Highway 50 and State Highway 101, east of La Junta, lies the community of Las Animas with its historical and recreational attractions.

KIT CARSON MUSEUM (ages 5 and up)

On the corner of 9th and Bent Streets; P.O. Box 68, Las Animas 81054; (719) 456–2005. Open daily Memorial Day through Labor Day, 1:00 to 5:00 P.M. (during winter by appointment; call 719–456–0802). Children under age 14 Free. *Donations appreciated from those ages 14 and older.*

This museum is housed in a complex originally built for German prisoners of war captured in World War II. Here you will find the first Las Animas city jail, built in 1882, with plank walls and a dirt roof. Check the inside back wall for charred boards where two prisoners tried to burn their way out. Also of interest is the circa-1860 stage station. Made of logs and primitive in design, it supposedly served as lodging for one night for Ulysses S. Grant during his travels out west. Your children will be intrigued by the one-room schoolhouse with its old wooden desks, blackboard, and books. Among the other buildings on the museum grounds are a blacksmith shop and a carriage house with a chuck wagon and a handsome carriage.

BOGGSVILLE (ages 5 and up)

Along the banks of the Purgatoire River, 2 miles south of Las Animas on State Highway 101; (719) 456–1358. Buildings open Memorial Day through Labor Day, 10:00 A.M. to 4:00 P.M.; site and walking trails open year-round. **Free.** *Donations appreciated.*

The historic settlement of Boggsville, once an agriculture and commerce center, was founded in 1862 by Thomas O. Boggs and his wife, Rumalda Luna Bent; L. A. Alien; and Charles Rite. Kit Carson and his family lived here for one year before the untimely death of both Carson and his wife. Boggs and Bent raised the Carsons' seven children. A work in progress, the site now includes the restored circa-1866 Boggs house and one of the three wings of the John Prowers home. Excavations are being conducted to determine the former locations of other structures that once stood here. With sufficient donations and volunteer help, plans are to eventually reconstruct the Kit Carson home, the schoolhouse, and the general store.

JOHN MARTIN RESERVOIR AND HASTY LAKE (all ages)

10 miles east of Las Animas off U.S. Highway 50. Open year-round. **Free** *entry.*

You can swim, picnic, camp, jet-boat, water-ski, sail, and windsurf at John Martin Reservoir and Hasty Lake. Especially convenient for families, Hasty Lake provides marked-off swimming areas, rest rooms, a playground, a fishing pier, and an enclosed picnic shelter with fireplace on the west side of the lake. Fishing at Hasty Lake is considered good to excellent. The lake is stocked annually with rainbow trout, walleye, and channel catfish.

For More Information

Trinidad–Las Animas County Chamber of Commerce, *309 Nevada Avenue, Trinidad 81082; (719) 456–0453; www.ruralnet.net.*

Cañon City

U.S. Highway 50 leads west from Pueblo to Cañon City, a distance of 38 miles. This small town and vicinity harbor several attractions worth checking out.

DINOSAUR DEPOT AND GARDEN PARK FOSSIL AREA (all ages)

330 Royal Gorge Boulevard, Cañon City 81215; (719) 269–7150 or (800) 987–6379; www.dinosaurdepot.com. Open daily Memorial Day through Labor Day, 9:00 A.M. to 5:00 P.M.; the rest of the year, Wednesday through Saturday 10:00 A.M. to 4:00 P.M. and Sunday noon to 4:00 P.M. $, children 3 and younger Free.

Jurassic dinosaurs inhabited the Cañon City region 150 million years ago. Dinosaur Depot and the Garden Park Fossil Area facilities make learning about them fun. The museum is designed to stimulate an interest in science, instill an appreciation for the vast time spans in the earth's past, recapture the excitement when dinosaur remains were discovered here in the 1870s, and foster awareness for the importance of protecting fossil resources. Among its exhibits is a stegosaurus skeleton in the process of being removed from rock that has held it captive for more than 150 million years. Knowledgeable guides, regularly scheduled programs geared toward children and adults, a gift shop, and tours of the Garden Park Fossil Area make this a worthwhile stop.

ROYAL GORGE CANYON AND BRIDGE (all ages)

South of U.S. Highway 50, 12 miles west of Cañon City; P.O. Box 549, Cañon City 81215; (719) 275–7507 or (888) 333–5597; www.royalgorgebridge.com. Open daily 8:30 A.M. until dusk. Entry fees include unlimited rides, shows, and attractions. Some attractions are seasonal, but the bridge, shops, eateries, and several attractions are open daily, weather permitting. $$–$$$, children under 3 Free.

The Royal Gorge Bridge, the world's highest suspension bridge, spans the Royal Gorge Canyon. Stretching for nearly a quarter of a mile, 1,053 feet above the rushing Arkansas River, this man-made marvel is truly a remarkable sight. Visitors can ride a trolley or walk across. Those who want an eagle-eye view of the bridge and the massive granite-walled cliffs can take the thirty-five-passenger aerial tram across the chasm. Or you can ride the world's steepest incline railway for a thrilling descent to the river's edge at the very bottom of the canyon.

A 360-acre park surrounds the Royal Gorge Bridge. Here your children can ride a vintage miniature train, go round and round on the carousel, see the friendly mule deer that frequent the area, visit the trading post, and spend time at Kids Krazy Korner to play on the slides and climbing apparatus. They might even meet Gorgeous the chipmunk, Robin the deer, Little John the bear, and Stryker Rick the old gold prospector, all costumed characters that wander the park amusing visitors with their antics. A full-service restaurant and several snack bars stand by to handle big and little appetites.

THE CAÑON CITY AND ROYAL GORGE RAILROAD (all ages)

Trains depart from Santa Fe Depot, 401 Water Street, Cañon City 81212; (303) 569–2403. Open daily Memorial Day through Labor Day, tours 9:30 A.M. and 12:30 P.M.; September through mid-October, tours 12:30 P.M.; mid-October to Memorial Day, Saturday and Sunday only, tours 12:30 P.M. Closed in January. Reservations highly recommended. $$$–$$$$

A two-hour, 24-mile, round-trip journey along the Royal Gorge Route, aboard the only passenger train with access through this remarkable natural wonder, will take you deep into the canyon beside the mighty Arkansas River. From the open-air observation deck, your children can watch for bighorn sheep and red-tailed hawks. Look up along the way and you will see, 1,000 feet above the tracks, the Royal Gorge Suspension Bridge spanning the chasm and clinging precariously to the edge of the gorge.

As you glide along, the conductor will call your attention to the Hanging Bridge, at a point where the gorge narrows to 30 feet. Here the railroad had to be suspended over the river due to the sheer rock walls that go straight down into the surging water on both sides. Built in 1879, this unique structure has served on a main rail line for more than a century.

The train consists of former Canadian National Railway passenger cars built in the mid-1950s. Two former Chicago & Northwestern Railroad locomotives power the train. Food and beverages are available in the concession car. All coaches are heated in the winter and air-conditioned in the summer.

BUCKSKIN JOE (all ages)

8 miles west of Cañon City on U.S. Highway 50, in the Royal Gorge Park Area; (719) 275–5149; www.buckskinjoes.com. Open May through last Sunday in September, 9:00 A.M. to 6:00 P.M. $–$$$

Buckskin Joe is one of Colorado's most unusual "towns." An authentically reconstructed gold-mining camp, it is modeled after an actual mining town that once thrived 90 miles northwest of this location. The original town and this rebuilt version were named after a legendary character who, in 1859, along with several other miners, made a rich placer strike on a small creek near the present-day community of

Fairplay. His real name was Joseph Higgenbottom, but he was called "Buckskin Joe" due to his mode of dress.

With vintage buildings resembling those of the original settlement, gathered from several ghost towns throughout the state, today's namesake is similar to a living-history museum, with a general store, blacksmith shop, livery stable, saloon, print shop, "Mystery House," barn and corral with farm animals, and perhaps a few too many gift shops.

Kids can ride a pony through town, pan for gold, explore a make-believe gold mine, take a horse-drawn wagon ride, and view a magic show. If you stop for lunch at the Gold Nugget restaurant, consider ordering a buffalo burger.

 ROYAL GORGE SCENIC RAILWAY AND ANTIQUE STEAM TRAIN AND CAR MUSEUM (all ages)
Adjacent to Buckskin Joe; (719) 275–5485; www.buckskinjoes.com. Open daily March through May, 10:00 A.M. to 5:00 P.M. (weather permitting); June through Labor Day, 8:00 A.M. to 7:00 P.M.; after Labor Day through October, 9:00 A.M. to 5:00 P.M. $–$$

The Royal Gorge Scenic Railway takes passengers on a 3-mile, thirty-minute excursion around the town of Buckskin Joe and to the very rim of the spectacular Royal Gorge Canyon. When you return to the depot, don't overlook the Antique Steam Train and Car Museum. Here you will see, among other exhibits, a dandy 1915 Model T Highboy Speedster and a cute-as-can-be 1929 Model A.

Where to Eat

Harvest House Restaurant. *1925 Fremont Drive, Cañon City 81212; (719)* *275–3377.* Menu with kid-friendly choices. $–$$

Where to Stay

Best Western Royal Gorge Motel. *1925 Fremont Drive, Cañon City 81212; (719) 275–3377 or (800) 780–7234; www.bestwestern.com.* Family suites with microwave ovens and refrigerators. Seasonal swimming pool, enclosed hot tub, guest laundry, playground, picnic area with barbecue. $–$$, children under 12 stay **Free**.

Comfort Inn. *311 Royal Gorge Boulevard, Cañon City 81212; (719) 276–6900.* **Free** continental breakfast. Indoor heated swimming pool and spa. Guest laundry. Pets allowed with deposit. Nearby playground and picnic area. $–$$

"Are We There Yet?"

Traveling as a family can result in memories that last a lifetime or, unfortunately, can create some nightmares you'd rather not recall. A successful trip depends on involving each member of the family in the planning. For some great ideas for designing your next family adventure, log onto www.bestwestern.com, then click on "Tips for Traveling with Kids."

For More Information

Cañon City Chamber of Commerce, *403 Royal Gorge Boulevard, Cañon City 81212; (719) 275–2331 or (800) 876–7922; www.canoncitychamber.com.*

The chamber of commerce is located in a lovely old home once occupied by former Colorado governor James Peabody.

Llama Trekking

If you and your family would like to experience Colorado's backcountry but would prefer not to pack in your supplies, you might want to consider llama trekking. Terrain varies from easy walking to moderate hiking, and ventures range in length from half-day jaunts to weeklong journeys. Some outfitters provide camping gear, day packs, heated tents, solar showers, and gourmet meals; others offer the animals and the expertise, but you bring your own gear. To provide you with an enjoyable initiation into llama trekking, several outfitters have a "Lunch with a Llama" program, whereby you take an easy half-day or daylong walk to and from a wildflower-strewn meadow or wooded picnic area for lunch (transported by the company's llamas). This would be great fun for families with young children. Remember, though, your kids must be able to walk the distance or be packed in on your back, not on the llama's. These congenial critters are pack animals and are not ridden.

Some outfitters plan trips for special interests, whereby an archaeologist or naturalist may accompany the trip. On other outings instructors in photography, art, or fly-fishing may come along.

Contact the Colorado Llama Outfitters and Guides Association at 30361 Rainbow Hill Road, Golden 80401 or call (303) 526–0092 for more information and a list of professional, fully licensed and insured guides and outfitters.

Silver Cliff

 MISSION: WOLF (ages 4 and up)

Between Cañon City and Cotopaxi, State Highway 69 curves south and leads to the towns of Silver Cliff and Gardner. From State Highway 69 in Gardner, go north 13½ miles on the Gardner Road (dirt). Turn right at Blue Spring (cattle tank on right) and follow driveway 1½ miles along fence to Mission: Wolf; P.O. Box 211, Silver Cliff 81249; (719) 859–2157; www.missionwolf.com. Open daily 9:00 A.M. to 6:00 P.M. **Free**, *but donations are desperately needed.*

Mission: Wolf is a nonprofit facility dedicated to caring for captive-born timber wolves and wolf-dog hybrids. Thirteen packs live in fenced enclosures on thirteen acres of primitive land.

Mission: Wolf's first priority is to provide a natural, comfortable life for the resident wolves. The prime objective is to educate the public as to the tragedy that occurs when wild animals are confined to a life of captivity. The focus is to dispel the fears people have of the wolf, discourage private ownership of wild animals as pets, and support wild habitat protection. The dream and ultimate goal is to get the public to realize that wolves and humans can coexist so that places like Mission: Wolf will no longer be necessary.

According to Mission: Wolf directors, there are an estimated 250,000 wolves and wolf-dog hybrids living in captivity today. Bought as pets, most eventually end up homeless due to their wild and independent nature. When released on their own, three-fourths die from auto accidents, gunshot wounds, poison, and other human-related causes. This facility receives an average of four requests every week to take in another homeless animal. Because of a lack of funds, Mission: Wolf has had to turn away more than 3,000 wolves and wolf-dogs since 1997.

Come spend a few hours or a few days in outrageously beautiful wilderness while experiencing the thrill of a close-up encounter with these exquisite animals. Staff educators are present at all times to care for the wolves, give tours of the premises, and answer questions. Drop-in visitors are welcome daily from 9:00 A.M. until 6:00 P.M.

Campers who are willing to bring in all their necessities, including water, are welcome also but must be prepared for primitive conditions. Inquire about the intern and volunteer programs. The dirt access road is especially difficult after recent snow or rain. Following inclement weather, it is best to phone first to find out if the way is passable.

Walsenburg

The small town of Walsenburg lies south of Pueblo, on I–25. This community, with a population of 3,700 residents, is surrounded by majestic scenery—the legendary Spanish Peaks to the south, the magnificent Sangre de Cristo Range to the west, and rolling prairie lands to the east. Walsenburg is the gateway to the Highway of Legends, a Colorado Scenic and Historic Byway. The circular route loops around the base of the Spanish Peaks and travels through the small mountain towns of La Veta, Cuchara, Stonewall, and Segundo to Trinidad and back to Walsenburg.

    LATHROP STATE PARK (all ages)

3 miles west of Walsenburg on U.S. Highway 160; 70 County Road 502, Walsenburg 81089; (719) 738–2376; www.parks.state.co.us/lathrop/index.asp. $ per car.

This 1,100-acre recreational area encompasses Martin Lake and Horseshoe Lake. These two regularly stocked lakes provide good fishing for rainbow trout, bass, walleye, and tiger muskies, Colorado's version of the Loch Ness Monster. These huge predatory fish are said to pop out of the water to glare at fisherfolk, chase boats to shore, and gobble up ducks and other waterfowl. Additional Lathrop State Park activities include windsurfing, water-skiing, boating, hiking, cross-country skiing, camping, and golfing.

La Veta

Seventeen miles west of Walsenburg on State Highway 12, La Veta is home to many artisans. Painters, poets, photographers, and writers are continually inspired by the spectacular mountain vistas.

 FRANCISCO FORT MUSEUM (ages 4 and up)

306 South Main Street, La Veta 81055; (719) 742–5501; www.hchstoc.org. Open Memorial Day through early October, Monday through Friday 10:00 A.M. to 5:00 P.M. $, children 9 and younger Free.

Stop at La Veta's Francisco Fort Museum to view Indian artifacts, ranching items, and period clothing. Kids will want to check out the old schoolhouse, post office, and blacksmith shop.

OLD LA VETA PASS ROAD (all ages)

For directions inquire at the La Veta Chamber of Commerce (719–742–3676) or at one of the local shops.

Excellent hiking exists in the La Veta area. The summertime trekking trails become outstanding cross-country ski routes during winter. The Old La Veta Pass Road was originally a narrow-gauge railroad route, and several old structures, including the historic train depot, remain along the way.

For More Information

La Veta/Cuchara Chamber of Commerce, *124 North Main Street, P.O. Box 32, La Veta 81055; (719) 742–3676; www.lavetacucharachamber.com.*

Southeastern Colorado Annual Events

JUNE

Pikes Peak International Auto Hill Climb. *At Pikes Peak Highway, south of U.S. 24 at Cascade, June; (719) 385–7325; www.pikespeakcolorado.com.* This mid-summer auto extravaganza thrills onlookers as race cars exceed 130 miles per hour over the 12½-mile course to the top of Pikes Peak via a dirt road with 156 turns and an altitude gain of nearly 5,000 feet. Be advised that the loud noise from the cars' engines could frighten little tykes. $$$$, children under 12 𝐅𝐫𝐞𝐞.

Donkey Derby Days. *Cripple Creek, late June; (719) 689–3021 or (719) 689–2169.* At this event, said to be the longest-running annual festival in Colorado, your kids can gobble watermelon in the watermelon-eating contest, and you can all watch the Firemen's Follies, where firehoses are used to push back the opposing team in a spirited game of tug-of-war. The biggest draw is the donkey races, when local businesspeople attempt to guide (push?) their furry friends for 1 block, all uphill, to see who is master, human or beast. 𝐅𝐫𝐞𝐞 admission.

JULY

Santa Fe Trail Encampment. *La Junta, late July; (719) 383–5010.* This event celebrates fur-trading days at Bent's Old Fort by showcasing the bustling activity that was common there in the mid-nineteenth century. $

Hornbeck Homestead Days. *Florissant, late July; (719) 748–3253.* The wonderful aroma of baking bread emanates from the kitchen woodstove, and old-time games are played in the yard during this celebration. $

AUGUST

Colorado State Fair. *Pueblo, late August; (800) 876–4567.* This seventeen-day affair features top-name country-western entertainers, amusement-park rides, a petting zoo, stock exhibits, craft and food booths, and a rodeo. $–$$$

SEPTEMBER

Chile and Frijole Festival. *Pueblo, late September; (719) 583–0453.* This "hot and sassy" celebration features fiery mariachi music that will have your little ones dancing like Mexican jumping beans. Here you can smell the roasting chilies, taste genuine frontier food, learn how to make adobe blocks, and check out the arts and crafts booths. **Free** admission.

Aspen History Tours. *Cripple Creek, late September/early October; (719) 689–2634.* Take a tour on a guided four-wheel-drive vehicle to mining areas that are usually off-limits to travelers because they are on private property. While passengers admire the golden aspens in their fall splendor, a guide provides information on the region's famous gold rush days. Donations go to charity. **Free**.

Northwestern Colorado

World-renowned ski resorts; fascinating dinosaur digs; warm, soothing natural hot springs; and some of the country's dandiest dude ranches make northwestern Colorado a delightful destination for families.

Doris's Top Picks
in Northwestern Colorado

1. Cross Orchards Historic Site, Grand Junction
2. Dinosaur Discovery Museum, Fruita
3. Fraser Valley Tubing Hill, Fraser/Winter Park
4. Georgetown Loop Railroad, Georgetown
5. Glenwood Springs Hot Springs Pool, Glenwood Springs
6. Phoenix Mine, Idaho Springs

Idaho Springs

If you travel 32 miles west of Denver on I–70, you will come to the historic town of Idaho Springs. Gold was discovered here in 1859. The community has retained its mining-era heritage by preserving its gingerbread-trimmed Victorian homes and old-time storefronts and providing tours of mining facilities.

NORTHWESTERN
COLORADO

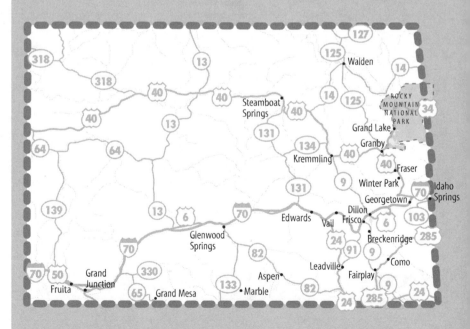

ARGO GOLD MINE (ages 4 and up)

North of I–70 (you can see it from the highway); (303) 567–2421; www. historicargotours.com. Open daily mid-April through mid-October, 9:00 A.M. to 6:00 P.M. $$

The Argo Gold Mine stands in the heart of Idaho Springs's historic mining district. Visitors interested in the process of removing gold from the remainder of the ore walk 500 feet into one of the mine tunnels and then proceed from level to level of the museum buildings to view the rock-crushing apparatus and grinding equipment. The one-hour tour of this National Historic Site is partially underground, so it's important to wear warm clothing.

PHOENIX MINE (ages 4 and up)

4 miles west of Idaho Springs (take the Stanley Road west for 1 mile, then turn left onto Trail Creek Road); (303) 567–0422; www.phoenixmine.com. Open daily year-round, 10:00 A.M. to 6:00 P.M. $–$$

Here is an opportunity to visit a working underground gold mine. With a seasoned Colorado hard-rock miner as your tour guide, you will get a realistic idea of what it's like to mine gold. Watch as miners push tons of gold and silver ore in small railcars just as their predecessors did more than one hundred years ago. Your kids can try out the antique tools, listen to fascinating stories about the "Tommyknockers" (mine ghosts), and pan for gold in a mountain stream after the tour. Any gold you find is yours to keep. Bring your camera!

INDIAN SPRINGS RESORT (all ages)

302 Soda Creek Road, P.O. Box 1990, Idaho Springs 80452; (303) 989–6666; www.indianspringsresort.com. Open daily 7:30 A.M. to 10:30 P.M. Hours vary for pool, geothermal cave baths, and restaurant. $–$$

Long before gold was discovered in the Rocky Mountains, both Ute and Arapahoe Indians considered the hot springs that bubble endlessly from the earth at this rather rustic resort to be sacred. Later, miners soaked their tired muscles in the hot pools. The famous, as well as infamous, came as well. The Roosevelt and Vanderbilt families took to the waters here. Notorious outlaws Frank and Jesse James and Billy the Kid dropped in for a spell. Clint Eastwood, James Caan, and other movie greats have also been guests of the resort.

The Indian Springs Resort features an indoor swimming pool, outdoor hot tubs, private bathing rooms, cave hot pools, lodging, a restaurant, and a campground.

Especially popular with families is the large, mineral water–fed swimming pool, covered with a translucent dome and surrounded by banana and palm trees and lush tropical foliage. The pool's water is kept at a comfortable ninety degrees, so kids can splash about as long as they please. The underground cave pools are much hotter, and children ages twelve and under are not allowed in this area.

Knowing that kids and dirt just naturally go together, it comes as no surprise to find whole families sloshing about in the resort's "Club Mud," a large sunken tub filled with mushy mineral-rich clay that reportedly absorbs toxins from the body. You can spread the gooey muck on one another and then shower it off, or sit back and let the mud dry in order to obtain the maximum effect. Your kids won't soon forget the time they had parental permission to wallow in the mud. Definitely a photo moment.

Where to Eat

Beau Jo's. *1517 Miner Street, Idaho Springs 80452; (303) 567–4376; www.beaujos.com. Open daily for lunch and dinner.* Find out what makes Colorado-style pizza special. Beau Jo's has been feeding happy customers for more than twenty-five years. The hand-rolled white or wheat crust is very thick, but it's never left—they serve honey so that you can enjoy it for dessert. Look for Beau Jo's in seven other locations along the Front Range. $

Winter Park

This town's name is a little misleading because Winter Park is both a winter and summer community with loads of family activities throughout the entire year. Summertime brings hiking, fishing, mountain hiking, horseback riding, and white-water rafting to this resort, a favorite of Coloradans. And wintertime provides its own plethora of activities.

Located 67 miles northwest of Denver, Winter Park is best reached by traveling west on I–70 for approximately 42 miles to U.S. Highway 40 at exit 232. Follow U.S. Highway 40 north over Berthoud Pass and into Winter Park.

WINTER PARK SKI RESORT IN SUMMER (all ages)

(970) 726–5514; www.skiwinterpark.com. $–$$$, depending on activity.

ALPINE SLIDE (ages 4 and up)

Open daily June through Labor Day, 10:00 A.M. to 5:30 P.M.; September, weekends only, 10:00 A.M. to 6:00 P.M. $$, seniors 70 or older and children 5 or younger ride **Free**.

This is Colorado's longest alpine slide. Located beneath the Arrow Chairlift, it thrills sledders along a winding 3,030-foot-high, nearly 1½-mile-long concrete track with twenty-six linked turns. No special skills are necessary to operate the sled, so this is an ideal family activity. Kids soon learn to speed up or slow down by pushing or pulling on the joystick. Children 45 inches tall or shorter must ride in a sled with an adult.

ZEPHYR EXPRESS CHAIRLIFT (all ages)

Open daily mid-June through Labor Day, 10:00 A.M. to 5:30 P.M.; September, weekends only, 10:00 A.M. to 5:00 P.M. $$–$$$, seniors 70 or older and children 5 or younger **Free**. *Additional charge for transport of bikes, available for rent at the base of the mountain.*

Bikers, hikers, and sight-seers can take the Zephyr Express Chairlift to the summit of 10,700-foot Winter Park Mountain, accessing a massive network of biking and hiking trails. Consider picking up picnic supplies in the village and then spreading a blanket at the top of the mountain for a meal with spectacular views of the Continental Divide and the valley below. If you somehow get to the summit without vittles and the fresh air has everyone complaining about the hungries, treat yourselves to a delicious repast at the mountaintop Lodge at Sunspot, open daily for lunch from June 15 through Labor Day and on weekends only through September.

HUMAN MAZE (ages 4 and up)

Open daily mid-June through Labor Day, 10:00 A.M. to 5:30 P.M. $, seniors 70 or older and children 5 or younger **Free**. *Discount rates for repeat visits.*

Located at the base of the Zephyr Express Chairlift, this is a fascinating challenge for the young and not-so-young. The Human Maze, an enormous wooden network of passages that wind and twist into wrong turns and dead ends, is sure to delight. Time your entry, get your hand stamped at the four checkpoints, and race to see which member of your family can get out the quickest. Afraid you might lose someone? Not to worry. An observation tower lets you give helpful route directions if any of your little "mice" get confused or lose their way in this life-size puzzle.

MOUNTAINSIDE MINI GOLF (ages 4 and up)

Open daily mid-June through Labor Day, 10:00 A.M. to 5:30 P.M. $

This eighteen-hole mini golf course, located at the bottom of the Alpine Slide, depicts historic aspects of the Fraser Valley. You can hit the balls through the legendary Moffit Tunnel, down the Mogul Run, and through the Mary Jane Mine Shaft. Along the way you'll meet up with water hazards, banked fairways, and a miniature Alpine Slide.

CLIMBING WALL AND ZIP LINE (ages 4 and up)

The indoor Climbing Wall features a variety of simulated rock formations, providing novice and experienced climbers with a place to learn and perfect their climbing skills. An outdoor climbing wall appeals to youngsters ages four and up. The Zip Line is a 70-foot-long cable that propels riders on an exciting ride through space while attached by a full body harness. Cost for full- and half-day passes varies, depending on the combination of activities. This attraction is located within the West Portal Station and is an excellent activity for inclement weather. $-$$$$

Plenty of Paths for Pedaling

Mountain bikers, novice or advanced, will be happy to know that the Winter Park and Fraser Valley area encompasses more than 250 miles of single track and more than 600 miles of interconnected trails and four-wheel-drive roads ideal for this popular sport. You can pick up a mountain-bike map for free at any bike shop or at the Winter Park Visitors Center.

WINTER PARK SKI RESORT IN WINTER (all ages)

(970) 726–5514; www.skiwinterpark.com. $-$$$$, depending on activity.

Wintertime is the peak season in Winter Park. You'll find many choices for family fun at the Winter Park Ski Resort, which is the closest major ski resort to Denver and one of the largest in the state. The four mountains that comprise the area's ski terrain—Winter Park, Mary Jane, Vasquez Cirque, and Vasquez Ridge—are interconnected by ski trails and lifts. The twenty lifts, including seven high-speed express quads, five triples, and eight doubles, have an uphill capacity of 34,910 skiers per hour.

WINTER PARK SKIER AND RIDER IMPROVEMENT CENTER (ages 3 and up)

The Winter Park Skier Improvement Center has developed the perfect program for families that want to learn to ski or snowboard together rather than splitting up for individual lessons. It doesn't matter if each member of the family has different skill levels, or if the parents are just seeking tips on how to teach and encourage their children in the sport. The instructor will design the lesson to meet the needs of the entire family. The program is called "Family Private," and the cost runs $200 for three hours.

CHILDREN'S CENTER

Child care, nonski programs, ski school, and ski rentals are all conveniently located at the Children's Center. The child-care facility accepts infants as young as two months. And potty-trained three- and four-year-olds can ride the Magic Carpet, a nonlift moving sidewalk, up the gentle pitch of their own private "mountain" to practice sliding down the hill and pushing their tiny skis into their first snowplow stop.

Older kids ride the lift to Discovery Park, an enclosed ski park with miniature race courses and animal adventure trails, and explore trails that lead to Rendezvous Flats and a tepee village hidden in the woods. Children from ages three through thirteen can sign up for snowboarding lessons. Phone for lesson times, cost, and registration information (970–726–5514).

NATIONAL SPORTS CENTER FOR THE DISABLED (NSCD) (all ages)

For more details phone (970) 726–1540, extension 2.

NSCD was founded more than twenty-five years ago and is recognized as the world's finest ski program for the disabled. In addition to skiing, it provides snowshoe and Sno-Cat tours, moonlight snowmobile dinner rides, daytime snowmobile tours, and the "Sunspot StarRide," a moonlit gondola ride to the Lodge at Sunspot for a four-course dinner, plus a sleigh ride.

NSCD's summertime recreation includes white-water rafting, mountain biking, hiking, camping, fishing, rock climbing, and scenic hayrides.

BONFILS-STANTON FOUNDATION WINTER PARK OUTDOOR CENTER (all ages)

This center, part of NSCD's nationally acclaimed program, offers people with disabilities and their families the opportunity to experience the beauty of the Rocky Mountains via a universally accessible nature trail system. The pathway accommodates those using wheelchairs, leg braces, guide dogs, crutches, and canes. All campsites feature accessible picnic tables and fire rings. Wooden tent platforms have been built to wheelchair height so that individuals in wheelchairs can more easily pitch their tents.

During spring, summer, and fall, the visually impaired are offered an eight-day technical rock-climbing program designed to conquer fear and to teach rope handling, knot tying, rules, and responsibilities. Throughout the course, students spend many hours rock climbing with experienced climbers.

During winter, under the direction of Hal O'Leary, the world's leading authority on ski programs for the disabled, the NSCD provides recreational and competitive skiing to thousands of children and adults from all over the world. All disabled persons are welcome, from the first-time skier to the elite-level competitor. To assist in catering to the needs of more than forty-five different disabilities, an extensive adaptive equipment lab, staffed by trained technicians, modi-

Need a Lift? In Winter Park, the Lift, a local shuttle service, provides Free transportation between lodging properties and activities to the Winter Park Ski Resort base area. The Smart Shuttle (also Free of charge) serves local restaurants and bars on Friday and Saturday nights and takes passengers right to their doorsteps. For information call (970) 726–4118.

fies, develops, and creates ski equipment on site. The NSCD maintains that everyone, regardless of disabilities, should have the opportunity to enjoy the outdoors.

Where to Eat

Carvers Bakery Cafe. *93 Cooper Creekway, Winter Park 80482; (970) 726–8202. Open daily.* For a hearty breakfast or lunch, this is the place. Be forewarned, though. Carvers is as popular with locals as it is with visitors, so there could be a bit of a wait. $

Hernando's Pizza and Pasta Pub. *78199 U.S. Highway 40, Winter Park 80482; (970) 726–5409. Open daily for dinner.* Well known for its original pizza pies, this restaurant is a good choice for families. $

Where to Stay

Winter Park Central Reservations. *(800) 729–5813.* This is your best bet for accommodations. Be prepared to tell them the number of people in your family, ages of children, what your needs are, and what your price range is. They no doubt will be able to find you a suitable place to stay. Ask about the four-night, learn-to-ski package for families.

For More Information

Winter Park/Fraser Valley Chamber of Commerce, *P.O. Box 3236, Winter Park 80482; (970) 726–4118 or* *(800) 903–7275; www.winterpark-info.com.*

Fraser

The resort community of Fraser lies just north of Winter Park along U.S. Highway 40. Families interested in cross-country skiing will find lots of options in this area.

High Country Stampede Rodeo Series The John Work

Arena, located 1 mile west of Fraser, hosts this Old West extravaganza, featuring the "Best Little Rodeo in Colorado," every evening from early July through August. The Junior Rodeo gets under way at 5:30 P.M. and showcases wranglers ages nine to seventeen who participate in some of the same events as their older counterparts: calf roping, barrel racing, and pole bending. The adult bareback, saddle bronc, and bull-riding events follow at 7:30 P.M. Only the most rugged of cowpokes can hang on to a one-ton Brahma bull with one hand while being tossed from side to side and hither and yon for the eight seconds required to receive a score and qualify for prize money. For information call (800) 903-7275.

DEVIL'S THUMB RANCH (ages 5 and up)

(970) 726–8231; www.devilsthumbranch.com. $$$

Located north of Fraser, this recreation area is a popular Nordic center with a scenic network of 65 miles of groomed trails. Lessons and rentals are available.

SNOW MOUNTAIN RANCH/YMCA (all ages)

Ten miles northwest of Fraser via U.S. Highway 40. Mailing address: P.O. Box 169, Winter Park 80482; (970) 887–2152 or (303) 443–4743; www.ymca rockies.org. Open year-round. $–$$$

Snow Mountain Ranch is an affordable family destination in all seasons with overnight lodging in cabins that sleep five to twelve people, in lodge rooms berthing four to six, and at campsites (summer only). Primarily set up for conferences and large groups, the mountain setting with its varied activities is an ideal choice for a family reunion.

Hiking, mountain biking, miniature golf, tennis, fishing, canoeing, horseshoes, hayrides, and horseback riding fill the slate for sunny days, while plenty of other options, including an indoor swimming pool, a sauna, a skating rink, a library, Bible studies, and a homestead museum, occupy kids and their parents during times of rare bad weather.

You'll also find 50 miles of groomed Nordic trails for all abilities. Three miles of lighted track provide an invigorating evening sport. Cross-country ski lessons and rentals are available, as well as lodging and rentals for downhill skiing at nearby Winter Park and Silver Creek.

FRASER EXPERIMENTAL FOREST RANGER STATION (all ages)

Call (970) 887–4100 for details. **Free**.

Located 3 miles south of Fraser on County Road 73, this ranger station provides marked trails suitable for beginning, intermediate, and expert cross-country skiers. There are no food facilities here, and the nearby vault rest room is sometimes locked. In the summer, the trails provide mountain biking courses, and campgrounds are available.

FRASER VALLEY TUBING HILL (ages 3 and up)

Behind the Alco Shopping Center in Fraser. Open late November through mid-April, depending on snowfall, Monday through Thursday 2:00 P.M. to 8:00 P.M. and Friday through Sunday 10:00 A.M. to 10:00 P.M.; (970) 726–5954. $$–$$$, seniors 60 or older may use a tube at half price.

Snow tubing allows you to take an exhilarating ride down a snow-covered slope on an inner tube, spinning and yelping for joy all the way to the bottom. Then you lie down on your inner tube and hold on for dear life to a minilift that drags you back up to the top of the hill. When fingers and toes begin to feel like icicles, gather your kids and traipse into the warming hut for a hot beverage. Children must be at least three years old to participate, and those ages three through six must ride with an adult. Be prepared for the cold by bringing earmuffs or stocking hats, heavy gloves or mittens, insulated jackets, and snowpants. A change of outfits is also a good idea, because you are apt to get rather wet from snow spray and from tumbling off your tube into the snow.

For More Information

Winter Park/Fraser Valley Chamber of Commerce, *P.O. Box 3236, Winter Park 80482; (970)* *726–4118 or (800) 903–7275; www. winterpark-info.com.*

Grand Lake

Sequestered between the western boundary of Rocky Mountain National Park and Grand Lake, the state's largest natural lake, is Grand Lake village, the mountain community that bears the lake's name. The town is small, with hospitable lodging, good eateries, and the ever-present souvenir and gift shops.

The lake provides numerous water sports. You can rent a canoe or bumper boat at one of the two marinas. Or perhaps your family would prefer a rowboat or motorized craft in order to try your luck fishing for rainbow trout, kokanee salmon, or Mackinaw. Trolling and inlet fishing usually bring the best results. Fishing licenses are required for those age seventeen or older and can be bought at the marina.

Because Grand Lake village borders Rocky Mountain National Park, the hiking trails are seemingly endless. And if you visit Grand Lake during winter, you will find that those same trails that were so wonderful for summertime treks have become outstanding cross-country skiing and snowmobiling routes. Do remember, though, that appropriate cold-weather clothing is a must, and if you plan to go snowmobiling, it is important to reserve your machine in advance. Other wintertime activities in the Grand Lake area include ice fishing, dogsledding, and snowshoeing.

Grand Hikes

Grand Hikes Due to its close proximity to Rocky Mountain National Park, the Grand Lake region offers excellent wilderness hiking.

A 1-mile round-trip hike begins at the Never Summer Ranch parking lot, located within the national park north of Grand Lake village on U.S. Highway 34, and leads along level ground and through a lovely meadow endowed with a carpet of wildflowers.

The trailhead for Coyote Valley Trail, a 2-mile round-trip trek along the Colorado River and through a wetlands area, is located 6½ miles north of Grand Lake village on U.S. Highway 34.

If your kids are experienced hikers, you might want to try the Colorado River Trail. Located about 12 miles north of Grand Lake village, the nearly 4-mile-long (one way) trail ends at the abandoned mining camp of Lulu City.

For more information about these and other hikes, inquire at the Kawuneeche Visitors Center.

KAWUNEECHE VISITORS CENTER (all ages)
Located 1½ miles north of Grand Lake village, on U.S. Highway 34; (970) 627–3471. Open daily 8:00 A.M. to 4:30 P.M. **Free** *guided hikes.*

This visitors center hosts several family-oriented programs each day throughout the summer. One of the most popular with kids is the "Come Bug a Ranger" session, where participants learn about the insects that inhabit Rocky Mountain National Park.

"Skins and Things" teaches children and adults about the animals that live in the park—deer, elk, bighorn sheep, bears, mountain lions, otters, squirrels, and rabbits, as well as raptors such as peregrine falcons, hawks, golden eagles, and bald eagles.

HOME, HOME ON THE RANCH

One would be hard pressed to find a better family vacation than that spent on a dude ranch. Horseback riding, gold panning, llama trekking, square dancing, rafting, fishing, hiking, swimming, and relaxing are some of the activities families can enjoy together on dude ranches.

Because most dude ranches provide counselors and programs for children and teens, and in some cases even baby-sitting for infants, parents can spend time alone if they wish without feeling guilty about not including their children. For the single parent, dude ranching may be especially attractive. While children indulge in their own activities, Mom or Dad is free to pursue adult interests. Or parent and child can spend all their time together. The choice is theirs. This outdoor experience allows for complete freedom, because all needs are provided for and you can participate in group activities as much or as little as you please.

Another important plus is knowing the total cost before leaving home. Very little money is spent after arrival. In addition, there is no repeated unpacking and repacking; no getting up in the morning and climbing back behind the wheel for another day of dodging semis and breathing exhaust fumes; no more taking chances on unfamiliar eating places and searching for lodging every evening; and no roar of traffic going by your window all night long. Rates vary according to ranch selected and facilities provided. A ballpark figure would be from $950 to $2,000 per week per adult. Reduced rates are available for children. It's best to call individual ranches for exact costs.

Dress on a guest ranch is casual. Pack a good pair of jeans along with a couple of western shirts for "dress-up" affairs, but be sure to bring along everybody's favorite, most comfortable grubbies, too. Take jackets and sweatshirts, even in summer, and a pair of boots for horseback riding. Forest insects seem to get as hungry as riders, hikers, and anglers, so repellent is a must.

For More Information

The Colorado Dude and Guest Ranch Association *(970–887–3128; www.coloradoranch.com)* has forty participating ranches. Each one is regularly inspected for cleanliness, facilities, hospitality, and honest representation. Phone for a brochure describing member ranches.

Grand Lake Chamber of Commerce, *14700 Highway 34; P.O. Box 57, Grand Lake 80447; (970) 627–3402 or (800) 531–1019; www.grandlakechamber.com.*

Granby

The hamlet of Granby lies along U.S. Highway 40 northwest of Fraser.

DROWSY WATER RANCH (all ages)

County Road 2, P.O. Box 147, Granby 80446; (970) 725–3456 or (800) 845–2292; www.drowsywater.com. Open from early June to mid-September.

Snuggled in a lush valley along Drowsy Water Creek, on the western side of the Continental Divide, this ranch is a family-run operation whose aim is to provide a memorable dude ranch experience. Owners Ken and Randy Sue Fosha welcome you to their home and vow to "treat your children as we do our own: with understanding, patience, love, and respect. Our ranch is for children. Our counselors and program supervisors are college students selected for their attentiveness, experience, and interest in child development and recreation."

Kids aren't likely to linger over breakfast at the Drowsy Water Ranch. Too many ways to have fun await them. Programs and activities abound for little ones, ages five and under, and for older youngsters age six through teens.

Families can spend the day together swimming in the heated outdoor swimming pool or enjoying ranch activities, or they can go their separate ways. While parents take to the trail on the back of a trusty steed or read a book under a shady tree, kids are receiving riding instruction, going on nature hikes, taking part in arena activities, making crafts, listening to storytellers, and fishing the stocked ponds. They participate in their own hayride and campfire cookout and then join parents in the Tepee Dancehall for an evening of down-home square dancing. Rates include accommodations in attractive log cabins, all meals, and all activities.

Kremmling

Kremmling is located approximately 100 miles northwest of Denver, off U.S. Highway 40.

LATIGO RANCH (all ages)

Box 237, Kremmling 80459; (970) 724–9008 or (800) 227–9655; www. latigotrails.com. Open year-round, except October, November, April, and May.

Latigo Ranch encompasses 450 acres and has access to more than 50,000 acres of the Arapahoe and Routt National Forests. Horsemanship is taken seriously here, and careful instruction is provided by experienced wranglers. Novices may choose walk-only rides, while more accomplished equestrians may engage in trotting and cantering. Little cowpokes new to the sport are carefully guided along level paths by qualified wranglers.

Guests at Latigo Ranch can participate in cookouts, hayrides, nature walks, fly-fishing, and volleyball. They can dance to lively country-western music (kids are encouraged to join in), play Ping-Pong, shoot a game of pool, swim in the outdoor swimming pool, and go on wiener roasts. Family rides are arranged so that all members of your family ride together, sometimes joining up with other moms and dads and their kids.

Six- to seven-year-olds ride as frequently as older children, but their treks are shorter in duration. Counselors also take them swimming, fishing, and hiking and play educational games with them.

Three- to five-year-olds are supervised while parents are horseback riding. They learn about mountain animals, plants, and rocks; hear stories about Native Americans and horses; create crafts; and feed ranch pets Charlie the lamb, Charcoal and Smokey the rabbits, and Wilbur the pig. They ride Papoose the Shetland pony and play stick-toss with Stormy the dog.

Winter activities at Latigo Ranch include cross-country skiing on 55 kilometers of groomed track, sliding down a tubing hill, dogsled rides, snowshoeing, and wildlife viewing.

Rates include accommodations in nicely appointed log cabins, all meals, and all activities. Cost varies with season. Baby-sitting for infants is available at extra charge if arranged at the time you make your reservations.

Walden

The small town of Walden, located in what is referred to as the North Park region of Colorado, about 150 miles northwest of Denver, is surrounded by unequaled wildlife-viewing possibilities. In 1995 the Colorado Senate designated tiny Walden (population 1,000) as the "Moose-Viewing Capital of Colorado." You are most likely to see moose in the early morning or late afternoon and early evening. Because other wildlife is also abundant, you may see more furry and feathered critters in these parts than people.

The moose are here year-round, but the roads are often impassable during late fall, winter, and spring. The best time to go is from Memorial Day through mid-October. And it's always a good idea to call (303) 639-1234 for road conditions.

COLORADO STATE FOREST (all ages)
If seeing and photographing a 7-foot-tall, 1,400-pound bull moose sounds exciting, take State Highway 14 south from Walden 20 miles to County Road 41 near the KOA Campground, and then go north on CR 41 for approximately 7 miles to the viewing platform. The deck overlooks a prime moose habitat, and moose are regularly seen in the creek bottom below. A wildlife interpretive trail is across the road from the platform.

STATE PARK MOOSE VIEWING SITE (all ages)
Moose—along with deer, elk, coyotes, small game, and birds—are frequently seen at this site, located at mile marker 58, which is 24 miles southeast of Walden on State Highway 14. From the parking lot walk about 300 feet to the edge of a large meadow; the Nokhu Crags in the distance provide an outstanding backdrop for your photos.

ARAPAHO WILDLIFE REFUGE NATURE TRAIL (all ages)
This is another significant spot for wildlife viewing. Take State Highway 125 south from Walden for 8 miles, turn east on County Road 32, proceed for about ½ mile, and turn south to the trailhead parking lot. This ½-mile trail, accessible to strollers, wheelchairs, and the physically challenged, loops through a variety of wildlife habitats where you are apt to see a combination of moose, deer, beavers, porcupines, songbirds, and waterfowl. Interpretive stations along the way provide information and suggest what to watch for. The trail is open from early April to late

October, weather permitting. Parking and rest rooms are located at the trailhead. For more information call (970) 723–4600 or (970) 723–8202.

 NORTH PARK PIONEER MUSEUM (ages 3 and up)
365 Logan Street, Walden 80480; (970) 723–4600. Open mid-May through mid-September, Thursday through Tuesday 10:00 A.M. to 4:00 P.M. **Free.** *Donations are greatly appreciated.*

"Everybody is welcome, and bring the kids," is the motto of this museum, opened in 1963 in a three-room ranch house built in 1882. Today the complex encompasses twenty-seven rooms packed with treasures. The kitchen has a coal range, a hand-operated dishwasher, and a "square skillet to cook a square meal." Other chambers include the Country Store and the Post Office, the Laundry Room with old-time washing machines and hand irons, an Army Room with Red Cross and U.S. Army and Navy uniforms from World Wars I and II, and the Buggy Shed, sporting a buggy and a mint-condition 1936 Dodge.

Your children will especially like the Toy Room, with old-fashioned dolls, games, and toys; and the School Room, showcasing antique desks along with old books, slates, sewing cards, lunch pails, and report cards.

Steamboat Springs

Steamboat Springs, located in the Yampa Valley 166 miles northwest of Denver along U.S. Highway 40, skillfully blends an Old West influence with a ski resort ambience, resulting in a compatible mix of down-home hospitality and exuberant vitality.

In 1913 Norwegian Carl Howelsen introduced recreational skiing to this valley. The Steamboat Springs Ski Resort continues to attract skiers, novice to Olympic-caliber, with ideal "Champagne Powder" and world-class facilities. Lodging, dining, shopping, and four-season recreation and festivals draw visitors to Mt. Werner year-round.

Cowboys have always played an important role in Steamboat Springs. Long ago the downtown streets were built wide enough to handle large herds of cattle, driven north from Texas. These days cowhands continue to drive their cattle, sheep, and horses to the high meadows for summer grazing, and ranching, farming, and coal mining are still practiced by area residents. According to a chamber of commerce resource, "It oughta have a Western mystique. It's been a cowboy town for more than one hundred years."

HOWELSEN HILL (ages 4 and up)

(970) 879–8499. Open daily during winter months, weather permitting. $$ to ski; watching is ᖴree.

Skiing was a necessary mode of travel for the early settlers due to heavy snowfall in this mountainous region. Then in 1913, when Carl Howelsen built a ski jump and proceeded to hurl himself 100 feet into the air, the Steamboat Springs townsfolk realized that skiing could be fun, too. These days, Howelsen Hill, in downtown Steamboat Springs, maintains 15-, 20-, 30-, 70-, and 90-meter jumps and "bump jumps" used by future Olympians as a training site.

DOWNTOWN (all ages)

A pleasant mix of restaurants, shops, galleries, and historic buildings line the streets of downtown. You'll enjoy the small-town ambience. Here are a few standouts for families. Hours vary by season.

OFF THE BEATEN PATH

56 7th Street, Steamboat Springs 80487; (970) 879–6830. Open daily winter and summer, 7:00 A.M. to 9:00 P.M.; spring and fall, 7:00 A.M. to 7:00 P.M.

A great bookstore with an in-house bakery—what a terrific combination! Your whole family will love the books, magazines, puzzles, and games. An *Alice in Wonderland* scene decorates the floor of the children's section upstairs where a sign advises: Look at the books any time of the day. Be sure to be kind and put them away. The selection is awesome!

The small coffeehouse offers breakfast, lunch, and snacks. Their decadent desserts and gourmet coffee drinks are difficult to resist. Why try?

FELIX AND FIDO

635 Lincoln Avenue, Steamboat Springs 80487; (970) 870–6400. Open Monday through Saturday 10:00 A.M. to 6:00 P.M. and Sunday 10:00 A.M. to 5:00 P.M.

Did you leave your dog or cat at home? This is where you'll find just the perfect souvenir for him or her. Anything you'll ever need to pamper Spot or Puff is right here. And there are also canine and feline items for you—jewelry, calendars, note cards, etc. Even if you don't have a pet, you'll have a great time perusing the incredible selection.

F. M. LIGHT & SONS

830 Lincoln Avenue, Steamboat Springs 80487; (970) 879–1822. Hours vary greatly according to season.

Remember all those signs leading to South Dakota's Wall Drug Store? You see advertisements for F. M. Light & Sons long before you get here; there are more than 250 signs within a 150-mile radius. This western-wear store has been in business since 1905, and the fourth generation of the founding family operates it now. Kids love to have their picture taken next to the life-size plastic horse out front. Inside, there are $4.98 straw cowboy hats and lots of authentic western gear. For $3.98 youngsters can scoop a bag full of polished rocks; "You must be able to close the bag." Get discount tickets to the rodeo while you're here.

LYON'S CORNER DRUG AND SODA FOUNTAIN

9th Street and Lincoln Avenue, Steamboat Springs 80487; (970) 879–1114. Open daily; hours vary.

Everyone knows where Lyon's is—it's been on the same corner for more than seventy years. Drop in for a treat at their old-fashioned ice-cream fountain. You may have to wait—there are only ten stools. For a quarter, play golden oldies in the vintage jukebox.

YAMPATICA (all ages)

Outdoor activities in many locations. Store: 10th Street and Lincoln Avenue; (970) 871–9151. Open Monday through Saturday 9:00 A.M. to 6:00 P.M. Free.

Their motto is "Leave town with more than a T-shirt." This non-profit group leads enjoyable, educational hikes—wildflower hikes, bird walks, history walks through downtown—and holds campfire programs in state parks and at the ski area. Programs are designed to encourage family participation. "Nature Detective" and "Young Naturalist" are two sessions designed for kids only, ages seven to eleven years. During the winter they offer "Ski with a Ranger," a one-hour educational run down the mountain.

Call for a current schedule or visit their store, where books, puzzles, games, posters, maps, and all other items have a cultural or natural history theme.

STEAMBOAT SPRINGS HEALTH AND RECREATION CENTER (all ages)

3rd Street and Lincoln Avenue; (970) 879–1828. Open daily year-round, Monday through Friday 5:30 A.M. to 10:00 P.M., Saturday 7:00 A.M. to 9:00 P.M., and Sunday 8:00 A.M. to 9:00 P.M. $

A family swim in the pool or a soak in the hot mineral pools that range in temperature from 98 to 102 degrees at this facility is a great way to end a day of outdoor adventure. If you crave more exercise, there is an Olympic-size lap pool. And your kids are sure to love the center's water slide.

STEAMBOAT SPRINGS TRANSIT

Look for white metal signs designating the route; (970) 879–3717. Operates daily, at least every thirty minutes. **Free**.

Enjoy the scenery; leave driving to the locals. The SST bus line runs through downtown, out to the ski area and back. Buses are marked CONDOS or DOWNTOWN. Ask the driver for a complete schedule. Don't worry about having correct change—it's always **Free**.

 STEAMBOAT SPRINGS PRCA SUMMER PRORODEO SERIES (all ages)

Howelsen Hill Rodeo Grounds; (970) 879–0880. Mid-June through August, Friday and Saturday 7:30 P.M. $, kids under 12 **Free**.

Bareback riding, steer wrestling, calf roping, barrel racing, and bull riding: It's big-time rodeo with a small-town feel. Your kids can even get in the act—the Calf Scramble challenges six- to twelve-year-olds, and even younger cowpokes can attempt the Ram Scramble. This rodeo is a great combination of serious sport and good fun. An hour before the show, there's a barbecue dinner and entertainment. Discount tickets are available at F. M. Light & Sons downtown.

 RIVER TUBING (ages 2 and up)

On the Yampa River through town. Rentals $$.

The minute they see all those tubers floating down the river, your kids will want to jump right in. The gentle Yampa flows right through town with easy access from many spots. You'll discover a multitude of outfitters who rent tubes and include drop-off and pick-up services in their modest fees. The big black inner tubes have mesh across the middle so that no one falls through. Toddlers can ride double with an adult. Tubing companies require footwear for this activity.

PERRY-MANSFIELD PERFORMING ARTS CAMP (ages 8 and up)

One- to six-week courses run from mid-June to late August. Call (970) 879–7125 or (800) 430–2787 for a brochure, rates, and seminar and performance dates; www.perry-mansfield.org. $$$–$$$$

For the creative members of your family—would-be thespians; ballet, modern, and jazz dancers; musical theater and voice aspirants; creative writers; and those interested in stage management and production—this camp may be just the incentive needed to start a career in the arts.

Established in 1913 by Charlotte Perry and Portia Mansfield, this unique institution is the oldest performing arts school and camp in the country. Agnes de Mille choreographed her *Rodeo* ballet after attending a local square dance nearby. Dustin Hoffman helped perfect his acting in the studios and theaters at Perry-Mansfield. Other distinguished alumni include Julie

> **Pretty Neat Playgrounds** Some playgrounds are definitely better than others. Steamboat Springs has two great play places, both the work of community volunteers. Located at elementary schools, they are unsupervised but open to the public until dark. You'll find them next to Strawberry Park and Soda Creek Elementary Schools.

Harris, John Cage, and Lee Remick. A limited number of scholarships are available by audition each year.

The Perry-Mansfield Performing Arts Camp presents several performances each season open to the public at nominal cost.

FISH CREEK FALLS (all ages)

North on 3rd Street from Lincoln Avenue to Oak Street. Follow the signs; it's about 3 miles from town. Open dawn to dusk. $ for parking. Free admission.

Taller than Niagara, Fish Creek Falls impresses visitors—more than 250,000 of them each year. It's an easy, scenic ⅓-mile walk to the overlook. Or take the ¼-mile path down to the base of the falls. From here you can continue hiking 3 miles to Upper Fish Creek Falls. But remember, it's 3 miles back again!

The falls got its name because homesteaders around 1900 caught their winter's supply of fish here, using pitchforks, hooks, and gunnysacks.

MOUNTAIN SPORTS KAYAK SCHOOL (ages 8 and up)

In the Ski Haus store on U.S. Highway 40 between town and Mt. Werner; (970) 879–8794. Morning and afternoon sessions daily, weekend evening sessions. $$$$

This is the kind of experience that families fondly remember long after their vacation is over. Try kayaking together in a beautiful mountain setting. All equipment and kayaks are provided. The half-day "Never-Ever" class begins on shore, moves to ponds, and closes with a paddle down a gentle stretch of the Yampa River. Owner Barry Smith is an expert at instilling confidence as he teaches. Half-day

Fun Facts Steamboat Springs has produced more winter Olympic medal winners—a total of thirty-six and counting—than any other town in the United States, thus earning it the title of Ski Town U.S.A.

to five-day intermediate and advanced classes also are available. If you have three- to five-year-olds, they ride in the kayak with you. Children nine and older can take the lesson without you, but you don't want to miss this.

VERTICAL GRIP CLIMBING GYM (ages 4 and up)

South of U.S. Highway 40 at Pine Grove Road, next to the bike path; (970) 879–5421. Open daily; hours vary by season. $$$ and up.

Challenging, exciting, and safe in this controlled environment, indoor climbing is a sport that parents and children can do together. Come to learn new skills, practice techniques, or just watch. You need only a sense of adventure—equipment and instruction are provided. Vertical Grip's well-trained staff gives private or group lessons for all abilities. Take advantage of their late evening hours. If the kids haven't been exhausted by their daytime activities, an after-dinner climb might be just the ticket.

STEAMBOAT LAKE STATE PARK (all ages)

North of Steamboat Springs, 26 miles on County Road 129; (970) 879–3922; camping reservations (800) 678–2267; www.parks.state.co.us/steamboat/. Open year-round. $ per car.

Sunset magazine includes campgrounds here on their list of "The West's Top Ten." With many sites near the shoreline and most shaded by aspen or lodgepole pine, it's no wonder. Summer reservations for campsites or cabins are strongly advised.

There's a sandy swim beach, not easy to find in Colorado. The park boasts premier fishing—anglers catch rainbow and cutthroat trout year-round. Water-skiers and boaters also enjoy the reservoir and full-service marina. Picnic areas are located throughout the park. In the winter activities change to ice fishing and cross-country skiing. With more than 100 miles of trails nearby, snowmobiling attracts many enthusiasts.

Fun Facts The name Steamboat Springs is said to have been chosen for the town in 1865 when three French fur trappers were traveling down the Yampa River. One of the men heard a chug-chug sound like that of a paddle-wheel steamer. Excited, the men rushed toward the rhythmic noise they perceived to be a steamboat and discovered instead a bubbling mineral spring. The town was named for the nonexistent steamboat.

ON MT. WERNER—SUMMER SEASON

SILVER BULLET GONDOLA (all ages)

Daily mid-June through Labor Day, 10:00 A.M. to 4:00 P.M.; early June and September, open weekends only; (970) 879–6111. $$$, one **Free** *child with each paying adult.*

Enjoy spectacular scenery as the eight-passenger gondola carries your family up to Thunderhead Peak, elevation 9,080 feet. Get a snack or a meal and spend some time shopping for souvenirs at the Top Shop. Soak up some rays while you take in the view from the sundeck. You can hike back to the base, rent a mountain bike and glide down, or catch the gondola for the return trip.

Fun Facts The snow here is so special that it has a trademarked name. "Champagne Powder" describes incredibly light and fluffy snow for exceptional skiing. The term originated in Steamboat Springs.

HIKING (all ages)

More than 40 miles of trails on Mt. Werner offer something just right for everyone. Here are two good routes for families, both from the top of Thunderhead.

VISTA NATURE TRAIL

This 1-mile trail starts and ends at Thunderhead. Along the way you'll find signs about wildlife and native vegetation. The scenery is fantastic, and there are picnic areas along the route. Guided nature walks are scheduled here throughout the summer.

THUNDERHEAD HIKING TRAIL

This 3-mile route takes you back down to the base on roads and trails. Allow one and a half hours hiking time, and be sure you all have water bottles and proper shoes. Remember that weather changes rapidly in the Colorado mountains, so bring a jacket.

KIDS' ADVENTURE CLUB (ages 3–12)

In the Kids' Vacation Center, first floor of the gondola building; (970) 879–6111, extension 5390 or (800) 299–5017. Open early June through late August, Monday through Friday 9:00 A.M. to 5:30 P.M. Reservations are a must. $$$$

Need a little break from one another? Give your kids a chance to meet new friends and enjoy some Steamboat activities without you. Short hikes, outdoor games, arts and crafts, picnics, and water activities engage three- and four-year-olds. Older campers enjoy those activities plus mountain biking, kayaking, swimming, scavenger hunts, and tennis. Single- or multiple-day rates are available. This is a very popular program with Steamboat residents and visitors. Necessities include sunscreen, a swimsuit and towel, and a raincoat.

 ### MOUNTAIN BIKING

(970) 879–6111, extension 3524 or (800) 299–5017. Open daily mid-June through Labor Day, 10:00 A.M. to 3:45 P.M. $$–$$$$

Bikes are permitted on the gondola, so you can ride downhill all day. Forty miles of trails challenge all levels with varying elevation changes. Bring your own bike and helmet, or rent at the base or top of the gondola. Helmets are required on the mountain—they're included with rentals.

An easier option for casual riders is the Yampa River Core Trail, a 4-mile paved path along the river that connects the ski area with town. Stop along the way to watch tubers and kayakers or visit the Yampa River Botanic Park.

*S*teamboat's Celebrities

The winner of the first U.S. gold medal in Alpine skiing is a Steamboat Springs resident. In fact, Billy Kidd is Director of Skiing and has been since 1970. Every day that he's in town, Kidd offers a free clinic to guests. Look for him in his signature pheasant-feathered Stetson.

The first American female to win an Olympic medal in snowboarding also lives here. Shannon Dunn earned a bronze in the half-pipe at Nagano, Japan, in 1998.

ON MT. WERNER—WINTER SEASON

 SKI PROGRAM FOR KIDS

Steamboat offers a full range of child care, lessons, and facilities for kids 6 months to 18 years; $$$$. Reservations are required for all programs; (970) 879–6111 or (800) 299–5017. Here are a few standouts:

BUCKAROOS (ages 2 years through kindergarten)

All ski resorts offer child care, but not many offer ski lessons for two-year-olds! Buckaroos combines all-day or half-day child care with a one-hour private ski clinic.

KIDS' SKI FACILITIES

Rough Rider Basin is a kids-only zone—adults are not allowed unless they're with a child. This Wild West area with tepees, log cabin playhouse, mine shaft, and picnic spot has its own lift.

Beehive Terrain Park is a kids-only zone for pint-size snowboarders.

Kids-only beginner lifts include three magic-carpet conveyor lifts.

BILLY KIDD PERFORMANCE CENTER (ages 7 and up)

(970) 879–6111 or (800) 299–5017. Two- to three-day programs. $$$$

Top-notch coaches provide personalized, intensive clinics that challenge youngsters ages seven to twelve with moguls and racing; includes video analysis.

KIDS' ADVENTURE CLUB AT NIGHT (ages 4–12)

In the Kids' Vacation Center; (970) 879–6111, extension 5390. Tuesday through Friday 6:00 to 10:00 P.M. $$ per hour; family rates available.

Supervised games and movies along with pizza and snacks entertain children. On Activity Night, eight- to twelve-year-olds visit Vertical Grip Indoor Climbing Gym or Hot Springs Pool.

SNOW TUBING (ages 5 and up)

At the base of Preview lift. Nightly 5:00 to 10:00 P.M. Tickets are available from the Ski and Sport Shop across from the lift. $$

If you're at least 36 inches tall, you are eligible to participate in this old-fashioned winter fun.

Where to Eat

Giovanni's Ristorante. *127 11th Street; Steamboat Springs 80477; (970) 879–4141. Open Thursday through Tuesday for dinner.* Linguine? Scampi? Veal piccata? Giovanni's serves fine Italian cuisine. Watch for summertime special offers like "two-for-one Tuesday." $$

The Shack Cafe. *740 Lincoln, Steamboat Springs 80477; (970) 879–9975. Open daily for breakfast and lunch until 2:00 P.M.* Wait in line along with the locals for hearty food in a casual log cabin atmosphere. Breakfast is served all day. Enjoy homemade soups and fresh-baked pies. $

Steamboat Yacht Club. *811 Yampa Street, Steamboat Springs 80477; (970) 879–4774. Open daily for lunch and dinner*

December through September. In the summer dine outside on the large deck overlooking the river. Your children will be entertained watching the tubers float by. On winter evenings the dining room has a great view of ski jumping at Howelsen Hill. Soups, salads, sandwiches, seafood, and meat dishes—all delicious. $–$$$

Winona's. *617 Lincoln Avenue, Steamboat Springs 80477; (970) 879–2483. Open daily for breakfast; lunch Monday through Saturday.* Here you'll find healthful and delicious food at a reasonable price. Peruse the bakery case of homemade treats. The cinnamon rolls are hard to ignore, and the cheerful atmosphere is just right for families. There are outdoor tables, too. $

Where to Stay

Rabbit Ears Motel. *201 Lincoln, Steamboat Springs 80477; (970) 879–1150 or (800) 828–7702; www.rabbitearsmotel. com.* You won't miss their neon sign! Owned and operated by the same fam-

ily since 1969, this sixty-five-room motel offers lots of conveniences without a fancy price tag. Location, location, location—on the river, walking distance to town, directly across from the hot springs pool, next to the park. The *Free* city bus stops right outside the door.

Rooms vary in size and amenities, but most have microwaves and refrigerators. Discount passes to the pool and water slide and *Free* continental breakfast make Rabbit Ears a real find. $$

Steamboat Central Reservations. *(970) 879–0740 or (800) 922–2722; www.steamboat-ski.com.* Their motto is "One call does it all." They'll help you find a motel, hotel, condo, cabin, guest ranch, or inn and arrange ski rentals, lessons, dining, or airfare.

Steamboat Grand Resort Hotel and Conference Center, *2300 Mt. Werner Circle, Steamboat Springs 80487; (970) 871–5500; www.steamboatgrand.com.* Steamboat Springs's newest grand hotel's use of native stone and natural woods, indoor streams, and two-story-high fireplaces creates a comfortable western-themed mountain lodge ambience. Located at the base of the ski mountain, it features beautifully appointed studios and one-, two-, and three-bedroom units; a state-of-the-art fitness center; an outdoor year-round heated swimming pool, and an on-site child care center. $$$-$$$$

For More Information

Steamboat Springs Chamber Resort Association, *1255 South Lincoln Avenue, Steamboat Springs 80477; (970)* *879–0880; www.steamboat-chamber.com or www.steamboatsummer.com.*

Georgetown

Located 50 miles west of Denver on I-70, historic Georgetown is surrounded by the Arapahoe National Forest and spectacular mountain peaks. This small mountain town (population 900) is home to more than 200 Victorian structures that date back to the late 1800s and early 1900s.

You will find two parks in town with picnic tables and playground equipment. A marked nature trail (easy climb) leads from Georgetown Lake toward the Saxon Mine, with marvelous views of the valley. Boutiques, art galleries, historical museums, antiques shops, and cafes crowd the narrow streets.

 GEORGETOWN LOOP RAILROAD (all ages)
1111 Rose Street, Georgetown 80444; (303) 569–2403 or (800) 691–4386; www.georgetownloop.com. Open daily late May through September. $$–$$$
It's difficult to say who loves trains more, children or grown-ups. It doesn't really matter—everyone aboard the Georgetown Loop Railroad can be a kid, at least for a day.

Powered by a steam locomotive, the excursion train huffs and puffs between the towns of Georgetown and Silver Plume, over the reconstructed, 95-foot-high Devil's Gate Bridge, and through spectacular vistas of forests and mountaintops.

"Tis the Season to Be Jolly . . . " During the first two full weekends in December, Georgetown welcomes the Christmas season with its annual Christmas Market, an old-fashioned outdoor celebration in the European tradition.

At noon each day of the fest, a Swedish Santa Lucia processional, led by the Queen of Lights followed by local children, winds its way through the village streets. Craft and food booths provide Christmas gift ideas, strolling carolers add to the merriment, and an Old Country-style St. Nicholas hands out candies to the children. When you get chilled through and through, head for the bonfire, buy a bag of fresh-roasted chestnuts, and sip a cup of hot cider, guaranteed to warm your heart as well as your tummy. For more information call (303) 569–2840 or (800) 472–8230. 𝐅𝐫𝐞𝐞 admission.

LEBANON SILVER MINE TOUR (all ages)

1106 Rose Street, Georgetown 80444; (303) 569–2403 or (800) 691–4386. Open daily late May until early September. $

Accessible only via the Georgetown Loop Railroad, the abandoned Lebanon Silver Mine presents tours guided by members of the Georgetown Historical Society. You and your family will see the blacksmith shop, the tool shed, the manager's office, and the mine itself.

OLD GEORGETOWN STATION

1106 Rose Street, Georgetown 80444; (303) 569–2403 or (800) 691–4386. Open daily late May through September. 𝐅𝐫𝐞𝐞.

This historic landmark is where you purchase tickets for both the Georgetown Loop Railroad and the Lebanon Silver Mine. Besides the ticket window, the station also contains a restaurant, a gift shop, and rest rooms.

Where to Eat

The Happy Cooker. *412 6th Street, Georgetown 80444; (303) 569–3166.* This casual cafe is an old standby in Georgetown, a favorite of locals and visitors in-the-know. They serve breakfast favorites such as quiches and Belgian waffles, and for lunch you might try their homemade soups and hot-from-the-oven breads. During the summer months you can dine on the patio. $

Where to Stay

Mountain Memories Resort Service. *(303) 569–2772.* Several bed-and-breakfasts and motels offer accommodations in Georgetown, but perhaps the best bet for families would be to stay in one of the lovely, no-host historic homes, ranging from Victorian cottages and Bavarian chalets to luxury cabins and modern condos, available for short-term rental. All guest houses come fully equipped with kitchens, linens, breakfast "makings," refrigerated staples, fireplaces or Franklin stoves, firewood, and china. Rates vary, depending on season and number of guests in your party. Minimum stay is two or three nights, again depending on season. Discounted weekly and monthly rates are available. $$$$

For More Information

Georgetown Information Center, *612 6th Street; P.O. Box 444, Georgetown 80444; (303) 569–2888 or (800) 472–8230. Open daily year-round.*

Quick Cookie Stop Whether you've just finished a train ride on the Georgetown Loop or you're headed along I-70 to further adventures, stretch your legs in Silver Plume, an old mining town at exit 226.

Thursday through Sunday head to Sopp and Truscott, combination general store and bakery, at the east end of Main Street. You'll find Ann, the proprietor, baking bread and cookies. **Free** samples of all the varieties of bread that she has baked that day await your approval. You'll probably need a loaf or two for the road—cinnamon fruit bread is the most popular. Take a close look—not too close!—at the old slicing machine in action. If your timing is excellent, Ann will be pulling a tray of cookies out of the oven. While you munch on your treat, look for mountain goats on the hillside across the road.

Summit County

Summit County's four major ski areas—Arapahoe Basin, Breckenridge, Copper Mountain, and Keystone—attract visitors from far and wide. Each area offers excellent family experiences year-round. During the summer season Lake Dillon provides a water playground.

To give you some idea of the scenery, the county's lowest town sits at 9,000 feet. Take advantage of Summit County's paved bike path system, more than 400 miles of off-road, paved trails connecting each town and resort.

Dillon

Located 26 miles west of Georgetown, just off I-70 on U.S. Highway 6.

  ### DILLON RESERVOIR (all ages)
The main reason folks come to the tiny community of Dillon is to enjoy the outdoors. Here they can picnic beside the lake; rent a boat and fish for rainbow, cutthroat, and brook trout and kokanee salmon; and walk or ride the bike path that runs along the shoreline.

Dillon Down Under Dillon is quite a survivor. The original town was located at the bottom of the current Lake Dillon. This idyllic spot was at the confluence of three rivers, but in 1960 construction began on Dillon Dam and the entire town was forced to move. All the residents and some original buildings were relocated, including several restaurants that are still in business today.

Frisco

Once a favorite camp of Ute Indians due to the large population of bison, elk, and deer and later a booming silver- and gold-mining community, the small town of Frisco is perfectly located for an abundance of outdoor activities. The town is accessible from I-70 and lies west of Dillon.

 ### FRISCO NORDIC CENTER (all ages)
Located less than a mile south of Frisco on east side of State Highway 9; (970) 668–0866. $$–$$$

During winter the Frisco Nordic Center provides cross-country ski rentals for adults and children and sleds for kids who would rather slide than glide. Forty kilometers of beginner, intermediate, and advanced trails are groomed daily, and 20 kilometers of packed snowshoe trails await. Group lessons are available in both cross-country skiing and snowshoeing.

TWO BELOW ZERO (all ages)

Rides leave from the Frisco Nordic Center; (970) 453–1520 or (800) 571–6853. Open Monday through Saturday, approximately Thanksgiving through March. The "Cocoa Ride" begins at 5:30 P.M., and the "Dinner Ride" begins at 7:00 P.M. It is mandatory that participants arrive at least fifteen minutes before departure time for check-in. Departures are always on time. Sleigh space is limited, so reservations are necessary. $$–$$$$

Two Below Zero is a family-owned and -operated business providing dinner rides on mule-drawn sleighs. Three fourteen-passenger, hand-crafted red oak sleighs pulled by pairs of winsome mules (either Jack and Nel, Jake and Ed, or Agnes and Ada) will take you for a twenty-minute ride to a warm and comfortable dining tent with a wooden floor and two heating stoves. You will be served top sirloin steak and marinated chicken cooked on a gas grill and baked potato, French bread, fresh vegetables, and homemade dessert. Following dinner you will be entertained with live music. Warm hats, gloves, shoes, and coats are a must for the ride to and from the camp.

For More Information

Summit County Chamber of Commerce, *P.O. Box 2010, Frisco 80443; (970) 262–2866 or (800) 530–3099; www.summitchamber.org.*

The Summit County Chamber of Commerce Guest Assistance Center, *(970) 262–0817 or (970) 668–2051.*

Breckenridge

Breckenridge is 85 miles west of Denver, south from Frisco on State Highway 9. This pretty little mountain town began as a mining camp in 1859. Many a boom and bust followed until the early 1940s when, during World War II, the search for gold ceased and the town's population dwindled. Then in the 1960s "white gold" replaced the yellow kind, and the Breckenridge Ski Resort brought new life to the community.

International Snow-Sculpture Championships

International Snow-Sculpture Championships This event attracts competitors from all over the world. Past participants have included artisans from China, Switzerland, Russia, Poland, Canada, England, Morocco, France, and, of course, the United States. Using only hand tools, four-person teams begin with identical twenty-ton blocks of tightly packed snow. After five days, including two evenings working until midnight and one around-the-clock stint, the snow sculptors will have transformed the mountain community into a glorious, though temporary, outdoor art gallery with works worthy of the best of museums (if only they wouldn't melt!).

Highly qualified artists, the likes of world-renowned Loveland, Colorado, sculptor George Lundeen—whose 16-foot bronze statue of aviation pioneer Elrey Jeppesen stands in the Jeppesen Terminal at Denver International Airport—serve as judges. Festivities take place in late January. Call (970) 453–6018 for exact dates and more details. **Free.**

Breckenridge is a picture-postcard-perfect Victorian-style village with more than 120 restored structures listed on the National Register of Historic Places. Six blocks of shops, boutiques, and restaurants adorn Main Street, while year-round activities for families vie for your attention.

In summer you can go white-water rafting, stream and lake fishing, hiking, horseback riding, mountain biking, and four-wheeling. You might try sledding on the Superslide or attempt to find your way out of the delightful Amaze'n Breckenridge labyrinth, Colorado's largest human maze (much like the one in Grand Lake). Your family can ride the Superchair, a four-person chairlift that takes passengers to an elevation of 12,000 feet for hiking, mountain biking, or lunch at the Vista House Restaurant.

Wintertime in Breckenridge brings Alpine and Nordic skiing, snowshoeing, ice fishing, dogsledding, snowboarding, snowmobiling, and ice-skating on Maggie Pond.

 ## ON THE MOUNTAIN

Breckenridge Ski Resort boasts four interconnected mountains with 139 downhill trails serviced by twenty-two lifts. The vertical drop varies from 1,277 to 3,398 feet, and the average snowfall is 255 inches.

Professional snowboarders rave about Breckenridge's terrain garden known for its air, hits, slides, and gigantic half-pipes. The resort has a Pipe Dragon for building and maintaining the two half-pipes that meet Olympic specifications.

The children's ski school is located at both Peak 8 and Peak 9 Village Base areas. Alpine skiing lessons are available for those ages three and up, and snowboard instruction begins at age eight.

THE BRECKENRIDGE OUTDOOR EDUCATION CENTER

This center provides daily half-day or full-day ski instruction for children and adults with disabilities or serious illnesses. The cost of $55 per half day or $90 per full day includes equipment, lift ticket, and instruction.

Ullr Fest Immediately following Breckenridge's snow sculpting championships comes the weeklong, riotous Ullr (pronounced "OOO-lur") Fest, an annual wild-and-woolly event in which amateurs compete beside world-class athletes in what is known locally as the "Ullympics." While festivities include such wacky events as snowshoe volleyball, this is also the opportunity to see freestyle skiing experts perform daring inverted aerials and observe ballet and mogul disciplines. The zany, outrageous parade; the ice-skating party; and the kids' concert are sure to please. All this activity takes place in honor of Ullr, Norse god of winter. Call (970) 453-6018 for more information. **Free**.

Where to Eat

Fatty's Pizzeria. *106 South Ridge Street, Breckenridge 80424; (970) 453-9802. Open daily for lunch and dinner.* Fans of Fatty's say this casual pizza place puts out the best pizza pie in town. They also have daily specials such as pasta or Mexican dishes. $-$$

Helpful Hints

In resort and mountain towns, pick up free local papers, such as *Steamboat Today* or *Vail Trail*, for daily and weekly information on what to see and where to eat. You might even find discount coupons.

Where to Stay

Accommodations at Breckenridge range from B&Bs to posh resort lodging. Your best bet is to call the Breckenridge Resort Chamber's Central Reservations System at (800) 221-1091.

For More Information

Breckenridge Resort Chamber, *311 South Ridge Street, P.O. Box 1909, Breck-* *enridge 80424; (970) 453–2913; www. gobreck.com.*

Fairplay

Gold was discovered in this area in 1859, and what is now the small town of Fairplay, with only about 450 year-round residents, was then a wild-and-woolly mining camp. Located south of Breckenridge, at the juncture of U.S. Highway 285 and State Highway 9, the hamlet boasts a few artisan shops, two historic hotels that have seen better days, a picturesque old church, and a wonderful outdoor museum.

 SOUTH PARK CITY MUSEUM

Follow the signs from the center of town; (719) 836–2387; www.southparkcity. org. Open daily 9:00 A.M. to 7:00 P.M., Memorial Day through Labor Day; 9:00 A.M. to 5:00 P.M., mid-May to Memorial Day and after Labor Day to mid-October. $, children 5 and younger **Free**.

A visit to Fairplay's South Park City Museum reveals nineteenth-century life in a Colorado mining town. Seven structures stand on their original sites, and twenty-seven other weather-worn buildings that would have decayed and ultimately disappeared have been restored and moved to the museum location from abandoned mining camps and area ghost towns. Now filled to the rafters with more than 60,000 artifacts, the vintage structures represent life as it was between 1860 and 1900.

Your kids will delight in dashing from doorway to doorway to see the one-room schoolhouse; the general store filled with old-time canned goods, hardware, and clothing; and the stagecoach and wagon barn and livery. They may even appreciate their own dentist a little more after viewing the crude instruments used by the dentists of days long past. The museum has a railroad station and an old narrow-gauge train engine with a bell kids can clang.

Como

The hamlet of Como lies a few miles northeast of Fairplay, just off U.S. Highway 285. Once a major railroad terminus, the area is steeped in rail and mining history.

WILDERNESS ON WHEELS FOUNDATION

Just off U.S. Highway 285 along Kenosha Gulch, 60 miles southwest of Denver, 15 miles west of Bailey; (303) 751–3959; www.wildernessonwheels.org. Open mid-April to mid-October, weather permitting. **Free.** *Donations appreciated.*

The Wilderness on Wheels Foundation, with volunteer help and donated materials, has built a wonderful wilderness facility. A little more than 1 mile of boardwalk on twenty acres of land offers wheelchair access to campsites and stocked fishing ponds. In addition to the ponds, Kenosha Creek provides anglers with rainbow and brook trout. This facility also works well for families with small children. There's easy walking for little tykes and the boardwalk is stroller friendly, so you can go for a family hike without packing your baby on your back.

Reservations are suggested for the campsites. Disabled campers are welcome to bring along their able-bodied friends and relatives.

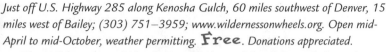
Leadville

From I-70 turn south on State Highway 91 at Copper Mountain; continue 24 miles to Leadville.

MATCHLESS MINE (ages 5 and up)

Located 1¼ miles east of Harrison Avenue on East 7th Street; (719) 486–1899. Open daily year-round, 9:00 A.M. to 4:45 P.M. $, children 5 and younger **Free.**

Leadville's history is nearly as rich as the fortunes extracted from its gold, silver, and lead mines during the 1800s. Horace Tabor and his wife, Augusta, dry goods merchants who became millionaires through mining investments, and "Baby Doe" Tabor, for whom Horace divorced Augusta, thus creating a national scandal, are among the most colorful of Leadville's former residents.

On his deathbed Horace bade Baby Doe never to sell or leave his Matchless Mine. Thirty years later, penniless but faithful to her promise, she was found in the mine's ramshackle cabin, frozen to death. Today visitors can visit Baby Doe's cabin and the exterior of the mine.

TABOR OPERA HOUSE (ages 5 and up)

308 Harrison Avenue, Leadville 80461; (719) 486–3900 or (800) 933–3901; www.home1.gte.net/tabor. Open daily 9:00 A.M. to 5:30 P.M., Memorial Day through Labor Day. Inquire about occasional stage performances. Tours, $; performances, $$–$$$.

You won't want to miss a tour of Leadville's historic Tabor Opera House. Built for Horace Tabor in 1879, it is now a museum extraordinaire. Lillian Russell, Florenz Ziegfeld's *Mamselle Napoleon,* and Sousa's Marine Band played to packed audiences during the opera house's prime. Here you will see the original cashier's cage, its counter worn from all the silver dollars that passed over its surface, and the mint-condition, signed and framed photographs of well-known actors and actresses that line the walls. You will be allowed backstage and on the stage itself

Unsinkable Molly One of Leadville's famous former residents was the "Unsinkable Molly Brown." Molly married mine superintendent James Brown, who owned a one-eighth interest in a mine that eventually made the couple extremely wealthy. They then moved to Denver, where Molly tried unsuccessfully to fit into high society. Her acts of heroism while a passenger on the ill-fated *Titanic,* however, won her international recognition, ultimately forcing the city's hoity-toity crowd to include her in their social circle.

to gaze upon Horace and Baby Doe's private box seat and the trapdoor used by Houdini. Then follow your guide down the dusty steps to the lower-level dressing rooms, still endowed with antique furniture, actors' trunks, and stage props.

The survival of the Tabor Opera House is solely due to Florence Hollister and her daughter, Evelyn Furman, who in 1955 pooled their life savings and rescued this irreplaceable piece of history from demolition. Evelyn Furman continues to cherish the old building and to share it with guests.

 ### NATIONAL MINING HALL OF FAME & MUSEUM (ages 4 and up)

120 West 9th Street, Leadville 80461; (719) 486–1229; www.leadville.com/ miningmuseum. Open daily 9:00 A.M. to 5:00 P.M., May through October; Monday through Friday 9:00 A.M. to 3:00 P.M., November through April. $, children 5 and younger Free.

To discover the romance and excitement of the glory days of mining, stop in at this museum, located in an expanded circa-1896 schoolhouse. Here you will see twenty-two miniature dioramas meticulously created by artist Hank Gentsch, the "Wheelchair Woodcarver." The Crystal Room showcases outstanding mineral specimens on loan from the Smithsonian Institute in Washington, D.C. The Gold Rush Room contains gold specimens, photographs, artifacts, and documents relating to the nation's most prominent gold rushes, from Alaska to the Carolinas. Kids delight in the simulated underground mine.

LEADVILLE, COLORADO & SOUTHERN RAILROAD (all ages)

326 East 7th Street, P.O. Box 916, Leadville 80461; (719) 486–3936; www.leadville-train.com. Operates daily Memorial Day through September. Departures from Memorial Day to mid-June and from Labor Day through September are at 1:00 P.M., with weekend departures at 10:00 A.M. and 2:00 P.M. Departures from mid-June to Labor Day are at 10:00 A.M. and 2:00 P.M. Always safest to phone for exact departure times. $$$–$$$$

You won't find a more scenic railroad excursion than that aboard this train. In the shadow of spectacular Mt. Massive, the second-highest peak in Colorado at 14,421 feet, you will embark on a memorable two-and-a-half-hour journey, departing from the historic redbrick depot built in 1893. You will travel through aspen groves and pine and spruce forests, follow the headwaters of the Arkansas River, and stop at the French Gulch water tower for photos and a stretch.

Where to Stay

Historic Delaware Hotel. *700 Harrison Avenue, Leadville 80461; (719) 486–1418 or (800) 748–2004; www.delaware hotel.com.* There are several motels on the edge of town, but for location and historical ambience, plan to spend the night at this more-than-a-century-old, redbrick masterpiece with an elegant Victorian lobby and thirty-six guest rooms, including four two-bedroom suites. All have private baths and cable TV. Breakfast included in room rate. $–$$$

For More Information

Greater Leadville Area Chamber of Commerce, *809 Harrison Avenue, Leadville 80461; (719) 486–3900 or (800) 933–3901; www.leadvilleusa.com.*

Vail

A Tyrolean-inspired ski resort that's grown and grown and grown—that's Vail. In its nearly forty-year history, both town and ski amenities have become internationally known. Host to World Alpine Ski Championships, it is also part-time home to former president Gerald Ford. A mecca for the rich and famous, Vail also attracts Front Range residents with world-class skiing and snowboarding. Summer activities draw loyal fans from around the globe.

New in Town

Getting around Vail can be intimidating, especially if you have only a short time to stay. Here are a few hints to help you get oriented.

PARKING

Many areas in the village are pedestrian-only. Drive directly to a parking garage, east at Vail Transportation Center or west at Lionshead Parking Structure. There is a fee during the winter, $$$ per day, but in the summer it's Free.

INFORMATION

Stop at one of the visitors centers near the parking structures. They have maps and lots of literature. If you're in the area for a few days, be sure to get the weekly calendar of events. Free.

Another choice is the Activities Desk operated by Vail Associates, also a Free service. You'll find their office in Lionshead.

THE VILLAGE

From the visitors center see Vail on foot. Walk through the village and follow the path along the creek to Lionshead, or start at Lionshead and walk east. Explore shops and eateries along the way.

TRANSPORTATION

The City of Vail operates a Free continuous shuttle bus through the village. Hop on when you've had all the walking you can handle.

 COLORADO SKI MUSEUM AND COLORADO SKI HALL OF FAME (ages 6 and up)

231 South Frontage Road, in the Vail Village Transportation Center; (970) 476–1876; www.vailsoft.com/museum. Open Tuesday through Sunday 10:00 A.M. to 5:00 P.M. Closed May and October. Free.

Filled with memorabilia spanning 120 years of Colorado ski history, this museum includes among its treasures the largest collection of mementos from the famous Tenth Mountain Division, which trained alpine troops at nearby Camp Hale for European combat during World War II. The Hall of Fame recognizes those individuals who have contributed significantly to the sport of skiing.

VAIL RECREATION DISTRICT (ages 2½ and up)

700 South Frontage Road East, Vail 81657; (970) 479–2290.

Few tourists realize that the city's recreation department operates excellent programs that are open to the public by reservation or drop-in. They are convenient, fun, and reasonably priced. If you're looking for sports, ask about the tennis center and golf club—they're not just for kids. Vail Recreation District encourages visitors to see what they offer. Here are a few special programs.

CAMP VAIL (ages 5–12) and
PRE-KAMP VAIL (ages 2½–5)

June through August, Monday through Friday. $$$$ per day.

With a wide range of activities, arts to sports, there's something different every day. These camps are very popular, but you can make advance reservations. The winter program is an alternative to skiing.

Special evening events offered through Camp Vail include Night Hikes, an overnight on Vail Mountain (ages seven and up), and Movie Nights (ages five and up).

20 BELOW (ages 6–20)

Vail's Youth Center in Lionshead Parking Structure; (970) 479–2290. Open year-round (days and hours may vary with season), Sunday through Thursday 3:00 to 10:00 P.M. and Friday and Saturday 3:00 P.M. to midnight. Teens only after 6:00 P.M. $3.00 admission; activities Free.

It's called Vail's coolest hangout for good reason—it has an indoor skating ramp, pool tables, football, air hockey, big-screen TV, and videos in a supervised drop-in environment. 20 Below is equally popular with locals and visitors. It's a good place for your older kids to meet new friends and get away from their "boring family" for a few hours.

PLANET FUN (ages 4–15)

In the Vail Youth Center; summer only. $$–$$$$

Planet Fun has two- to three-hour activities that really appeal to kids, especially the hard-to-please middle schooler. Programs have included "Wacko Wednesdays," things you'd love to do at home but your mom would never let you. Supervised by experienced staff, it's good fun.

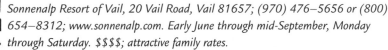

KIDVENTURES PROGRAM (ages 5–12)

Sonnenalp Resort of Vail, 20 Vail Road, Vail 81657; (970) 476–5656 or (800) 654–8312; www.sonnenalp.com. Early June through mid-September, Monday through Saturday. $$$$; attractive family rates.

"Gold Diggers and Train Riders" and "Jolly Ranchers" are just two themes kids can select at KidVentures. With alpine slides, mine tours, narrow-gauge trains, and pony and bike rides, days are packed with active participation. Program open to the public as well as to Sonnenalp guests. Reservations are required twenty-four hours in advance.

GONDOLA AND CHAIRLIFT RIDES

Single-ride or all-day passes are available for both lifts. $$$

EAGLE BAHN GONDOLA (all ages)

At Lionshead; weekends only, Memorial Day through late June, 10:00 A.M. to 4:00 P.M.; late June through Labor Day, Sunday through Wednesday 10:00 A.M. to 4:00 P.M. and Thursday through Saturday 10:00 A.M. to 11:00 P.M.

Enjoy an eagle-eye view of the Vail Valley and surrounding wilderness areas. At the top you'll find a restaurant, an outdoor eating area, bike rentals, and hiking trails. Walk the short path to the overlook. The vista makes a perfect backdrop for your Christmas card photo.

VISTA BAHN CHAIRLIFT

At Vail Village. Open daily late June through Labor Day, 10:00 A.M. to 4:00 P.M.

This high-speed, four-person chairlift whisks you to mid-Vail and back. Other choices? Take a hiking trail that connects to the gondola or hike down to the village.

HIKING (all ages)
Set off on your own or join a group—finding a great hike for your family won't be difficult.

HIKING MAPS

Pick up a hiking/biking map at the visitors center. Besides routes it gives descriptions of hiking trails on Vail Mountain and at Beaver Creek. Take an easy green trail (fifteen to thirty minutes) or a blue intermediate (one and a half to three hours). Choose a designated hiking trail (closed to mountain bikes) rather than a multiuse trail.

U.S. FOREST SERVICE HIKES

U.S. Forest Service on U.S. Highway 24 south of I–70; (970) 827–5715; or Activities Desk at Vail, (970) 476–9090. **Free**.
    The U.S. Forest Service leads hikes daily from Eagle's Nest in Vail. Conducted by a naturalist, the hikes vary in length and difficulty. Pick up their excellent brochure, which gives the schedule for both Vail and Beaver Creek hikes, directions to several self-guided hikes, and some information on plant and animal life along the routes.

VAIL NATURE CENTER HIKES

601 Vail Valley Drive, Vail 81657; (970) 479–2291. Open May through September; schedule varies. $
    Interpretive walks are scheduled daily and on several evenings. How about a Morning Bird Walk or Wildflower Walk?

 MOUNTAIN BIKING
Equipment for beginners, intermediates, and experts in adult and child sizes are available at rental shops throughout Vail Village and at the top of Eagle Bahn gondola.

ON VAIL MOUNTAIN

Mountain biking is not just for expert riders. Several trails are easy rides on gravel roads. For routes and descriptions pick up a map of Vail Mountain Biking Trails at the visitors center. Take bikes up the mountain on the gondola; $$$, all-day pass.

Rainy-Day Blues

Rainy-Day Blues On a rainy day you might be happy curling up with a book in the condo, but that won't keep the kids content for long. Here are a few other ideas.

INDOOR CLIMBING WALL

Vail Athletic Club (970–476–7960; www.vailmountainlodge-spa.com) has daily climbing programs for ages five to ninety-nine! Learn the ropes from experienced instructors. All equipment is provided.

INDOOR ICE-SKATING

Call Dobson Ice Arena (970–479–2270) for public skating hours. Hockey practice, clinics, and competitions also occur here.

INDOOR SWIMMING

Avon Recreation Center (10 miles west of Vail; 970–949–9191), with three pools and a Jacuzzi, will entertain your whole family. Kids love the water slides, fountains, and lazy river.

GORE TRAIL

Paved trails weave throughout Vail Village, following Gore Creek east to the Alpine Garden, amphitheater, playground, Tennis Center, and Nature Center. Continue on this trail, which parallels I-70 for 20 miles to Copper Mountain and Frisco in Summit County. There you can connect to Breckenridge.

BETTY FORD ALPINE GARDEN

In Ford Park west of the amphitheater; (970) 476–0103. Open spring through fall, dawn to dusk. **Free**.

For a respite from active days, stroll through this beautiful formal alpine garden, the highest botanical development in the nation. You'll all appreciate the colorful displays, which include more than 2,000 varieties of flora. If the kids tire of the beauty before you do, there's a great playground just up the hill.

FORD AMPHITHEATER (all ages)

In Ford Park; (970) 476–2918.

On Tuesday evenings, June through July, a group called Hot Summer Nights presents a series of concerts. There is some covered seating and plenty of lawn to spread out a blanket and enjoy a picnic. Kids love to dance to the music and scramble on the large rocks scattered throughout the grass. **Free**.

VAIL NATURE CENTER (all ages)

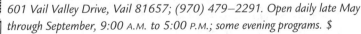

601 Vail Valley Drive, Vail 81657; (970) 479–2291. Open daily late May through September, 9:00 A.M. to 5:00 P.M.; some evening programs. $

A short trail along Gore Creek leads to an interpretive center/natural history museum. Informal, hands-on displays teach about local plants and animals. Kids love to crawl into the bubble window to watch birds at the feeder. Even the toilet is interesting here. Be sure to ask about it.

Special programs include day camp by the day or week. Or bring your family to an evening talk around the bonfire. The guided walk to a beaver pond on Monday and Wednesday nights is popular.

PINEY RIVER RANCH (all ages)

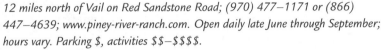

12 miles north of Vail on Red Sandstone Road; (970) 477–1171 or (866) 447–4639; www.piney-river-ranch.com. Open daily late June through September; hours vary. Parking $, activities $$–$$$$.

Piney River Ranch offers horseback riding, fishing, and boating in a rustic setting surrounding an alpine lake. Although it's just 12 miles from Vail, you won't get here in twelve minutes. Miles of dirt road force everyone to adopt a more leisurely pace. Along the way watch for the trailhead to Lost Lake. It's a beautiful hike in the mountains, nothing commercial about it.

PINEY RIVER RANCH STABLES (ages 6 and up)

One-hour rides scheduled from 10:00 A.M. to 4:00 P.M. $–$$

Ride in a small group, one wrangler with eight riders. Pony rides for those under age six require Mom or Dad to hold the lead. Make reservations before you arrive so that you won't be disappointed.

BOATING AND FISHING (all ages)

A sixty-acre lake beckons. Rent a canoe or rowboat; fishing gear is also available. Bring your camera—this lake is surrounded by beautiful scenery. Fishing is **Free**; $$ rental fee for kid's gear.

VAIL WINTER ACTIVITIES

Vail Resorts' Web site offers up-to-date snow conditions, information on all programs, and "Cool Deals"—last-minute specials on lodging and other promotions: www.snow.com.

SKIING LESSONS AND CHILD CARE
(ages 2 months–14 years)

Children's Ski and Snowboard Center, (970) 476–3239 or (800) 475–4543; Small World Play School, (970) 479–3285. $$$$

Skiing, snowboarding, lessons, and child care are available at three Vail Associate (VA) resorts in this valley: Vail, Beaver Creek, and Arrowhead. VA also owns Breckenridge and Keystone in Summit County. Uniform standards at all VA ski schools ensure continuity in instruction even if you ski at more than one area. Lift tickets from Vail are valid at all resorts. Children's Centers operate at Golden Peak, Lionshead, and Beaver Creek. Small World Play Schools provide alternative activities for those too young to ski. The Children's Ski and Snowboard School serves children ages three to fourteen. An introduction to snowboarding is offered for five- to seven-year-olds. Boarders must be at least eight years old for regular lessons. Reservations are required for all programs.

SKE-COLOGY

This ski school program combines environmental education with ski lessons. Developed in cooperation with the Colorado Division of Wildlife and the U.S. Forest Service, the program helps kids learn ecology while exploring designated on-mountain trails.

KIDS' MOUNTAIN ADVENTURE ZONES
Free *with lift ticket.*

Ski-through attractions in several locations on the mountain delight kids with bumps, jumps, and tunnels. Thunder Cat Cave, Chaos Canyon, and Dragon's Breath Mine—some are animated and educational; all are fun.

ADVENTURE RIDGE

On Vail Mountain at the top of Eagle Bahn gondola; some activities open at noon, others later in the afternoon. **Free** *gondola access to Adventure Ridge for non-skiers after 2:00 P.M. Activity fees $$–$$$.*

Vail's winter playground is a family delight. Start with the eight-lane tubing hill, complete with tow rope. There's an outdoor skating rink and two snowboarding half-pipes. Find out about sled dogging (a fast slide down the mountain on special footwear) and give it a try. Take a guided snow-bike tour. There are also five restaurants.

Arrowhead As the smallest, least resortlike area in the valley, Arrowhead, near Edwards, is a wonderful choice for families new to skiing. The lessons at Arrowhead are the same that you'll get at Vail or Beaver Creek. The runs are just right for parents who want to ski together with young children. If you decide you want more of a challenge, ski from Arrowhead to Beaver Creek. Your lift tickets are good there, too. One more plus: Parking is Free at Arrowhead.

NORDIC CENTER
When the snow falls, Vail's championship golf course becomes the Nordic Center, home to cross-country skiing and snowshoeing enthusiasts. In the evening take a horse-drawn sleigh ride to dinner at Season's restaurant.

HOT WINTER NIGHTS
On Golden Peak. Weekly during ski season; check schedule at visitors center. Free.

A synchronized skiing demonstration choreographed to music lights up the nights. The show ends with a spectacular fireworks display.

Business as Usual? If you've brought your family on a ski vacation but can't leave your work at home, Vail can help. You won't be staying at the hotel while the family hits the slopes. Vail Associates, in partnership with Sprint, operates a business center atop Vail Mountain. Take a few runs, then stop at the center to get your work done. You'll pay only for long-distance and video conferencing fees. Phones, fax, computers, e-mail—all gratis.

VAIL PUBLIC LIBRARY

292 West Meadow Drive, Vail 81657; (970) 479–2185. Open Monday through Thursday 10:00 A.M. to 8:00 P.M., Friday 10:00 A.M. to 6:00 P.M., and Saturday and Sunday 11:00 A.M. to 6:00 P.M. Story hours on Tuesday and Wednesday, 10:00 A.M. for toddlers, 11:00 A.M. for preschoolers. **Free**.

Summer or winter, you'll find carpeted nooks, interactive toys, books on tape, and a puppet theater besides a great selection of books in the glass-enclosed Children's Room. Check for special programs—evening story hours, a puppet show, etc. Story hour includes a follow-up activity.

In the main library older children gravitate toward the high-tech computers with games and Internet access. Parents appreciate the peaceful, pleasant ambience and, of course, the books and magazines. Even if it isn't raining, the library is worth a stop.

Help for Mom and Mr. Mom

Several businesses in the Vail Valley offer services that make traveling with children much easier. Ask at a visitors center for specific information about these and other services:

A call to Baby's Away, specializing in baby supply rentals, may eliminate having to cart along equipment; (970) 926–5256 or (800) 369–9030.

Baby-sitting services abound. The going rate is $12 to $15 per hour. Contact your hotel concierge for recommendations.

Where to Eat

Kaltenberg Castle. *600 Lionshead Mall, Vail 81657; near the Eagle Bahn gondola in Lionshead; (970) 479–1050. Open daily November to mid-September for lunch, après-ski, and dinner.* It looks like a castle and it's headed by royalty, the great-grandson of the last king of Bavaria. Large Bavarian-style meals are served in a large Bavarian-style dining room. Even the children's menu has Bavarian choices, a nice break from the usual chicken nuggets or burger. The grand deck is an excellent place to relax with views of Vail Mountain.

The castle is also a brewery where Prince Luitpold and his brewmasters continue a 700-year-old tradition of producing Royal Bavarian Beer. $–$$$

Where to Stay

Sonnenalp Resort of Vail. *20 Vail Road, Vail 81657; (970) 476–5656 or* *(800) 654–8312; www.sonnenalp.com.* In the heart of Vail Village, this elegant yet comfortable resort can't be missed in summer when the window boxes overflow with blooms—they're award winners. Attention to detail applies to all facets of your stay at Sonnenalp. Kids are not only welcome but stay **Free** if under age twelve. All-inclusive packages include coupons for KidVentures day camp programs. There's also an indoor/outdoor pool, a rarity in the area. $$$$

For More Information

For information on activities, lodging, and dining in Vail, there are two major resources:

Vail Valley Chamber & Tourism Bureau, *100 East Meadow Drive, Suite 34, Vail 81657; (970) 479–1385; www.visitvailvalley.com.*

Vail Activities Desk, *(800) 525–2257.* Vail Associates provides free information on lodging, dining, and activities in the valley, including places not owned by the corporation. They describe themselves as a "concierge service to the whole valley." You are welcome to use their help even if you are not staying in Vail.

Vail Valley

Stretching for 15 miles west of Vail, known to locals as Down Valley, the communities of Avon, Beaver Creek, and Edwards offer summer and winter activities geared to families. From the very commercial to totally natural, ultra-expensive to free, it's all here.

AVON

AVON RECREATION CENTER (all ages)

325 Benchmark Road, Avon 81620; (970) 949–9191. Open Monday through Friday 6:00 A.M. to 9:00 P.M. and Saturday and Sunday 8:00 A.M. to 9:00 P.M. $$

A lap pool, slide pool, leisure pool, and whirlpool fit the bill for families. Kids will love the slide, sprays, fountains, and lazy river. Fitness and conditioning equipment are also available.

NOTTINGHAM PARK

In Avon, west of the Recreation Center. Water activities open late May through Labor Day.

Kids are delighted by the amenities in this forty-eight-acre open-space park. They'll enjoy running off steam and playing at the playground if this is just a quick stop. But if you can stay longer, there are paddleboats and canoes, or you can rent a mountain bike (adult, child, and trailers) for a half hour or more. Croquet, volleyball, soccer, basketball, or in-line skating? Equipment is for rent in the log cabin. For something new, try out the nine-hole disc golf course. It's free; disc rental is $2.00. Keep this park in mind when you need an after-dinner activity.

Winter at the lake brings ice-skaters, from twirling ballerinas to hockey players.

BEAVER CREEK

Self-described as sophisticated, Beaver Creek exudes resort atmosphere. Upscale lodging, dining, and shopping cluster at the base of the ski area. Among the ultraposh amenities, you'll find a few family-oriented treasures, and you may enjoy browsing a bit—looking is free!

Beaver Creek is a full-service ski area with ski school, child care, and rental facilities. It's owned and operated by Vail Associates.

To drive to Beaver Creek, you must first stop at the security gate at the base of the mountain to obtain a day pass. During ski season visitors must park in Avon and take a free shuttle.

 ### BEAVER CREEK CHILDREN'S MUSEUM (all ages)
In Beaver Creek village; (970) 926–5855. Open late June through Labor Day, Wednesday through Sunday 10:00 A.M. to 4:00 P.M. **Free**.

Just the spot for some indoor fun, the Children's Museum entertains kids with hands-on interactive exhibits. Fun at One, special events, and Friday workshops at 1:00 P.M. are **Free**, but advance registration is required.

 ### BEAVER CREEK ICE-SKATING (ages 4 and up)
Outside in the center of the village. Open daily, weather permitting, 6:00 to 9:00 P.M. $$ for skating and rental.

This experience might go in your family record book—there are not many places where you can ice-skate outside in the summertime! It's also fun in the winter.

 ### FIVE SENSES TRAIL (all ages)
Wander at your own pace along this 1½-mile self-guided trail beginning at Beaver Creek Chapel and ending at Flood's Ponds. **Free**.

For More Information

Beaver Creek Information Center,
(970) 845–9090.

Edwards

 VAIL VALLEY RODEO

The Ranch at Berry Creek, I–70 at the Edwards exit; mid-June through early September; every Thursday, barbecue at 5:30 P.M., rodeo at 6:30 P.M. $$

Sitting on wooden bleachers at this weekly community event, you'll feel a million miles away from the glitter of Vail. It's perfect family entertainment—not too long, not too expensive, but, oh, so western.

Come early to get a good seat. Chow down on barbecue dinner. Meet the mountain man and his burro. Bull riding, bronc busting, team roping, and barrel racing—all are exciting. But the Mutton Busting and Calf Scramble are the evening's highlights, especially if your kids decide to participate. Those younger than age fourteen can chase calves around the arena, trying to remove five-dollar bills wrapped around tails. Cowpokes under fifty pounds can try riding a ram. There are no seat belts. Make sure the battery on your camcorder is charged!

*B*udget Stretchers Spend an evening in Edwards. On summertime Wednesday evenings, free outdoor concerts liven up the square. Toddlers romp in the grassy area, and families spread their picnic dinners on blankets. It's all very casual.

For diversions before, during, or after the concert, check out Bookworm, a cozy bookshop with an all-ages inventory. And just around the corner, don't miss the candy store.

Where to Eat

There are hundreds of restaurants, delis, markets, and snack stops in the Vail Valley. Those in Vail and Beaver Creek tend to be quite pricey—okay for that special meal but cost-prohibitive for three meals a day. Also, crowded restaurants with leisurely paced dining can be one frustration too many for worn-out youngsters. To save both time and dollars, consider arranging lodging that includes some kitchen facilities. And remember, there's also takeout.

Here are a couple of suggestions away from the main resort areas.

Fiesta's. *In Edwards Plaza, Edwards 81632; (970) 926–2121. Open daily for lunch and dinner; also open for weekend breakfast.* The Marquez sisters share their family secrets here—their great-grandparents' recipes from New Mexico. Fiesta's continually earns the Best Mexican Food award from Vail Valley residents, so count on a crowd. $

Markos. *In Edwards Plaza, Edwards 81632; (970) 926–7003. Open daily for lunch and dinner.* Tasty Italian food in a relaxed atmosphere makes Markos appealing. Choose from grinders to made-to-order Fettucine Royale. And there's always pizza. $

Where to Stay

The Lazy Ranch Bed & Breakfast. *0057 Lake Creek Road, Edwards 81632; (800) 655–9343.* This century-old farm is the recipient of the coveted Colorado Centennial Farm Award. Guests stay in four nicely decorated guest rooms, one of which has a fireplace and a private bath. The other three share two baths. The innkeepers serve a complimentary ranch hand–size breakfast of fruit, ham-and-cheese crepes, and fried potatoes or, perhaps, homemade biscuits and gravy. Dinners are available at additional charge if requested at the time you make your reservations. $$–$$$

For More Information

The Chamber of Commerce, *south end of the City Market grocery store in Avon; P.O. Box 1437, Avon 81620; (970) 949–5189; www.vailvalleychamber.com.* Serves Avon, Beaver Creek, and Edwards.

*S*eeking Doc Holliday Both Wyatt Earp and Doc Holliday eventually made their way to Glenwood Springs, where Holliday hoped that the healing waters of the mineral springs would eradicate his advanced tuberculosis. A short hike from the Glenwood Springs Chamber of Commerce office, at Grand Avenue and 11th Street, takes the curious to Linwood Cemetery and Holliday's gravestone, which reads simply, HE DIED IN BED; 1852–1887.

Glenwood Springs

Glenwood Springs was fated to become a popular destination for travelers. Drawn to the mineral-rich springs, the Ute Indians were the first to come to the area. Considering the springs to be sacred, they took to the waters for spiritual cleansing and physical healing. When white settlers came the Ute moved on, and soon weary miners were soaking away their aches and pains in the warm revitalizing waters. The word spread quickly, bringing notables such as Presidents Theodore Roosevelt and William Taft, followed by members of high society.

Glenwood Springs is situated at the confluence of the Colorado and Roaring Fork Rivers, thus creating excellent rafting, kayaking, and canoeing. Diverse river conditions allow adventurers to float peacefully past scenic vistas or shoot white-water rapids with names like "Man-eater" and "Panic Alley."

GLENWOOD SPRINGS HOT SPRINGS POOL (all ages)

415 East 6th Street, P.O. Box 308, Glenwood Springs 81601; (970) 945–6571 or (800) 537–7946; www.hotspringspool.com. Open daily, 7:30 A.M. to 10:00 P.M. during summer, 9:00 A.M. to 10:00 P.M. during winter. All-day pass to pool, $–$$; water slide, $.

With water kept at a comfortable ninety degrees, the Glenwood Springs Hot Springs Pool is the largest outdoor hot springs swimming pool in the world. Measuring 405 feet long and 100 feet wide, it contains 1,071,000 gallons of constantly filtered water. An adjacent 100-foot therapy pool is kept at 104 degrees. The lap lanes, diving boards, and especially the water slide appeal to all ages.

If you visit in winter, brave the run from the dressing rooms to the pool, hop in, and hope for a snowstorm. Could anything be more invigorating than to soak in the toasty water while watching feathery snowflakes sifting down from the sky?

The complex features parklike grounds, a full-service restaurant, a snack pavilion, swimsuit and towel rentals, lockers, showers, and a health and fitness center.

GLENWOOD CAVERNS (ages 6 and up)

Located at 508 Pine Street, Glenwood Springs 81601; (800) 530–1635; www.glenwoodcaverns.com. Open May 1 through October, weather permitting. Tour begins at the Glenwood Caverns Gift Shop & Museum, located next to the Hotel Colorado at 508 Pine Street. Call ahead for tour times and reservations.

(Reservations are not required but are highly recommended.) $$–$$$, children 5 and younger are **Free** *when accompanied by an adult.*

Whimsically called the Fairy Caves, these caverns are surrounded by mystery. No one seems to know exactly who discovered them or when they were first found.

Formed in limestone deposited approximately 325 million years ago, the caves are located on top of Iron Mountain, just north of Glenwood Springs. The property on which they dwell was homesteaded in the 1800s by the C. W. Darrow family, who opened the caves for public tours around 1886. A pathway providing access via horseback, horse and carriage, or foot was formed, electric lights were installed, and a tunnel was blasted through the rock to expose a spectacular view of Glenwood Canyon. Even though the caves were eventually closed, private caving expeditions discovered more caves over the years.

Reopened to the public in May 1999, the caves offer several levels of touring. The "Family Tour" covers a distance of ½ mile and takes approximately two hours. Participants make their way through subterranean caverns, grottos, and a maze of corridors; visit a cliffside balcony with panoramic views of Glenwood Canyon; and stare in wonder at newly discovered areas where formations remain untouched by man. Unusual crystalline formations, unique cave bacon, and fragile soda straws enhance the Barn, a towering, five-story chamber. "Oohs" and "aahs" accent the culmination of the tour as viewers exclaim in delight at the glittering stalactites and gleaming stalagmites that line the entire length of the Kings Row cavern.

For those in your family who crave adventure, there is the "Wild Tour," consisting of a three- to four-hour journey to rarely visited areas deep within the caves. Cavers are provided with necessary equipment, including lighted helmets. Participants must be age thirteen or older. This is a challenging undertaking, and a previous tour of the Fairy Caves to observe how your children react to caving is highly recommended before venturing on this one.

Bring sweaters and jackets. Cave temperature consistently remains at fifty-two degrees Fahrenheit. Elevation is 7,100 feet.

 CANYON BIKES (all ages)
526 Pine Street, Glenwood Springs 81601 (in Hotel Colorado); (970) 945–6605; www.canyonbikes.com. Open May through September. Hours vary, as do rates; best to phone. $$$–$$$$

These folks specialize in rental bikes for self-guided rides along the Glenwood Canyon bike trail that include a detailed, printed map to the route, bike locks, helmets, and packs. If your children are small, you can rent Burley trailers and trailer bikes here, too.

Where to Eat

Daily Bread. *729 Grand Avenue, Glenwood Springs 81601, downtown; (970) 945–6253. Open daily for breakfast; open for lunch Monday through Saturday.* Nine varieties of bread, puffy fragrant cinnamon rolls, and fantastic granola—all made here—are just a few reasons why Daily Bread has such loyal customers. There are always lots of families. Count on a crowd on weekends. $

Where to Stay

Because the Hot Springs Pool is such a draw, Glenwood Springs hotels, especially those nearest the pool, fill quickly during summer. Many Colorado families return year after year. Make reservations early.

Hot Springs Lodge. *415 East 6th Street, Glenwood Springs 81601; (970) 945–6571 or (800) 537–7946; www.hot springspool.com.* If you're planning to spend your time in the Hot Springs Pool, the Lodge can't be beat for location. Right across the street from the pool, you can walk back and forth easily; no need to join the parade looking for a parking place. Another bonus— Lodge guests receive discount passes for the pool.

Many rooms have refrigerators, and there are laundry facilities—always appreciated by those with kids. Octo-ber through mid-March, $; mid-March through September, $$.

Hotel Colorado. *526 Pine Street, Glenwood Springs 81601; (970) 945–6511 or (800) 544–3998; www.hotelcolorado.com.* Sleep where U.S. presidents have slept! Theodore Roosevelt and William Taft were guests here. So was Al Capone. In business more than a hundred years and now a National Historic Landmark, the Hotel Colorado is a good stop whether you stay here or not. Walk through the grand lobby and check out the legendary birthplace of the "Teddy Bear." Gift shop, restaurant, and Legends Trading Company are open to the public.

If you want to spend the night, call ahead to reserve a Family Room: two bedrooms connected by a bathroom. $$

For More Information

Glenwood Springs Chamber Resort Association, *1102 Grand Avenue, Glenwood Springs 81601; (970) 945–6589; www.glenwoodsprings.net.*

Aspen

The well-known resort community of Aspen is located on State Highway 82, 40 miles southeast of Glenwood Springs.

Walk down Main Street in Aspen and you are apt to glimpse at least one celebrity. Stay in one of the luxury hotels and frequent the ski slopes, and you will run into several. Stroll out of the main shopping area just a few blocks, however, and you'll be in a small-town neighborhood of mining-era Victorian houses.

Once a rowdy silver-producing town, Aspen fell into near ruin with the crash of the silver market in 1893. The present-day glitz and glamour are still tinged with a bit of the town's rough-and-tumble past—and that's the charm of Aspen.

ASPEN IN SUMMER

Although Aspen may be best known for its stellar ski slopes and winter beauty, its summer season also has lots to offer outdoor enthusiasts—hiking, fishing, mountain biking, rafting, backpacking, llama trekking, golfing, tennis, jeep tours, and music festivals, to mention a few.

ON THE MOUNTAIN

The town is surrounded by four outstanding ski mountains: Aspen Mountain, Aspen Highlands, Tieback/Buttermilk, and Snowmass. Besides world-class downhill skiing, the resort community offers outstanding cross-country skiing, snowshoeing, dogsledding, and sleigh rides. And then there are Sno-Cat tours, snowmobiling, ice climbing, ice-skating, and ice fishing. The ski schools provide lessons for all skill levels. The Aspen Highlands Snow Puppies program offers instruction for children as young as three and a half years old. Nursery care is available for those ages six weeks to four years old. Children as young as age eight can participate in snowboarding lessons.

Where to Eat

Boogie's Diner. *534 East Cooper Avenue, Aspen 81611; (970) 925–6610.* This casual restaurant features generous servings at affordable prices. $

Main Street Bakery Cafe. *201 East Main Street, Aspen 81611; (970) 925–6446.* Good, inexpensive meals. Great bakery for picking up snack items for later. $

Where to Stay

Stay Aspen-Snowmass. *425 Rio Grande Place, Aspen 81611; (888) 290–1324.*

For More Information

Aspen Chamber Resort Association, *425 Rio Grande Place, Aspen 81611; (970) 925–1940 or (800) 262–7736.*

Aspen Skiing Company, *(970) 925–1220 or (800) 525–6200.*

Snowmass Resort Association, *(970) 923–2000 or (800) 766–9627.*

Grand Junction

Grand Junction is located on the western edge of the state along I-70, southwest of Glenwood Springs. With a population of approximately 28,000, the town is family friendly, and the area is teeming with wonderful attractions and activities. The streets are easily maneuvered; a downtown, outdoor pedestrian mall makes shopping a pleasure; and tree-shaded residential neighborhoods lend a comfortable, down-home atmosphere to the city.

Art on the Corner This unique outdoor art show, located in Grand Junction's Downtown Shopping Park, hosts a variety of sculptures from many artistic approaches. Sculptors loan their work for one year. All pieces, featuring some of the country's best artisans, are for sale. Free.

DOO ZOO (ages 1–10)

241 Colorado Avenue, Grand Junction 81501; (970) 241–5225. Open Monday through Friday 9:00 A.M. to 4:00 P.M. and Saturday 10:00 A.M. to 5:00 P.M. $

This wonderful children's museum, with plenty of hands-on play areas, contains 8,000 square feet of interactive exhibits designed to stimulate curiosity, imagination, and gross and fine motor skills. Kids will find a play supermarket with cash register, scanner, scale, grocery carts, and shelves of canned and boxed goods; a post office; a bank; and a playhouse with dress-up clothes, hats, and shoes. A large wooden fire truck invites them to don firefighter jackets and hats and climb aboard. There's a theater, a room of balls to jump in, and a building-block room for the wee ones with rocking chairs for Mom and Dad.

LINCOLN PARK (all ages)

Located at North Avenue and 12th Street; (970) 254–3866. Pool is open daily late May through Labor Day, Thursday through Tuesday 1:30 to 8:00 P.M. and Wednesday 9:30 A.M. to 8:00 P.M. $–$$

If the kids need a break from car travel, this city park is a great place to get rid of the wiggles. It has picnic tables under shade trees and an outdoor pool with a 351-foot water slide.

CROSS ORCHARDS HISTORIC SITE (all ages)

3073 F (Patterson) Road; (970) 434–9814. Open May 1 through mid-October, Tuesday, Friday, and Saturday 10:00 A.M. to 3:00 P.M. $

Once one of the largest apple orchards in the state, from 1896 to 1923, this farm features self-guided tours through the remaining orchard to the six-sided summer house and through the pantry, kitchen, dining room, and sleeping quarters of the workers' bunkhouse. Meander over to the old barn and you are likely to see Rock and Spud, the two beautiful, brown-eyed mules, along with Cider the pig, and a few turkeys, chickens, and ducks.

Docents in period clothing answer questions and explain the history of the farm. Sit for a while under a shade tree or on the bunkhouse porch, try one of the cook's hot-from-the-oven cookies, visit the blacksmith in his work shed, and stop by to watch as the carpenter creates simple old-fashioned wooden toys. Lovely flower beds grace the grounds, and a picnic area is perfect for those who choose to bring along their lunch. And don't forget the Country Store for gift items and locally produced food products.

Dino Find In 1993, during a Family Dino Camp session sponsored by the Dinosaur Discovery Museum, a fourteen-year-old resident of Boulder, Colorado, discovered an egg from an armored *Mymoorapelta maysi*. It was the first egg ever found in the Mygatt-Moore Quarry. The egg is being studied by the world's foremost expert on dinosaur eggs, Dr. Karl Hirsch, at the University of Colorado–Denver.

Dinosaur Hiking Trail

Rabbit Valley *(970–244–3000),* located 30 miles west of Grand Junction on I–70, features a 1½-mile "Trail through Time," a self-guided walking tour rich in fossils. Several species of dinosaurs, including apatosaurus, diplodocus, and brachiosaurus, have been found in Rabbit Valley.

Scientific research is ongoing here, and you can see paleontologists at work on Monday and Tuesday during the summer months (best to phone to confirm days and times). The iguanodon fossils discovered here in 1982 are considered the oldest of this type ever found.

Grand Mesa

Billed as "The World's Largest Flat-Topped Mesa," the Grand Mesa (970–242 8211), with entry located 23 miles east of Grand Junction off I–70, encompasses 200 lakes stocked with rainbow, lake, and brook trout; mile upon mile of hiking trails; and bear, deer, and elk viewing. The 10,000-foot-high plateau comprises 53 square miles of aspen groves, pine forests, and spectacular valley views.

Fruita

Located just west of Grand Junction, off I–70.

DINOSAUR DISCOVERY MUSEUM (ages 4 and up)
Located on State Highway 340, just south of I–70 at exit 19; (970) 858–7282 or (888) 488–3466; www.dinosaurjourney.org. Open daily year-round, 9:00 A.M. to 5:00 P.M. $–$$

If you come anywhere close to Grand Junction, a stop at this fascinating museum is an absolute must. This is one of those attractions that is worth going out of your way to experience.

Prepare your littlest ones by telling them to expect growls and roars and giant (some are full-size) moving dinosaurs with big teeth and huge claws. Then turn them loose and anticipate an argument when it's time to leave.

Kids love this place. The 22,000-square-foot museum encompasses remarkably realistic, robotic reproductions of dinosaurs, including a

Utah raptor called "The Super Slasher" in the process of eating another dinosaur and a gigantic, fuzzy, long-furred, long-tusked woolly mammoth. Perhaps the most popular with kids is the dilophosaurus from the early Jurassic Period that periodically spits a stream of "venom" toward squealing kids. Children can make dinosaur footprints in wet sand with plastic dino feet, trace shapes of prehistoric beasts onto paper with crayons, watch as little plastic dino babies hatch from their eggs (all the while chirping and looking anxiously from side to side), and sweep away sand to expose simulated bones hidden in a large tray. Also a big hit with kids is the earthquake simulator, where they stand on a surface that shakes and quakes while the sounds of an earthquake rumble around them.

COLORADO NATIONAL MONUMENT
Reached by taking the Fruita exit off I–70 and following the signs leading to the west entrance; (970) 858–3617. **Free**.

This 20,000-acre natural museum of geologic splendor—featuring sheer-walled canyons, arched windows, rock spires, massive domes, and natural monoliths—provides peaceful sanctuaries for visitors. Desert bighorn sheep, coyotes, bobcats, mountain lions, mule deer, antelope, squirrels, and rabbits call this majestic place home. You are likely to see canyon wrens, turkey vultures, ravens, and, hopefully, the magnificent golden eagle.

Two good hikes for families with younger children are the Window Rock Trail, an easy, ½-mile round-trip ramble over level ground, and Otto's Trail, a gently sloping, 1-mile round-trip walk. Use caution at overlooks and steep drop-offs.

Where to Stay

Country Inns of America. *718 Horizon Drive, Grand Junction 81506; (970) 243–5080 or (800) 990–1143.* Guest laundry, a swimming pool, and a wading pool make these accommodations popular with families. Apartment-style rooms with one, two, and three bedrooms available. $$-$$$$

For More Information

Grand Junction Visitor and Convention Bureau, *740 Horizon Drive, Grand Junction 81506; (970) 244–1480 or (800) 962–2547; www.visitgrand junction.com.*

Annual Events in Northwestern Colorado

JANUARY

International Snow-Sculpture Championships. *Breckenridge, late January; details at Daniel's Cabin Activities Center; (970) 453–6018.* Skilled artisans come from around the world to compete in this event. Plan to stay for several days so that you can see the sculptures in the making and in their magnificent finished state. **Free.**

JUNE

Strawberry Days. *Glenwood Springs, mid-June; (970) 945–6589.* Colorado's longest running civic celebration began as a one-day picnic and developed over the years into an almost weeklong celebration. There's a Kidsfest, a parade, live music, craft and food booths, and a carnival. Reserve lodging far in advance for this one.

JULY

Steamboat Springs Cowboy Roundup Days. *Steamboat Springs, early July; (970) 879–0880.* This family-friendly event has been an ongoing tradition since 1876, when only a few settlers and Native Americans attended. The festival includes an all-you-can-eat flapjack feed, footraces, a small-town-style parade, a PRCA ProRodeo, and a grandiose fireworks display.

Dinosaur Days. *Grand Junction, mid-July; (970) 242–0971 or (800) 962–2547.* This celebration includes a "Kids' Day at the Dinosaur Quarry" when youngsters can dig for replica fossils. Other events include a parade with floats depicting a prehistoric theme, the Stegosaurus Stomp Street Dance, and a Shoppasaurus Sidewalk Sale. Some events **Free.**

DECEMBER

Christmas Market. *Georgetown, early December; (303) 569–2840.* During the first two full weekends in December, Georgetown welcomes the Christmas season with an old-fashioned outdoor celebration in the European tradition. **Free** admission.

Southwestern Colorado

In southwestern Colorado you will find the state's highest concentration of ancient Native American ruins, an abundance of small friendly towns, and superb wilderness areas for outdoor recreation. This region also boasts excellent skiing, premium rafting, and legendary excursion trains.

Doris's Top Picks
in Southwestern Colorado

1. Bachelor-Syracuse Mine Tour, Ouray
2. Cumbres & Toltec Scenic Railroad, Antonito
3. Durango & Silverton Narrow Gauge Railroad, Durango and Silverton
4. Hiking, picnicking, skiing, Crested Butte
5. Jeeping, Ouray
6. Mesa Verde National Park, Cortez
7. Ouray Hot Springs Pool, Ouray
8. Vallecito Lake, Bayfield

S O U T H W E S T E R N
C O L O R A D O

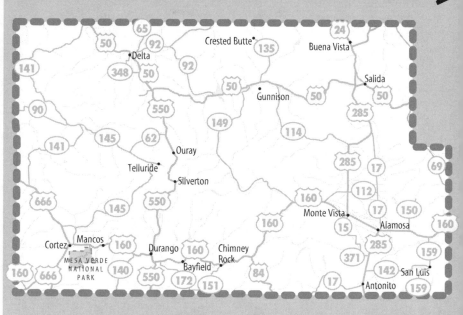

Buena Vista

This small town, a favorite of outdoor enthusiasts, is located on U.S. Highway 24, north of U.S. Highway 50, about a two-hour drive southwest of Denver.

 RIVER RAFTING

According to Mark Twain's Huckleberry Finn, "We said there weren't no home like a raft, after all. Other places seem so cramped and smothery, but a raft don't. You feel mighty free and easy and comfortable on a raft."

A great way to share in Huck's enthusiasm for rafting would be to run the Arkansas River, and the very best place to access the river is at Buena Vista. From exhilarating, wild white-water rafting to leisurely float fishing, you will "feel mighty free and easy and comfortable" on the Arkansas.

The Buena Vista area is home to numerous rafting outfitters. It is important, however, to choose your outfitter carefully. Inquire about the experience of the guides. Ask how long the operation has been in business and if the company is licensed with a government agency. Do those in charge seem to take passenger safety seriously, and are your questions being answered carefully? Call the Colorado River Outfitters Association at (303) 280-2554 or (303) 369-4632 for advice and more information.

Where to Eat

K's Dairy Delite. *223 South U.S. Highway 24, Buena Vista 81211; (719) 395–8695. Open March to mid-November.* "People live for K's to open in the spring." That's what residents say about this Buena Vista favorite. Stop in for a cone—vanilla, chocolate, or twist. There's also a fast-food menu—and plenty of local flavor. $

Casa del Sol. *303 North Highway 24; P.O. Box 1560, Buena Vista 81211; (719) 395–8810. Open daily, May through September, for lunch and dinner. Also open Thursday through Monday for lunch and dinner through winter months.* Traditional Mexican cuisine served in a charming setting attracts a loyal crowd, so reservations are advised. Dine inside or in the courtyard. $

Where to Stay

Plain Jane Sack & Snack. *P.O. Box 815, Ouray 81427; (970) 325–7313.* **Free** hearty continental breakfast, barbecue pit for guest use, kids' play area. Children are especially welcome. The B&B is close to the river, so keep a close watch on your children. $$

Salida

South of Buena Vista, U.S. Highway 24 and State Highway 291 lead to the small town of Salida.

 MOUNT SHAVANO FISH HATCHERY AND REARING UNIT (all ages)

7725 County Road 154, Salida 81201; ½ mile northwest of Salida; (719) 539–6877. Open daily 7:30 A.M. to 4:00 P.M. **Free**.

If you've ever wondered where all those kokanee salmon and rainbow, cutthroat, brook, and brown trout that you keep pulling out of Colorado's rivers, lakes, and streams come from, you might want to visit this hatchery. One of sixteen propagation units maintained by the Colorado Division of Wildlife, it hatches more than six million trout and salmon eggs each year and produces approximately 375,000 pounds of fish annually.

Kids can buy packets of fish food to feed the fish and obtain free posters and pamphlets here. Wildlife books and videos are available for purchase. There are self-guided tours (or guided tours upon request).

 CENTENNIAL PARK AND SALIDA HOT SPRINGS (all ages)

 410 Rainbow Boulevard (U.S. Highway 50), Salida 81201; (719) 539–6738; www.salidapool.com. Open daily Memorial Day through Labor Day, 1:00 to 9:00 P.M.; open Tuesday through Sunday the rest of the year with variable hours. $–$$

Centennial Park is home to the Salida Hot Springs, featuring a wading pool, a shallow pool, and a 4- to 10-foot-deep, 25-meter pool with two lap lanes. Collected underground and piped in from the mountains 5 miles away, the odorless, hot mineral water flows continuously into the various pools. Centennial Park also has tennis, volleyball, and basketball courts; horseshoe pits; a playground; and picnic tables.

Gunnison

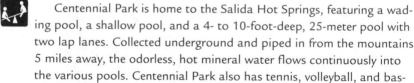

Located west of Salida on U.S. Highway 50, the town of Gunnison, home to Colorado's Western State College, is surrounded by 1,600,000 acres of the Gunnison National Park, with more than 700 miles of trout streams.

JORGENSEN PARK AND PACMAN LAKE (ages 3 and up)
Open daily. **Free.**

Jorgensen Park's PacMan Lake allows kids age fourteen or younger to fish free without a fishing license, and they may keep as many as four fish. The lake is stocked during the first week in June every year. Also at the park are two half-pipes for the skateboarders in your family.

 GUNNISON PIONEER MUSEUM (ages 4 and up)
Located at the east end of Gunnison, on U.S. Highway 50; (970) 641–4530. Open Monday through Saturday 9:00 A.M. to 5:00 P.M. and Sunday noon to 4:00 P.M., Memorial Day through Labor Day. $–$$, children 5 and younger **Free.**

Your children are sure to enjoy traipsing through the circa-1905 schoolhouse, the old post office, and the dairy barn with a hayloft. Here they can see a vintage narrow-gauge train engine, gondola, boxcar, livestock car, and caboose.

 CURECANTI NATIONAL RECREATION AREA (all ages)
Located along concurrently running U.S. Highway 50 and State Highway 92, between Gunnison and Montrose; (970) 641–2337. $$

 The Curecanti National Recreation Area encompasses 53 miles of the Black Canyon of the Gunnison and the 12-mile-long Black Canyon of the Gunnison National Monument, a spectacular gorge cut deep into the landscape over a two-million-year period of time by the raging Gunnison River.

Within the recreation area, 20-mile-long Blue Mesa Lake provides excellent fishing for kokanee salmon and brown, rainbow, Mackinaw, and brook trout. Those who fish these waters regularly say that the prime fishing times are early morning and late evening, when the fish are feeding, and that flies usually bring good results in the evening. Shore fishing is best in late spring and summer, when the lake levels are at their lowest. When the lake rises the fish are found in the deeper middle portion of the lake. A Colorado fishing license is required for all persons age fifteen or older. You can purchase a license at the marina or at area sporting-goods stores.

Many opportunities exist in the Curecanti National Recreation Area for hiking, camping, picnicking, and boating. Kids can earn Junior Ranger status by completing an activities booklet and interviewing a park ranger. They will receive an award certificate and a Junior Ranger badge.

For brochures and more information about the Curecanti National Recreation Area, write to or phone the U.S. Department of the Interior, National Park Service, Curecanti National Recreation Area, 102 Elk Creek, Gunnison 81230; (970) 641–0406.

Crested Butte

Approximately 28 miles north of Gunnison, State Highway 135 dead-ends in the middle of the Gunnison National Park at the historic town of Crested Butte and the ultramodern Crested Butte Mountain Resort. Located only 3 miles apart, the two communities are complete opposites. Crested Butte is an enchanting, circa-1870 former coal-mining camp with Victorian storefronts, art galleries, excellent restaurants, and charming boutiques. Crested Butte Mountain Resort boasts state-of-the-art skiing, luxury accommodations, and first-class amenities.

SUMMERTIME IN CRESTED BUTTE

During summer Crested Butte blossoms with exceptional hiking along paths bordered with acres of more than 300 species of wildflowers. The Colorado State Legislature has proclaimed Crested Butte the official Wildflower Capital of the state.

If your family enjoys mountain biking, there is bound to be a trail exactly right for your combined expertise levels. No need to transport your bikes to a trailhead, though, because you can take off in just about any direction from the center of town and find historic, scenic, easy, or challenging biking trails at the end of the street.

Other warm-weather activities include white-water rafting, horseback riding, four-wheeling, ghost-town exploring, hot-air ballooning, and horse-drawn carriage rides.

High-Altitude Hints

Parents are reminded that in Colorado, altitude will play an important part in your vacation. At Crested Butte you are at an elevation of more than 9,000 feet, and it may take a little time for your children to adjust. Recommendations include drinking much more water than usual, wearing sunscreen and sunglasses, and taking it easy the first day.

CHAIRLIFT RIDES (all ages)

Daily, mid-June through August, 9:30 A.M. to 2:30 P.M. $$$ for an all-day pass; children under 6 **Free**.

Two high-speed quad lifts whisk summer guests up the mountain. The Keystone Lift will also take your bikes. At the top you'll find hiking/biking trails and picnic areas. Or just ride round-trip, enjoying the spectacular scenery.

HIKING (all ages)

Peak Trail is a 1-mile round-trip hike that includes some fairly steep terrain. Silver Queen Trail follows a road from the top of the Silver Queen Lift (11,400 feet) to the top of the Keystone Lift. Or you could do it in reverse if you'd rather walk uphill!

MOUNTAIN BIKING (ages 8 and up)

Rent equipment at the base of the mountain to enjoy a day of riding for beginners and intermediates.

WINTER ON THE MOUNTAIN

If summers are spectacular in Crested Butte, then winters would have to be considered divine. When frosty-white snow ladens the roofs and hems the windowsills of the town's winsome little Victorian cottages, the ski slopes at Crested Butte Mountain Resort beckon. With an elevation of 12,162 feet at the summit and 9,375 feet at the base and fourteen lifts, including two high-speed detachable quads, the resort prides itself on tempting skiers of all levels. In fact, Crested Butte Mountain Resort leads the state in teaching first-time skiers.

An extensive children's program is maintained here. The nursery and day-care center accommodates babies up to six months old and has an infant-to-teacher ratio of two-to-one. Those age six months to potty-trained are provided with appropriate activities supervised by highly qualified early-childhood professionals. For the potty-trained to age seven years, a typical day includes snow play, structured activities, and rest time for those who require a nap. The learn-to-ski Mites program is for two- to three-year-olds, and the Miners program teaches kids ages four through seven to ski through an innovative teaching system that lets your child move through a series of stations at his or her own pace while mastering the basics of balance and how to ride the lifts.

*B*ubba Bear Your whole family will want to meet Bubba Bear. Fuzzy, huggable Bubba stands 7 feet tall and can ski like an Olympic downhiller. Crested Butte's official mascot and comedian, Bubba Bear lives in an igloo near the Children's Ski Center. Kids are welcome to drop in to play with Bubba whenever he is at home. He also has a clubhouse on the deck of the Twister Warming House where he visits with children and fans during lunchtime.

Bubba Bear loves hanging out with kids and skiing Crested Butte Mountain Resort's slopes. Although he's a cuddly, lovable bear, it's not easy to keep up with him when he decides to hit the "Extreme Limits." On the steeps, Bubba is one "extreme" bear.

If you spend your Christmas holidays at the resort, you'll see Bubba in his Santa suit handing out candy canes to all skiers. You will also find Bubba in the gift shops on T-shirts and as Bubba-cloned stuffed animals.

Bubba's beginnings are somewhat of a mystery, but legend has it that during the installation of the Paradise high-speed quad lift, an engineer came upon a massive piece of ice. Being a conservative soul, he decided to drag the slab to the Paradise Warming House to be recycled into ice cubes for beverages.

As the ice began to melt, however, a magnificent polar bear slowly emerged, opened his eyes, and smiled from ear to ear when he spotted some children skiing nearby.

Bubba Bear makes skiing fun for kids. Through him, the resort hopes to entice more children to give skiing a try.

 LIFT TICKETS FOR A FAMILY BUDGET (ages 3 and up)
Crested Butte sets itself apart from the rest of the skiing resorts with its almost unbelievable deals.

Free LIFT TICKETS
You can't beat this! Crested Butte opens each ski season with a gift—free lift tickets until mid-December. Free—for everyone. And then they do it again to celebrate the end of the season— free lift tickets for the last two weeks. And during those weeks, they also offer $15 lessons to first-time skiers over age twelve. If you haven't started skiing yet, this could be the time.

KIDS PAY THEIR AGE

It's just what it says. With the purchase of one adult lift ticket, all your kids ages six to sixteen pay their age for their ticket—no strings attached. The offer is good all season.

TAG A LONG LESSONS

This program encourages parents to get involved. Parents ski along with their child and an instructor. After the lesson you'll know just how to help your child.

Where to Eat

Donita's Cantina. *332 Elk Avenue, Crested Butte 81224; (970) 349–6674.* Donita's serves dinner only, Wednesday through Monday, from 5:00 to 9:30 P.M. This is the best Mexican fare in town, perhaps for miles around. No reservations taken except for groups of twelve or more, so it's best to plan to dine early.

Where to Stay

Crested Butte Mountain Resort Properties. *(800) 544–8448; www. crestedbuttemountainresort.com.*

For More Information

Crested Butte Chamber of Commerce, *601 Elk Avenue, Crested Butte 81224; (970) 349–6438 or (800) 545–4505; www.crestedbuttechamber.com.*

Crested Butte Mountain Resort, *17 Emmons Loop, Mt. Crested Butte 81225; (800) 544–8448; www.crested butteresort.com.*

Delta

Known more for corn, potatoes, and onions than as a tourist destination, Delta is a relatively undiscovered stop for travelers. Located between Grand Mesa and the Uncompahgre Plateau are orchards, wineries, and miles of interesting back roads to explore. As you walk or drive around town, take note of the colorful murals depicting the area's history, ring bells from the collection at the Delta Museum, and stop for cinnamon rolls at the Amish bakery.

CONFLUENCE PARK (all ages)

At U.S. Highway 50 and State Highway 92. Open daily, dawn to dusk.

You'll all enjoy this 265-acre multirecreational park. Confluence Lake is regularly stocked and has a handicapped-accessible fishing dike. An island accessed by bridge, a sandy swim beach, an instructional pond for learning and practicing water sports, and picnic sites along the lake make this a popular summertime spot.

Many come for the pageants, concerts, dances, and theater productions in the amphitheater.

Let your kids out of the car for a quick break at the skateboard park. Or try the 5 miles of trails (all wheelchair and stroller accessible) that wind through the park along the Gunnison and Uncompahgre Rivers and Confluence Lake. Interpretive signs highlight the wildlife—beavers, eagles, and blue herons—along the way.

BILL HEDDLES RECREATION CENTER (all ages)

In Confluence Park; (970) 874–0923. Open daily year-round, Monday through Friday 6:00 A.M. to 9:30 P.M., Saturday 8:00 A.M. to 8:30 P.M., and Sunday noon to 5:30 P.M. $

Indoor swimming pool, therapeutic pool, tot pool—all great family attractions after an active day or if less-than-perfect weather keeps you inside. There's also a sauna, weight room, two gyms, racquetball courts, and a snack bar.

Where to Eat

Daveto's. *520 Main Street, Delta 81416; (970) 874–8277. Open Tuesday through Saturday for lunch and dinner.* Nothing fancy here, but the home-cooked Italian dishes are worth a stop. Try the white pizza. $

Where to Stay

The Fairlamb House Bed & Breakfast. *700 Leon Street, Delta 81416; (970) 874–5158.* John and Elizabeth graciously welcome families to their beautifully restored 1906 home. Enjoy cold lemonade, spicy salsa, and chips while your kids play in the fenced backyard. Resident dog Nori will want to join in. Breakfast includes just-out-of-the-oven muffins, fresh fruit, and Elizabeth's special pancakes. $

Telluride

The mountain town of Telluride, on State Highway 145, is a National Historic District and has a reputation for having a festival of some sort nearly every weekend throughout the summer. From bluegrass to jazz, hot-air ballooning to mountain biking, and wine to mushrooms, there always seems to be something to celebrate in Telluride. And for those who can find nothing to pay homage to, there is an annual "Nothing Festival" held in mid-July.

THE TELLURIDE GONDOLA (all ages)
(970) 728–2711. Open daily 7:00 A.M. to 12:00 P.M. **Free**.

"The g" is the only transportation system of its kind in North America. This high-speed gondola links the town of Telluride with the Mountain Village. It operates year-round and is absolutely **Free** to foot passengers. Ride it for transportation or ride just for fun—it takes twelve minutes. There are special cars for handicapped passengers and four-footed friends.

HISTORIC WALKING TOUR (all ages)
Downtown. **Free**.

Not as boring as it sounds, this is a self-guided walk through town. The walking tour is printed in the *Official Visitor's Guide,* available at the Visitors Center. Learn some history of this Victorian mining town and get oriented to today's Telluride. Along the way you'll pass the old town jail, which is now the library (stop in for story hour), and the infamous Butch Cassidy Robbery Site. Too bad it doesn't include Robert Redford!

Just **Hop On** Telluride operates a **Free** shuttle bus down its main street (Pacific Avenue) to the town gondola station and back every twelve minutes.

CLIMBING WALL (ages 3 and up)
Telluride Middle/High School; (970) 728–4377, extension 153. Open year-round, Tuesday and Thursday 6:30 to 10:00 P.M.; also Sunday during ski season.

When you feel like climbing the wall, here's an activity for the whole family. There's staff on duty for assistance, and equipment is provided.

TOWN PARK (all ages)

At the east end of Pacific Avenue; (970) 728–2173. **Free**.

Everything you'd ever want in a park and more! It's worth a stop for the playground alone, but there's also a stocked fishing pond; a skateboard ramp; tennis, volleyball, and basketball courts; and a nine-hole disc golf course. Two great hikes, the San Miguel River Trail and Bear Creek Trail, start here.

If you want to stay longer at the park, there are forty-seven campsites. They're on a first-come, first-served basis; no reservations accepted.

IMAGINATION STATION

This outstanding community-built playground lives up to its name. Your kids will have a ball here on great climbing equipment and swings installed on a soft base of wood chips. The design is one of a kind.

SWIMMING POOL

In Town Park. Open Memorial Day through Labor Day, Tuesday through Friday 1:00 to 5:30 P.M.; weekends 10:00 A.M. to 6:00 P.M. $

Lifeguards are on duty. Adult lap swim held twice daily.

VOODOO LOUNGE YOUTH AND TEEN CENTER (ages 6 and up)

233 East Pacific Avenue, Telluride 81435; (970) 728–0140. Open year-round, Tuesday through Saturday; hours vary with season. **Free**.

Basketball/in-line skate court, games, crafts, big-screen TV—this is the place for kids to hang out and meet new friends. Supervision provided, brought to you by the Town of Telluride. Ask about their special activities.

BRIDAL VEIL FALLS (all ages)

East of downtown.

Its 450-foot drop makes Bridal Veil the highest unbroken waterfall in Colorado. You can hike or bike 2 miles on Bear Creek Trail or drive. Parking at the base of the falls is limited.

The Telluride Visitors Services operates a **Free** guided shuttle tour to Bridal Veil Falls Monday through Friday. Call (970) 728–3041 for information.

HIKING AND BIKING (all ages)

For information call Norwood Ranger Station, (970) 327–4261. **Free**.

Wildflowers in mid-July and fall colors at September's end are the high points. Many trails can be accessed right from town. Telluride Ski

214

Area offers additional choices from the gondola at Station San Sophia. Maps are available at shops in town.

BEAR CREEK PRESERVE

Access the Bear Creek Trail here. At this 320-acre preserve, owned by the Town of Telluride, children ages five to twelve can earn their Junior Ranger Certificate. Take a hike with the Bear Creek Ranger, help with a project in the preserve, and complete the Bear Creek Activity Book.

SAN MIGUEL RIVER TRAIL

This unpaved trail follows the San Miguel River through town and along the valley floor. The easy path is popular with walkers, runners, bikers, and in-line skaters. Beavers, muskrats, and birds live along the willow-lined river.

GEOLOGY TOURS OF TELLURIDE (all ages)

(970) 728–3391. $$$$

Rock hammers provided; just bring a backpack and camera. Local geologists take visitors on one-and-one-half- to three-hour tours to unearth crystals and ore samples or visit ghost towns and learn mining history. Here's your chance to learn some geology without a textbook.

FARAWAY ADVENTURE PROGRAM (ages 5 and up)

Faraway Ranch, twenty-five minutes west of town on Wilson Mesa; (970) 728–9386; www.farawayranch.org. Open daily for full-day programs. $$$$

It's worth the price. This is one adventure your family will remember forever. The 55-foot Tower of Empowerment, the 35-foot Wave Wall, and the 40-foot giant pendulum swing are all part of the Challenge Course. See confidence levels soar as your family builds new skills together. The tower is closed during the snow season.

TELLURIDE WINTER

SKIING (ages 3 and up)

565 Mountain Village Boulevard, Telluride 81435; (970) 728–7533 or (800) 801–4832; www.telski.com. $$$$

Telluride is a full-service ski area. Children's ski lessons begin at three years old, snowboarding lessons at age seven. Child care (no skiing) is available for children two months to three years. All programs require reservations. Check on bargain family packages offered January through mid-February.

SLEDDING AND TUBING (all ages)

Town Park. Open daily, daytime only, weather permitting. **Free**.

Bring your own sled or tube to Firecracker Hill. If yours didn't fit in the suitcase, there's a hardware store in town that sells what you need.

 ICE-SKATING (all ages)

In Town Park and on Mountain Village Pond. Daily, until dark, December through February, weather permitting. **Free**.

Bring your own skates or rent them at local ski shops. There's a warming hut with a fireplace. Schedules are posted for evening hockey and broomball games. They're lots of fun to watch, but bundle up.

Local Flavor To give you a flavor of this town:

- Thirty-minute "Puppy Parking" is available in two locations downtown.

- Take it or leave it. The Free Box, across from the post office, functions as a clearinghouse for no-longer-needed items.

Where to Eat

Floradora's. *103 West Colorado, Telluride 81435; (970) 728–3888. Open daily for lunch and dinner.* Onion rings with chipotle catsup—don't leave town without trying 'em. Friendly, noisy atmosphere is just right for families. The wraps and other entrees are huge, so consider sharing. Then you'll have room for onion rings and dessert. Floradora's has been family operated for more than twenty years. The owners started out as dishwashers right here. $

Maggie's. *217 East Colorado, Telluride 81435; (970) 728–3334. Open daily for breakfast, lunch, and snacks.* Maggie's Bakery and Cafe starts serving at 7:00 A.M. Locals congregate here for fresh baked goods and gossip. It's informal; everyone shares tables. $

Where to Stay

Both the town and Mountain Village can accommodate families in hotels, inns, and condominiums, budget-minded to luxury. More than 95 percent are within 3 blocks of a lift or the gondola.

Central Reservations. *700 West Colorado Avenue, Telluride 81435; (970) 728–3041 or (888) 355–8743; www.visittelluride.com.*

Telluride Visitors Services. *(970) 728–3041.*

Ouray

Ouray, on U.S. Highway 550 northeast of Telluride, prides itself on being a family town. Founded in 1876, it was settled by miners and prospectors but was never a tent city. By 1886 it had a school, several churches, a hospital, a four-star hotel, a smattering of restaurants, and several hardware and clothing stores. The focus was on families then, and it still is.

Affectionately called "Switzerland of the Rockies" by locals, and rightly so, this charismatic mountain town is flanked by the rugged San Juan Mountains. Deer, elk, bears, and rabbits inhabit these once-sacred hunting grounds of the Ute Indians.

There's a children's and beginner's ski hill with a free rope tow on 3rd Avenue, at the south end of town. A favorite spot of local kids, it is open daily after school and on weekends and holidays at no charge. There also is a free sledding hill on 5th Street.

JEEPING (all ages)

(800) 228–1876 or (970) 325–4746; www.ouraycolorado.com. $$–$$$
Excursions aboard roofless, sideless jeeps provide thrilling adventures along narrow gravel roads to ghost towns at elevations of 8,000 feet and above, and even to the crest of the Continental Divide.

OURAY ICE PARK (ages 5 and up)

Located in town on the Camp Bird Mine Road. Phone Ouray Mt. Sports for information, (970) 325–4284. **Free.**
This park offers ice climbing and instruction, an advanced cross-country skiing course, hiking and snowshoeing trails, and wonderful wintertime photo opportunities.

IRONTON PARK X-COUNTRY SKI PARK (ages 5 and up)

Located south of town on U.S. Highway 550. **Free.**
You can bring your kids here to teach them to cross-country ski on the beginner's trails. Trails for more advanced skiers also are available. All at no charge.

OURAY HOT SPRINGS POOL AND PARK (all ages)

(970) 325–4638 or (800) 228–1876. Open daily 10:00 A.M. to 10:00 P.M. during summer; shorter hours during spring, fall, and winter. $–$$

Once a gathering place for the Ute Indians, who enjoyed their revitalization and healing powers as early as the fourteenth century, Ouray's natural hot springs are still providing enjoyment to those who come to swim or just soak away stress and pamper themselves. Channeled from deep beneath the San Juan Mountains, the hot springs water now fills this beautiful 250-foot-by-150-foot oval, with lap lanes, diving area, children's splash pool, and a 104-degree "hot tub" soaking section.

The bathhouse contains showers, hair dryers, a playpen and changing table for infants, and secure lockers. You can purchase a sandwich and beverage at the SnackHaus and browse in the gift shop. The fitness center has workout equipment and offers weight training and aerobics classes. The adjacent park features a running track, a playground, and picnic tables.

BACHELOR-SYRACUSE MINE TOUR (ages 6 and up)

Located on County Road 14, about a fifteen-minute drive from Ouray; (970) 325–0220. Open daily from mid-May to mid-September, 9:00 A.M. to 4:00 P.M.; open longer hours during the middle of summer. $$–$$$

If you've always wanted to go deep into a gold mine, here's your chance. You will board a mine train (called a "trammer") and travel a horizontal 3,350 feet into Gold Hill, accompanied by a thoroughly trained guide who more than likely once made his living mining at the Bachelor-Syracuse Mine. You will see rich veins of silver and other mineral deposits, visit the work areas to see how explosives are used (there are no explosives underground at this time), and hear the legends and lore of this very successful mine. Bring your camera (and your flash unit), because it's okay to take photographs. Take along a sweater or jacket, as the temperature within the mine is very cool.

Either before or after your mine tour, consider learning how to pan for gold and perhaps "strike it rich" in a stream that flows directly from the mine. An instructor will show you how the old-timers found many a gold nugget in this area. You can keep any gold that you find. The fee is $5.00 per person for a forty-five-minute session and includes use of a gold pan.

TREASURE CHEST GIFT SHOP

If your prospecting luck isn't so good, there are ore specimens from local mines and gold, silver, and gold-nugget jewelry for sale in the mine's Treasure Chest gift shop. Or if you want to strike out on your own following your gold-panning lesson and trial run, you can also purchase gold-panning supplies in the gift shop.

OUTDOOR CAFE
The Bachelor-Syracuse Mine's Outdoor Cafe serves reasonably priced breakfasts and barbecued lunch items. The cafe is open during mine-touring hours.

Where to Eat

Bon Ton Restaurant. *426 Main Street, Ouray 81427; (970) 325–4951 (also number for St. Elmo Hotel). Open year-round for dinner.* For that special night out, this is probably your very best choice. Terrific Italian and Continental cuisine, wonderfully prepared and beautifully presented. This is the perfect place for your children to put into action those good manners they've worked so hard on. $–$$$

The Outlaw. *(970) 325–4366. Reservations required. Open nightly "from when the snow melts to when the snow flies," which loosely translates to early June to late September.* For a memorable cookout, join the gang at the Outlaw for an evening of great food and congenial camaraderie beside a roaring canyon creek.

Your twelve-ounce rib-eye steak will be cooked over coals just the way you like it and served with fried potatoes, corn on the cob, baked beans, salad, and fresh-baked brown bread. All the while, your watermelon will be chilling in the stream. Following dinner, enjoy a mug of camp coffee while your kids toast marshmallows over the campfire. Guests are picked up between 5:30 and 6:00 P.M. at their hotels and motels and transported by four-wheel-drive vehicles to the Outlaw campsite. $$–$$$$

Timberline Deli. *803 Main Street, Ouray 81427; (970) 325–4958. Open daily year-round for lunch and dinner.* Serves sandwiches, soups, bagels, and desserts. $

Where to Stay

Alpenglow Condominiums. *215 5th Avenue, Ouray 81427; (970) 325–4664. Open year-round.* Offers one-, two-, and three-bedroom units with fully equipped kitchens, private decks, fireplaces, and cable TV. Off-season rates and package deals available. $$–$$$$

Ouray Victorian Inn. *50 3rd Avenue, Ouray 81427; (800) 846–8729.* This motel-style lodging has spacious rooms, two hot tubs, and a playground. Guests receive a free buffet breakfast during off-season (fall, winter, and spring). $$–$$$

For More Information

**Ouray Chamber Resort Associa-
tion,** P.O. Box 145, Ouray 81427;

*(970) 325–4746 or (800) 228–1876;
www.ouraycolorado.com.*

Silverton

Located south of Ouray on U.S. Highway 550 where it meets State Highway 110, the historic mining town of Silverton is so picturesque that it has been used as a setting for several motion pictures. Portions of *A Ticket to Tomahawk, Maverick Queen,* and *Across the Wide Missouri* were shot here. A walk through both the business and the residential districts reveals numerous structures and homes built in the 1880s.

CHRIST OF THE MINES SHRINE

The route to the Christ of the Mines Shrine is an easy walk, perfect for a picnic lunch hike. Beginning at the end of West 15th Street, southwest of town, the path is a gradual uphill climb. From the shrine you will have a wonderful panoramic view of Silverton.

The statue was constructed in Italy of Carrara marble and stands as a tribute to all those who worked the area mines. It also serves as a reminder of the town's mining heritage. Local volunteers built the alcove that houses the beautifully carved, twelve-ton figure of Christ.

OLD HUNDRED GOLD MINE TOUR (ages 6 and up)

From Silverton's courthouse take State Highway 110 east 4 miles to Howardsville. Turn right onto County Road 4 and go ¼ mile, then take the left fork up County Road 4-A for ¾ mile to the mine. Watch for blue-and-white mine-tour signs located along the way and at road forks starting ½ mile from Silverton on Highway 110; (800) 872–3009. Open daily mid-May through mid-October, 10:00 A.M. to 5:00 P.M. $$–$$$

A tour of this mine takes participants approximately ⅓ mile into the heart of Galena Mountain via a mine tram. Visitors don yellow slickers and white hard hats, travel to the Main Level Station, and then walk on level, gravel paths through well-lighted tunnels into the center of an actual gold vein. You will see a drilling demonstration performed by a miner using a hammer and steel and a "jackleg" air drill.

With the purchase of a tour ticket, your kids can pan for gold at no extra charge at the sluice box. They get to keep any gold they happen to find. Bring a lunch to eat in the covered picnic area. Drinks and snacks are available on the premises. The gift shop sells mine souvenirs, crystals, minerals, books, and postcards. The tour lasts approximately fifty minutes. Bring a jacket, because the underground temperature is a steady 48 degrees. Video and still cameras with flash are welcome. You'll no doubt want a photo of your children in their slickers and hard hats.

Where to Eat

Grand Imperial Hotel. *1219 Greene Street, Silverton 81433; (970) 387–5527.* This historic hotel, built in 1882, serves breakfast, lunch, and dinner year-round. A honky-tonk pianist entertains diners during summer months. $–$$

Where to Stay

Grand Imperial Hotel. *1219 Greene Street, Silverton 81433; (970) 387–5527.* Comfortable rooms in a variety of sizes; centrally located. $–$$$

For More Information

Silverton Chamber, *P.O. Box 565, Silverton 81433; (970) 387–5654 or (800) 752–4494; www.silverton.org.*

Durango

U.S. Highway 550 runs south into U.S. Highway 160 at Durango. This friendly town, with a population of approximately 16,000, makes an ideal jumping-off point for an almost endless number of family-oriented activities.

 ANIMAS VALLEY MUSEUM (all ages)
3065 West 2nd Avenue, Durango 81301; (970) 259–2402. Open mid-May through October, Monday through Saturday 10:00 A.M. to 6:00 P.M.; November to mid-May, Wednesday through Saturday 10:00 A.M. to 4:00 P.M. Minimal charge for adults. Children get in Free.

Kids can see what going to school was like in the late 1800s and early 1900s at this museum. They can also view a large collection of stuffed animals from that same era.

DURANGO & SILVERTON NARROW GAUGE RAILROAD (D&SNG) (all ages)

479 Main Avenue, Durango 81301; (970) 247–2733; www.durangotrain.com. Excursions are available year-round (except during November, when they make repairs) with numerous schedules. Phone for a brochure describing the various dates, times, and rates. Reservations are a must. $$$–$$$$

During your stay in Durango be sure to allow a full day to ride this vintage train through the spectacular San Juan Mountains from Durango to Silverton. Climb aboard one of the open or closed coaches for a three-hour journey to Silverton, two hours in town, and a three-hour ride back to Durango. Small kids, rocked to sleep by the swaying train, often snooze all the way back. You also have the option of either staying over in Silverton for the night and returning to Durango the following day or riding the train to Silverton and returning to Durango the same day by bus. During high season one train (with rest room) each day is equipped for wheelchairs. Keep in mind that this is a coal-fired steam train, so

End of the Trail North of Durango 3²⁄₅ miles, on the edge of the San Juan National Forest, is the Junction Creek Trailhead—official end of the Colorado Trail. For hikers completing the entire trek (more than 450 miles) from suburban Denver, it's a place for final pictures at the trail sign, crazed celebration, or retrospective contemplation.

you are likely to obtain a few black smudges before the day is over. It's best to wear washable, dark clothing. Especially if you choose to ride in the open cars, be sure everyone in your family has sunglasses, as much for protection from the occasional flying cinder as from the sun.

OUTLAW TOURS (all ages)

690 Main Avenue, Durango 81301; (970) 259–1800 or (877) 259–1800; www.outlawtours.com. Open year-round. $$$$

Enjoy superb mountain scenery while professional guides in specialized four-wheel-drive vehicles take you on a great adventure. Their combination jeep and train trip includes a van ride to the Silverton area, followed by four hours of jeeping to ghost towns and mines. They stop to do a little prospecting with the kids—"90 percent of the time we find rocks with silver or gold in them." Brunch is served along the way; then there's one and one-half hours of free time in Silverton before your return ride on the Durango & Silverton Narrow Gauge Railroad. Your kids may enjoy the train ride much more if it's only one-way.

Outlaw Tours also rents bicycles and will deliver you and the bikes (adult size, child size, carriers, and tagalongs) to a location that ensures that your ride is both scenic and downhill.

During winter months, take a sleigh ride or a tour on a snowmobile. They offer a one-hour ride, a two-hour lunch ride, and a dinner ride. Meals are served at their "cook-shack," accompanied by western entertainment.

DURANGO PRORODEO SERIES (all ages)

Located at the La Plata County Fairgrounds, 25th Street and Main Avenue, Durango 81301; (970) 946–2790. Mid-June to mid-August, Tuesday and Wednesday evening, 7:30 P.M. $–$$$

For rootin' tootin' buckin' bronco action, consider attending one of Durango's weekly summer rodeos. The Durango ProRodeo Series, a professional event sanctioned by the PRCA and the WPRA, features clowns, bull riders, trick riders, and a Wild West show. A barbecue at 6:00 P.M. precedes the rodeo. Cost for the barbecue ranges from $4.00 to $8.00 per person, depending on the items ordered.

COMMUNITY RECREATION CENTER (all ages)

2700 Main Avenue; (970) 375–7300. Open daily year-round, Monday through Friday 5:30 A.M. to 9:30 P.M., Saturday 8:00 A.M. to 8:00 P.M., and Sunday 8:00 A.M. to 6:00 P.M. $

This recreation center has a family emphasis, with a gym, lap pool, indoor track, racquetball, game room, climbing wall, cafe, and babysitting.

TRIMBLE HOT SPRINGS (all ages)

Off U.S. Highway 550 north; 6475 County Road 203, Durango 81301; (970) 247–0111; www.trimblehotsprings.com. Open daily 8:00 A.M. to 11:00 P.M. in summer, 9:00 A.M. to 10:00 P.M. in winter. Spa is open daily year-round, 9:00 A.M. to 9:00 P.M. $$

For extensive swimming and spa facilities, head for the Trimble Hot Springs. Here you will find an Olympic-size outdoor pool; a second, jetted outdoor pool; private indoor tubs; toddler gymnastics classes; and a picnic area with nicely landscaped grounds, tables, and a volleyball court.

They stay open late, so keep this in mind as an after-dinner activity. You'll all sleep well.

ROCKY MOUNTAIN CHOCOLATE FACTORY (all ages)

Make tour reservations, pick up tickets, and get directions at the downtown store; 561 Main Avenue, Durango 81301; (970) 259–1408. Days and hours vary. **Free**.

A thirty-minute tour of the Rocky Mountain Chocolate Factory is guaranteed to be a "sweet" stop. Sporting hairnets and safety goggles, you'll tour the production floor and pass copper kettles bubbling with English toffee, caramels cooling on marble slab tables, and rows of creamy centers heading for the chocolate waterfall. In the "Lucy Line," the finished product is weighed and packaged. Of course, you'll get to taste, and there is a gift shop filled with factory-fresh products.

 DIAMOND CIRCLE MELODRAMA (ages 5 and up)

In the Historic Strater Hotel, 699 Main Avenue, Durango 81301; (970) 247–3400. Early June through late September, nightly except Sunday. $$$

Families enjoy a fun-filled evening of vaudeville and Victorian melodrama. Order a big bowl of popcorn and beverages before you sit back to enjoy the show. Ragtime piano warms up the audience before the curtain rises. Practice hissing and booing the villain, and long swooning "ahhhhhhhs" for the handsome hero. A revue of skits, songs, and lively dance wraps up the performance. Kids enjoy seeing their waiter or waitress on stage and meeting the cast in the lobby after the show.

Where to Eat

Carver's. *1022 Main Avenue, Durango 81301; (970) 259–2545. Open Monday through Saturday, breakfast through dinner; Sunday, breakfast until 1:00 P.M.* Local vote says this is the best breakfast and bakery in town, and I concur. Bet you can't leave without buying a loaf of bread! Besides outstanding A.M. food, there's homemade soup, and Carver's is also a microbrewery. This is a good choice any time of the day. Weekend breakfast draws a crowd. Bring your sack of toys. $

Gazpacho. *431 East 2nd Avenue, Durango 81301; (970) 259–9494. Open daily for dinner, also for lunch Monday through Saturday.* Brightly colored furniture and Mexican folk art decorate the rooms of this multilevel restaurant. Steaming hot platters of smothered burritos, enchiladas, and stuffed sopapillas satisfy even hungry teens. $

Ken and Sue's Place. *636 Main Avenue, Durango 81301; (970) 259–2616. Open for lunch and dinner daily.* Ken and Sue understand what it's like dining with children—they have two preschoolers. A graduate of the Culinary Institute of America, Ken dishes up New American cuisine with a flair—

meat loaf with shiitake mushroom gravy, chipotle-honey glazed steak, or grilled tuna and oriental vegetables in Thai peanut sauce. Kids love his special twist on macaroni and cheese. The shaded patio is a popular summertime dining spot. $$

Mama's Boy. *27th Street and Main Avenue; (970) 247–0060. Open daily for dinner. Also at 550 North Hermosa; (970) 247–9053. Open Monday through Saturday for dinner.* You'll find New York–style Italian cooking here. "Delizioso!" is the recommendation of Fort Lewis College students and their families. Traditional choices, daily specials, and tempting desserts are authentic, ample, and awesome. $

Olde Tymer's Cafe. *1000 Main Avenue, Durango 81301; (970) 259–2990. Open for lunch and dinner.* They never alter their menu much. "We're a locals' place, and we know the traditions of Olde Tymer's should remain." Those traditions include Durango's best burger. You can also enjoy soups, salads, New Mexican green chili, and daily specials. $

Seasons. *764 Main Avenue, Durango 81301; (970) 382–9790. Open daily for dinner, Monday through Friday for lunch.* If your family is ready for a slightly more upscale dinner, Seasons is a great choice. Creative menu, delicious dining. The staff is very family friendly. $$

Where to Stay

Leland House. *721 East 2nd Avenue, Durango 81301; (800) 664–1920.* This inn nicely accommodates families. Its six attractive suites with small kitchens, private baths, bedrooms for parents, and living rooms with sofa sleepers for children are perfect for families that want to pack picnic lunches, heat baby bottles, and indulge in bedtime snacks. The Leland House is conveniently located close to shopping, restaurants, and the Durango & Silverton Narrow Gauge Railroad station. A complimentary breakfast is served across the street at the Leland House's sister inn, the Rochester Hotel. The morning repast includes fresh fruit, cranberry-raisin scones, and an entree such as Southwest Scramble, a combination of scrambled eggs, red peppers, black beans, sauteed corn, green chilies, and sausage topped with homemade salsa and served with flour tortillas and hashbrown potatoes. $$–$$$$

Strater Hotel. *699 Main Avenue, Durango 81301; (970) 247–4431 or (800) 247–4431; www.strater.com.* You'll get an automatic history lesson along with comfortable rooms in a great location. This Victorian-era hotel combines period decor with modern amenities. Be sure to check out the saloon. $$–$$$$

For More Information

Durango Area Chamber Resort Association, *Box 2587, Durango 81302; (970) 247–0312; www.durango.org.*

Purgatory/Durango Ski Area

Located 25 miles north of Durango, this ski area offers both summer and winter activities. Before the snow flies, your children age four or younger can ride the ponies. All your kids will enjoy Adventure Park with its miner's cabin and enchanting maze. Other activities and attractions include horseback riding, a volleyball court, horseshoe pits, a trout-fishing pond, an alpine slide, miniature golf, and mountain biking.

During the winter months this ski resort doesn't attract many glitzy, designer-tog types. Perhaps that's because it is so down-home friendly. The family-oriented resort receives an average of 300 inches of dry powder snow and many days of sunshine each year, resulting in outstanding skiing. It has a vertical drop of 2,029 feet and a good mix of novice, intermediate, and expert runs. You will find child care for youngsters ages two through twelve; ski lessons, plus day care when appropriate, are available for children ages three or older.

The Purgatory Ski Touring Center, located across the street from the resort, features touring and telemark lessons on more than 15 kilometers of groomed trails. Rental equipment is available. There is a nominal trail fee.

For More Information

Purgatory/Durango Ski Area, *(970) 247–9000; www.durangomountainresort. com.*

Mancos

"Where the Old West is Alive and Kickin' "—that's the town's slogan. Mosey up and down dusty Main Street; poke in the stores and shops. You are apt to see a couple of real cowboys, and you might even see a wainwright at work. It's all authentic.

MANCOS VALLEY STAGE LINE (all ages)

4550 County Road 41, Mancos 81328; (970) 533–9857 or (800) 365–3530. Go south on Main Street through Mancos, continue south 4 miles (road becomes County Road 41). $$$$, family rates available.

Ride through a secluded canyon in the first-class style of the 1860s—a stagecoach. As you roll along in the shadow of Mesa Verde National

Park, your kids will get a vivid picture of life one hundred years ago. The three-and-one-half-hour tour includes a stop at Native American ruins and lunch at a log cabin. One-hour rides are also available. Allow time to look at the collection of antique coaches and wagons.

 RIMROCK OUTFITTERS AT ECHO BASIN RANCH (ages 5 and up)
12175 County Road 44, Mancos 81328; (970) 533–7588. $$$–$$$$

This is the place to do cowboy things—breakfast rides or dinner rides on horseback or hay wagon, one- to four-hour rides, or all-day trail rides. Perry Lewis and his Rimrock Outfitters are based at Echo Basin Guest Ranch, 8,000 feet high in the LaPlata Mountains. Gentle horses, good grub, singing around a campfire—be Roy Rogers for an evening! When the snow flies, bundle up in your hats, coats, and snuggies, and hop aboard one of the ranch's nifty sleighs.

Read 'em Cowpoke Here's an entertaining, educational children's book that both sons and daughters can relate to: *Yipee-Yay: A Book about Cowboys and Cowgirls* by Gail Gibbons.

Cortez

Continue west 17 miles from Mancos on U.S. Highway 160 to its junction with U.S. Highway 666 to reach the historic city of Cortez.

Known as the "Archaeological Center of the United States," Cortez sits on the edge of the high Sonoran Desert surrounded by villages once occupied by the Ancient Pueblo People, who dominated the Four Corners area (where Colorado, Utah, Arizona, and New Mexico meet).

Long before the Spanish explorers discovered this region, the Ancient Pueblo People carved entire communities into the sandstone cliffs and along the mesas. Their culture was present until about the year A.D. 1300, when the Ancient Pueblo People suddenly disappeared from the area.

 MESA VERDE NATIONAL PARK (all ages)
P.O. Box 8, Mesa Verde 81330; off U.S. Highway 160, 7 miles east of Cortez;
 (970) 529–5036 or (970) 529–4631; www.mesaverde.national-park.com.
Open daily year-round; camping, lodging, and gasoline available seasonally. Most of

the ruins are inaccessible during winter months. Phone for information regarding schedules, rates, weather, and road conditions. $$ per car. Balcony House and Cliff Palace tours, $.

At Mesa Verde National Park you can see some of the world's largest, best-preserved cliff dwellings, including Cliff Palace and Balcony House. Be sure, however, to stop at the Far View Visitors Center (located within the park, 15 miles from the entry gate) to pick up your entry ticket, or you won't be allowed to enter the ruins. Obtain a map here, too, so that you can plan your exploration.

Cliff Palace, the largest cliff dwelling in the world, is reached via a ½-mile hike. Balcony House requires a bit of determination to reach, as it is located high up in the cliff. To explore this ruin you must climb 20-foot ladders and crawl through a small tunnel to gain access. Take heart, though. If you aren't into strenuous exercise, or if you have small children who can't maneuver ladders and rough trails, you can visit the many surface ruins or take the short walk that leads from the museum at Chapin Mesa Cliff Dwellings and Park Headquarters to Spruce Tree House in the canyon below. Here you can enter an excavated kiva to imagine the religious ceremonies that once took place inside this structure.

There are many possible routes to take throughout the park and numerous dwellings to explore, some with multiple rooms and chambers. Allow plenty of time for this adventure. There is so much to see here.

UTE MOUNTAIN UTE TRIBAL PARK (ages 6 and up)
On U.S. Highways 160/666, 20 miles south of Cortez; (970) 565–9653 or (800) 847–5485. Open year-round, weather permitting; reservations required. $$$$

The Ute Mountain Tribal Park encompasses approximately 125,000 acres and is part of the Ute Mountain Ute Indian Reservation. The tribe has set aside an area on their reserve for the preservation of the Ancient Pueblo People culture. Hundreds of cliff dwellings and surface ruins plus historic Ute wall paintings and ancient petroglyphs exist here. Many of the dwellings compare in size and complexity with those in Mesa Verde, and a select number of these have been stabilized for visitation. In order to protect this fragile environment, the park is accessible by guided tour only.

The park is operated as a primitive area, so there are no food, lodging, or other services available. Full- and half-day tours begin at Tribal Park Headquarters. One- to four-day mountain bike and backpacking trips also can be arranged.

This attraction is best suited for families with older children because the park can be a physically challenging experience, with several long ladders to descend and vigorous climbs necessary to reach some of the ruins. You may use your own car for transportation or pay an extra $5.00 per person for transport via van. Be sure the tank is full, because the main ruins are 40 miles off the paved roads. Tours are to remote areas, so bring adequate water, food, and comfortable clothing.

CORTEZ CULTURAL CENTER & MUSEUM (all ages)

25 North Market Street, Cortez 81321; (970) 565–1151; www.fone.net. cucenter. Center open year-round; dances daily (rain or shine), Memorial Day to Labor Day, 7:30 P.M.; cultural program at 8:30 P.M. Free.

On summer evenings in Cortez, the pulsating beat of Native American drums draws tourists to the dance ring a block north of downtown. Native American families in handmade dance regalia share their heritage, traditions, and stories. Your family can join travelers from around the world in the Friendship Dance.

After the dances, move inside for storytelling or demonstrations by sand painters or pottery artists. If you arrive a little early, walk through the museum and exhibits. The gift shop here has items affordable to youngsters' allowances.

NOTAH DINEH TRADING COMPANY AND MUSEUM (ages 6 and up)

345 West Main Street, Cortez 81321; (970) 565–9607 or (800) 444–2024; subee.com/nd/home.html. Open year-round, Monday through Saturday 9:00 A.M. to 6:30 P.M. Free admission.

An excellent selection of authentic Native American jewelry, pottery, and Navajo rugs is featured in this spacious gallery. Shelves encircling the sales floor hold an outstanding beaded-basket collection. (Items are very expensive, so you might want to have that "don't touch" discussion before entering the store.) Downstairs, the highlight of the museum is a 12-by-18-foot rug, one of the largest known Two Grey Hill weavings. More interesting to youngsters is the depiction of an early trading post with lots of artifacts to identify.

ANASAZI HERITAGE CENTER

On State Highway 184, 10 miles north of Cortez and 7 miles south of the town of Dolores; (970) 882–4811; www.co.blm.gov/ahc/hmepge.htm. Open daily year-round, 9:00 A.M. to 5:00 P.M. $

This center contains one of the world's major collections of artifacts that once belonged to the Ancient Pueblo People. Set into the hillside near the twelfth-century Dominguez and Escalante ruins, the facility includes a large exhibit hall, a 104-seat theater, a gift shop, and a gallery for temporary exhibits. Area archaeologists suggest that an introductory visit here will enrich your Mesa Verde experience.

View an entertaining orientation film, then head to the interactive exhibits. Use a floor weaving loom, microscopes, and computer stations. Make new discoveries at the "Touch me" drawers. Grind just a handful of corn with a metate to understand the effort required to feed a family. Try your skill at tree-ring dating or microanalysis of pottery shards.

A ½-mile walk takes you up the hill to the Dominguez and Escalante ruins. The paved path is handicapped accessible, but assistance is advised due to the trail's steepness. Along the way, signs identify native plants and their uses. A self-guiding booklet is available. Shaded tables make this a good picnic spot.

A Goat's Tale Set in the Southwest, this delightful story explains the process of rug making to children. Geraldine the Goat tells her own tale in *The Goat in the Rug*, by Geraldine (as told to Charles Blood and Martin Link).

LOWRY PUEBLO RUINS (all ages)

From U.S. Highway 666 at Pleasant View (20 miles north of Cortez), follow signs 9 miles west. Open daily, weather permitting. Free.

A country road, passing hay fields and row upon row of pinto beans growing in the rich red earth, leads away from crowds and organized tours to ruins in a different setting. There are no cliffs here. Structures sit atop a knoll with views extending into neighboring states. Inhabitants grew crops of corn, beans, squash, and tobacco; hunted small game; and made tools from animal bones. Skilled stoneworkers built a community of forty rooms and eight kivas (ceremonial chambers). The Great Kiva is one of the largest ever discovered. In the Painted Kiva you'll find ancient plastered walls decorated in bold designs. There is no museum or rangers on site; self-guiding booklets are available near the ruins. Facilities include picnic tables, fire pits, and latrines.

"ARCHAEOLOGY DETOUR" (ages 5 and up)
Crow Canyon Archaeological Center, 23390 Road K, Cortez 81321; (970) 565–8975 or (800) 422–8975; www.crowcanyon.org. All-day program offered June through August, Wednesday and Thursday. $$$$

Come here first, then go to Mesa Verde. In this one-day workshop for families, you'll learn about the Ancient Pueblo People who lived in this area hundreds of years ago. Spend a half day at an active excavation, learning by walking through the site and talking to archaeologists. You'll be ready for the great lunch waiting back at Crow Canyon Center. In the afternoon you'll learn how to think like an archaeologist through hands-on activities. Then tour their lab and visit the Curation Room to see artifacts previously excavated by Crow Canyon staff. When the day is done, you'll agree with them, "It's not what you find, it's what you find out."

> ## Four Corners Monument
> Tourists drive 40 miles into the high desert just to take a photo at this location. Here is the only place in America where four states—Colorado, Utah, Arizona, and New Mexico—meet. Watching as photographers arrange their family in all four states can be pretty entertaining. Native Americans from the area sell souvenirs, art, and snacks.

"Archaeology Detour" requires advance registration of at least one day, preferably one week.

Crow Canyon Archaeology Center is a nonprofit organization dedicated to research and education. They also offer weeklong Family Archaeology Adventures for moms and dads with teens. In addition, their staff leads Family Travel Adventures in the Four Corners region, and they operate a very popular program for school groups.

Where to Eat

Francisca's. *125 East Main Street, Cortez 81321; (970) 565–4093. Open Tuesday through Saturday for dinner, Thursday and Friday for lunch and dinner.* Features northern New Mexican–style dishes freshly prepared. Try the sopaillas served with local honey. $

Main Street Brewery & Restaurant. *21 East Main Street, Cortez 81321; (970) 564–9112. Open daily for dinner.* A relaxed western atmosphere, family-size booths, good service, and a game room for kids accompanied by an adult. A wide-ranging menu offers items from traditional sandwiches to bratwurst burritos. Warm apple strudel salutes the owner's German heritage. $

Nero's. *303 West Main Street, Cortez 81321; (970) 565–7366. Open daily for dinner.* Full Italian menu with nightly specials. Enjoy summertime covered-patio dining. $–$$

Quality Book Store and Earth Song Haven Tea Room. *34 West Main Street,* *Cortez 81321; (970) 565–9125. Open daily for breakfast, lunch, and desserts.* The breakfast menu, available all day, includes a dozen pancake choices, waffles, crepes, and quiches in addition to traditional bacon and eggs. Daily specials include vegetarian selections, homemade soups, and desserts. While you wait for your order, check out the excellent selection of books, especially regional titles, for all ages. $

Where to Stay

Lebanon Schoolhouse B&B. *24925 County Road T, Dolores 81323; (970) 882–4461; www.lebanonschoolhouse.com; 7 miles north of Cortez.* This fully restored 1907 schoolhouse makes a great base for family adventure in the Four Corners area. Children especially enjoy the two bedrooms with sleeping lofts. Common areas include games, puzzles, a large selection of books, television and video library, and an antique pool table. Guests have kitchen privileges, and a full breakfast is included. Outside, the original schoolyard merry-go-round awaits a spin from energetic youngsters. You can walk to the nearby llama ranch. $$–$$$

For More Information

Cortez Area Chamber of Commerce, *928 East Main Street, Cortez 81321; (970) 565–3414.* The center is open daily, May through September, 8:00 A.M. to 6:00 P.M.; October through April, 8:00 A.M. to 5:00 P.M.

Or call **Mesa Verde Country Visitor Information Bureau,** *(800) 253–1616; www.swcolo.org.*

Bayfield

Heading east from Durango, U.S. Highway 160 leads to the small community of Bayfield.

VALLECITO LAKE
15 miles north of Bayfield on County Road 501, off U.S. Highway 160; (970) 247–1573.

If you ask Coloradans where Vallecito Lake is, more than a few would have to admit that they don't know. Yet this beautiful mountain lake is easily accessed. With snow-capped mountains in the distance and surrounded by forests, dude ranches, lodges, and campgrounds, the secluded lake and valley offer an abundance of outdoor enjoyment: hiking, boating, four-wheeling, horseback riding, and just plain relaxing. As for fishing, Vallecito Lake holds the state record for northern pike—thirty pounds, one ounce, 48¼ inches. It formerly held the state record for German brown trout—twenty-four pounds, ten ounces, and 37½ inches. Full-service marinas can provide you with boats, motors, and bait.

 SAWMILL POINT LODGE

14737 County Road 501, Bayfield 81122; (970) 884–2669; located on Lake Vallecito. Open year-round. $–$$$$

This lodge is an ideal place to spend a few days, a week, or more. Here you can rent a one-, two-, or three-bedroom cabin that will nicely accommodate just about any size family.

The lodge also has motel-like rooms with kitchenettes. These accommodations will sleep from one to five persons. Also available are apartments that sleep from six to ten people. The main lodge overlooks the lake marinas.

Chimney Rock

If you continue east from Bayfield on U.S. Highway 160, you will arrive in Chimney Rock.

CHIMNEY ROCK ARCHAEOLOGICAL AREA (ages 6 and up)

All tours originate at the entrance cabin located 5 miles east of Chimney Rock on U.S. Highway 160, then 3 miles south on State Highway 151; (970) 883–5359; www.chimneyrockco.org. Open mid-May through September. Tours depart at 9:30 and 10:30 A.M. and 1:00 and 2:00 P.M. $

The mystical Chimney Rock Archaeological Area has long served as a landmark—first to missionaries, conquistadores, and prospectors and now to those seeking to view the ruins left by the Ancient Pueblo People and Chacoan residents who are thought to have lived here in the eleventh century. The high mesa site includes sixteen excavated areas. The High Mesa Village and the pueblo encompass structures that have been completely excavated and others whose treasures have only been partially unearthed. Some 200 other ruins exist throughout the 6 square miles of the Archaeological Area.

The site management tries to schedule Hopi dance performances and a Primitive Arts Festival each summer. In addition, they attempt to arrange evening full-moon tours during June, July, and August. Phone for exact dates and times.

The Chimney Rock tours are open for guided ventures only. They are led by members of the San Juan Mountains Association, Pagosa Chapter, a nonprofit volunteer group dedicated to promoting the interpretation and protection of priceless natural and cultural resources. No reservations are required for the daytime visits, but they are necessary for the evening full-moon tours.

Monte Vista

Monte Vista lies along U.S. Highway 160 at the intersection of State Highway 15.

Where to Stay

Best Western Movie Manor Motor Inn. *2830 West Highway 160 (2½ miles west of Monte Vista), Monte Vista 81144; (719) 852–5921. Open year-round, but movies are shown only from mid-May to mid-September.* If you are traveling between Chimney Rock and Alamosa, plan to spend the night in the world's only movie motel. Most of the guest rooms have picture windows that face a giant outdoor movie screen. While a few dedicated drive-in moviegoers insist on watching the film from their cars, you can stock up on popcorn from the snack bar, return to your room, prop yourselves up on bed pillows, turn up the sound on the built-in speakers, and watch the latest release. Kids bathed and already in their pajamas can nod off to sleep whenever they are ready. If the movie playing doesn't happen to be suitable for children, just pull your drapes and turn on the TV. $–$$

Alamosa

U.S. Highway 160 joins U.S. Highway 285 at Monte Vista and leads east to Alamosa.

SPLASHLAND HOT SPRINGS (all ages)

 Located 1 mile north of Alamosa on State Highway 17; (719) 589–6307. Open mid-May through September, 10:00 A.M. to 8:00 P.M. Open rest of year from noon to 6:00 P.M. Closed Wednesday year-round. $

This fun-filled complex features a geothermal-water outdoor swimming pool, a diving area, and a wading pool for toddlers. A concession stand sells snacks and beverages, and you can rent swimsuits and towels if you didn't bring them along or if you don't want to pack wet suits and towels back into the car.

ALAMOSA/MONTE VISTA NATIONAL WILDLIFE REFUGE (all ages)

Located 4 miles east of Alamosa on U.S. Highway 160 and then 2 miles south to El Rancho Lane; (719) 589–4021. Refuge is open daily year-round, sunrise to sunset. Headquarters building open year-round, Monday through Friday, usually from 7:30 A.M. to 5:00 P.M. **Free**.

The Bluff Overlook is open to the public and offers outstanding wildlife and wildlands viewing. Here you might see raptors, waterfowl, wading birds and shorebirds, sandhill and whooping cranes, and an occasional deer or elk. Early spring (mid-February to the end of March) would be the best time to view cranes and waterfowl, late April through summer to see wading birds and shorebirds, late September to hit the fall crane and waterfowl migration, and winter (November through February) to witness eagles. The headquarters building provides information and exhibits.

COLORADO ALLIGATOR FARM (all ages)

Located 17 miles north of Alamosa on State Highway 17, 9162 County Road 9, Mosca 81146; (719) 378–2612; www.gatorfarm.com. Open daily June through August, 7:00 A.M. to 7:00 P.M.; September through May, 9:00 A.M. to 5:00 P.M. $, children 5 and younger **Free**.

Alligators in Colorado, at 7,600 feet above sea level, in one of the coldest regions of the state? You bet. More than eighty alligators and millions of fish live at the Colorado Alligator Farm in southwestern Colorado's San Luis Valley. Ah, but you don't have to worry about these gators. They truly have it made. They lounge in an outdoor pen with a geothermal-heated pool kept at eighty-seven degrees, which makes it possible for the alligators to survive the cold winters. They gorge themselves on 300 to 400 pounds of fish parts each day. Happier alligators would be hard to find.

Brought to Colorado as 1-foot-long babies more than ten years ago, the gators were the ingenious idea of Erwin Young, owner of a fish-processing plant. He hoped they would be the answer to the disposal of tons of fish heads, bones, and by-products left over from his fish farm—and he was right.

Approximately 30,000 visitors tour the farm each year. Whole busloads of school kids come from several surrounding states to see the critters.

Besides alligators you will see thousands of Rocky Mountain white tilapia (a hybrid tropical perch), catfish, bass, and other species swimming in indoor and outdoor ponds. Plan to stay for several hours when you visit. You can enjoy warm-water fishing for largemouth bass, catfish, and tilapia, a picnic area, a gift shop, and several nature trails.

GREAT SAND DUNES NATIONAL PARK (all ages)

Located 38 miles northeast of Alamosa on State Highway 150; (719) 378–2312; www.nps.gov/grsa. The sand dunes are accessible year-round, twenty-four hours a day. The visitors center is open daily 9:00 A.M. to 6:00 P.M. Camping available year-round at $10 per site, per night. Access to the national park is Free *for those age 16 or younger. $*

"How far away is the beach?" is the question frequently asked of attendants at the National Park Service visitors center at the Great Sand Dunes National Park. No, there's no surf for swimming near these windswept masses that sometimes rise to heights of 700 feet, making them the tallest sand dunes in North America. And there isn't any snow, although often there are skiers at the sand dunes. Bring your old (very old) skis, join the hearty individuals who don't mind sand in their hair and down their necks when they lose their balance, and glide down the surface of dunes several hundred feet high. Keep in mind that it takes a lot of effort to ascend this "mountain." There are no lifts, and for every step you take, you seem to slide two steps backward on the soft sand. Don't have any old skis that you want sandpapered by this shifting "surf"? Not to worry. Stop at a grocery store in Alamosa and pick up some large boxes to construct makeshift sleds. Hang on tight to the edges of your cardboard sled and scoot down the dunes. Your kids will love this unique experience. Or just let them run, jump, roll, and slide on these ever-changing sand sculptures.

Stop at the visitors center for information on the dunes and other park features. You can obtain brochures, books, and maps here, and rangers will help you plan your visit. If you don't have much time, you can take a short hike along the Montvill Nature Trail or the Wellington Ditch Trail or have a picnic in the picnic area. If you have two to three hours, you might want to try hiking to the top of the highest dune, splash in Medano Creek, or take a ranger-guided hike. You can even spend the night on the dunes if you first obtain a free permit from the visitors center. Those intending to camp should be advised that the eighty-eight sites are first-come, first-served. They have drinking water and flush toilets but no shower facilities. Firewood is for sale at the visitors center.

Antonito

If you head south from Alamosa on U.S. Highway 285, almost to the Colorado and New Mexico border, you will reach the small town of Antonito.

CUMBRES & TOLTEC SCENIC RAILROAD (all ages)

(505) 756–2151; www.cumbrestoltec.com. Open daily Memorial Day through mid-October, with varying departure times. $$$–$$$$
    This historic excursion train travels from Antonito to Chama, New Mexico, and back. A Registered National Historic Site, the coal-fired, steam-powered train zigzags back and forth across the Colorado and New Mexico border, taking passengers over 10,015-foot Cumbres Pass, through two tunnels, and along the Toltec Gorge, which plunges 600 feet to the Los Pinos River. The Cumbres & Toltec operates the longest and highest narrow-gauge steam railroad excursion in the United States. It runs on a 64-mile segment of track built by the Denver & Rio Grande Railroad from 1875 to 1883. The line's original purpose was to carry passengers and mining supplies into the Silverton area and to bring the silver and gold out. It also carried lumber, livestock, and agricultural products originating at different points along the right-of-way.
    Passengers are taken aboard at either Antonito or Chama to ride to Osier, Colorado, for lunch. They then return to their departure points by train, or they can take the complete trip between Antonito and Chama (or vice versa) and return to their starting point via air-conditioned bus. Phone for a brochure listing a timetable, ride options, and current fares. Reservations are recommended.

Where to Stay

Conejos River Ranch. *P.O. Box 175, Conejos 81129; (719) 376–2464; www.conejosranch.com. Located 14 miles west of Antonito on State Highway 17.* This ranch is the perfect home base for those wanting to ride the Cumbres & Toltec train. In fact, ranch manager Ms. "Shorty" Fry is an agent for the train and can make all the arrangements for your rail journey.
    The ranch consists of eight bed-and-breakfast rooms in the main lodge

and six one-, two-, and three-bedroom housekeeping cabins. The Conejos River runs through the property, and the Rio Grande National Forest surrounds it. Nearby activities include hiking, horseback riding, wildlife viewing, snowmobiling, cross-country skiing, and, of course, the narrow-gauge train ride. Kids delight in fishing from the stocked children's pond and feeding the ranch goats, sheep, and horse. Shorty shares the story about one little girl who began to cry the night before her family was to depart the ranch. When asked what was the matter, the little girl replied, "Tomorrow we have to leave here and go to Disney World." How's that for a testimonial?

The ranch is open from May through December. A two-night minimum stay is required. The restaurant serves dinner seven nights a week at a reasonable cost. B&B accommodations, including breakfast, $$; cabins, $$-$$$.

San Luis

The small town of San Luis is accessible from Antonito by traveling north on U.S. Highway 285 and then turning east onto State Highway 142, which ends in San Luis. From Alamosa head east on U.S. Highway 160 and then turn south at Fort Garland onto State Highway 159 and continue for about 16 miles.

Established in 1851, the small village of San Luis is said to be Colorado's oldest town. Centered around the beautiful Sangre de Cristo Parish Church, the community reflects a laid-back way of life.

La Mesa de la Piedad y de la Misericordia
(Hill of Piety and Mercy)

Located on top of a mesa in San Luis is a series of stations of the cross depicting the last hours of Christ's life. Also included is a fifteenth station, representing the resurrection. The dramatic bronze sculptures found at each station were created by area resident Huberto Maestas, who has a studio in nearby San Pablo. For more information call (719) 672-3002. Free.

Where to Eat

Fabian's Cafe and Deli. *Located on Main Street, 3 blocks from Casa de Salazar; P.O. Box 10, San Luis 81152; (719) 672-0322. Breakfast and lunch served until 3:00 P.M. For wonderful Mexican food served* in a relaxed atmosphere, stop by this family-owned restaurant. The friendly, spotlessly clean cafe serves a terrific breakfast burrito with homemade, full-flavored, yet not *too* hot green chili. $

Where to Stay

Casa de Salazar. *603 Main Street, P.O. Box 674, San Luis 81152; (719) 672–3608.* Children are welcome at this circa-1906 bed-and-breakfast. The three guest rooms all have private baths, and a complimentary full breakfast is served each morning. $–$$

El Convento Bed & Breakfast. *512 Church Place, San Luis 81152; (719) 672–4223. Open year-round.* This bed-and-breakfast has four guest rooms, two with kiva fireplaces and all with private baths. $$

Southwestern Colorado Annual Events

JUNE

Spanish Fiesta. *(970) 264–2360; www.pagosa.com; mid-June.* Pagosa Springs throbs with the spirited music of mariachi bands during this celebration. Festivities include a community sidewalk breakfast, folkloric dancing, a children's parade and piñata party, a classic car show, and a grand parade.

Fat Tire Bike Week. *(970) 349–6438; late June.* During this festive celebration, Crested Butte hosts NORBA-sanctioned races, clinics, daily backcountry tours, bike polo, bicycle rodeo, and much more.

JULY

Cattlemen's Days. *(970) 641–1501; www.gunnisonchamber.com; mid-July.* Gunnison's annual Cattlemen's Days festival is said to be the oldest rodeo in the state. From horse, cattle, sheep, and swine shows to rodeos, a parade, a carnival, barbecues, and a hamburger fry, the activities are nonstop for the five-day celebration.

SEPTEMBER

Annual Southern Ute Tribal Fair. *(970) 563–0119; mid-September.* One of the oldest events of its kind, this fair is held on the Southern Ute Indian Reservation at Ignacio, on U.S. Highway 160, southeast of Durango. Powwows, with traditional dancing and drumming, are held daily. Most events are designated for Native American participants only, but a few are open to everyone. All are accessible for viewing. When you browse the craft and food booths, watch for fry-bread vendors. Fresh, hot fry-bread is delicious.

General Index

M

N

T

Table Mountain Inn, 52
Tabor Opera House, 177
Tattered Cover Book Store, 25
Telluride, 213–17
Telluride Central Reservations, 217
Telluride Ski Resort, 215
Telluride Visitors Services, 217
Timberline Deli, 219
Tiny Town, 44
Town Park (Telluride), 214
Trail Ridge Road, 80
Trail Ridge Store, 80
Trail through Time, 199
Trailhead of the Colorado Trail, 44
Travelodge, 96
Trimble Hot Springs, 223
Trinidad–Las Animas County Chamber
  of Commerce, 133
Trout Haven, 72
Two Below Zero, 173

U

United States Air Force Academy, 101
University of Colorado, 56–58
Ute Mountain Ute Tribal Park, 228

V

Vail, 180–89
Vail Activities Desk, 189
Vail Nature Center, 185
Vail Public Library, 188
Vail Recreation District, 181
Vail Ski Resort, 180
Vail Valley, 189–91
Vail Valley Chamber & Tourism
  Bureau, 189

Vail Valley Rodeo, 191
Vallecito Lake, 232
Vertical Grip Climbing Gym, 164
Victor Hotel, 124
Victorian Holiday Chalet Hotel, The, 33
Voodoo Lounge Youth and Teen
  Center, 214

W

Walden, 158–59
Walsenburg, 139
Washington Park, 24
Wells Fargo Culturefest, 35
Western Museum of Mining and
  Industry, 102
Westin Tabor Center, The, 33
White Fence Farm, 7
Wilderness on Wheels Foundation, 177
Wildlights, 36
Wildwood Inn, 77
Wings Over the Rockies Air & Space
  Museum, 27
Winona's, 168
Winter Park, 146–51
Winter Park Central Reservations, 151
Winter Park/Fraser Valley Chamber of
  Commerce, 151, 153
Winter Park Ski Resort, 146–51
Wool Market, 97
World Arena, 111
World Figure Skating Museum and Hall
  of Fame, 111
World's Largest Christmas Lighting
  Display, 36
WOW! Children's Museum, 64

Y

Yampatica, 161

Activities Index

HISTORIC STRUCTURES, SITES, AND LANDMARKS

MORE INFORMATION

MUSEUMS

OUTDOOR RECREATION

SHOPPING

SKI RESORTS

About the Author

Doris Kennedy has twelve travel guidebooks to her credit and is coauthor of five others. She and her professional photographer husband, Gary Kennedy, travel the world in search of stories and photographs. Their work appears in regional and national magazines and in the travel sections of major newspapers throughout the United States and Canada. Her weekly travel column has run in the *Denver Post* for the past ten years. She is travel editor for the monthly magazine *Colorado Woman News*. Doris and her family have traveled the state extensively. She still lives in Colorado and teaches travel writing in the Denver area.